# ALAN BLOOM'S HARDY PERENNIALS

## NEW PLANTS RAISED AND INTRODUCED BY A LIFELONG PLANTSMAN

# ALAN BLOOM'S HARDY PERENNIALS

NEW PLANTS RAISED AND INTRODUCED BY A LIFELONG PLANTSMAN

## ALAN BLOOM

B.T. Batsford Ltd, London

First published 1991

© Alan Bloom, 1991

Typeset by Florencetype Ltd, Kewstoke, Avon
and printed and bound by
Biddles Ltd, Guildford, Surrey

Published by
B.T. Batsford Ltd
4 Fitzhardinge Street
London W1H 0AH

A catalogue record for this book is
available from the British Library.

ISBN 0 7136 8039 3

# CONTENTS

# COLOUR PLATES

1 This geranium was named 'Laurence Flatman' in appreciation of his 40 years of devotion to the Nursery

2 *Potentilla* 'Blazeaway' enhances the range of colours in these already colourful plants

3 *Echinacea* 'Robert Bloom' was named after my eldest son in 1955; he is now Managing Director

4 *Achillea* 'Moonshine' has gained popularity far and wide, after being discarded for a time

5 The man who assisted greatly in raising new varieties chose this for his namesake as *Kniphofia* 'Percy's Pride'

6 I chose 'Gloaming' for this cultivar of *Campanula latifolia*. Its unusual colour keeps it always in demand

7 *Agapanthus* 'Bressingham Blue' was selected as the deepest colour from over 2000 seedlings on trial

8 *Pyrethrum* 'Bressingham Red' was the name suggested by a Yorkshire grower who wished me to launch it

9 *Helenium* 'Coppelia' is not too tall and just the right colour for blending with other colours

10 The tapering leafy spikes of *Aconitum* 'Bressingham Spire' are symmetrical and erect

11 From the origial batch of *Dicentra* Rokuju hybrids this selection – 'Pearl Drops' – has proved to be by far the best

12 In 1952 several *Erigerons* were raised from a deliberate cross – this one is 'Festivity'

13 *Heuchera* 'Red Spangles' was amongst those which gained premier awards in the Wisley Trials

14 Till this *Bergenia* appeared a pure white was needed and 'Bressingham White' filled that need

15 Named after my youngest daughter 'Jenny', this *Crocosmia* was her choice from among a dozen selections

16 I named this vigorous *Phlox* after 'Eva Cullum' when she retired from running the retail mail order section

17 The *Antholyza* parentage of *Crocosmia* 'Lucifer' gives extra hardiness and vigour

18 *Polygonum affine* 'Dimity' flowers freely and makes good ground cover with good autumn tints

19 For good summer brilliance *Kniphofia* 'Bressingham Comet'

20 The *Perovskia* is one of the few shrubby subjects which fits in with perennials – 'Blue Haze' is one of the best

# INTRODUCTION

It is not until one reaches at least the threshold of old age that the changes during one's lifetime become fully apparent. Before middle age, every advance in both manual practices and technology is accepted merely as progress in one way or another, calling for no special comment or celebration. However, from the standpoint of age, the comparisons between how things were and how they are now, 60 or 70 years later, hit one with almost frightening clarity; and in no aspect of basic endeavour have there been more radical changes than in the production and sale of nursery stock, hardwood or soft. Mechanisation has come in to supplement long-standing or traditional methods far beyond what I, for one, would have thought possible.

My working life began at barely 16, nearly 70 years ago. My first job on a nursery was to insert 8 cm clay pots in the soil between fairly short rows of strawberry plants. The rims had to be in rows at soil level, so that my skilled senior could insert the runners. It was late July and runners were plentiful with some beginning to make roots of their own. By September they would be independent plants fit for sale and commanding a higher price because they were pot grown. Other tasks I had to perform on that now extinct Wisbech nursery were almost all supervised by an older skilled worker; I was his assistant, fetching and carrying and in a general way being his dogsbody. I only weeded or washed pots on my own and even then was subject to frequent critical supervision. Once, however, with no one around I decided to dig a hole to bury some weeds instead of barrowing them away. I was – and always have been curious to know what lay beneath top soil, and there was just the chance that I might hit on King John's treasure which was said to have been lost in those parts. At 90 cm depth it was still fenland silt and there came a rasping, 'What the hell do you think you're doing?' followed by the foreman's sharp orders to do as I was told, no more, no less.

I stayed only ten weeks in Wisbech. The work was dull and the range of plants was narrow. A year at home was spent helping my father, initially to move his stocks of cut-flower perennials from Over to the newly bought 6-acre holding at Oakington. Transport once or twice a week for several weeks in the autumn of 1922 was by horse and trolley, the five miles taking just under the hour. Finding no real interest in market growing, I invested a few shillings in plants now and then. One purchase was 100 young seedling plants in 20 varieties for five shillings (25p) and included such alpines as *Alyssum saxatile*, *Tunica saxifraga*, mixed aubrietas etc. These I potted in the belief that I had begun to become a true nurseryman, for in addition I had raised some other kinds of plants of alpines from Thompson & Morgan's fourpenny packets of seeds.

By autumn 1923, however, I had agreed with my parents that I should work and train on a proper nursery and so began at Wallace's in Tunbridge Wells. There my wage was 15 shillings (75p) per week compared with only ten shillings at Wisbech, for only 50 hours, two less than at Wisbech; but the work was still close to drudgery, moving 200 frame lights (1·8 m x 1·2 m) night and morning for week after week, washing and crocking pots for my superiors, sifting and mixing soil and running errands. The sheds were draughty and without heat all winter. For a time I was put as helper to a man planting perennials, which were grown in beds 1·8 m wide. A line marked out the sides, leaving a 45 cm patch between adjoining beds and a shorter one across the bed for the rows of plants. As the bed was dug over, burying weeds, so a shallow trench was cut out with a spade close to the short lime, in which were placed the young plants, the soil returned and pressed with one's feet as each row was completed. The beds had to be a few centimetres higher than the paths on the edge and patted with a spade to give a neat finish.

Each kind of plant had to be labelled with its full botanical name. The labels were wooden strips, smoothly planed, about 45 cm long and pointed. Thick white lead paint was rubbed on one side, often with one's fingers, and the name written in pencil while the paint was wet, which then retained legibility much longer than if written on dried-off paint. The end of each bed abutted on to a much wider path so that a barrow, or even a pony cart could use it when lifting orders for plants, and as this service path or headland had beds on either side, labels needed always to face it.

This was the standard bed for perennials. Trees and shrubs were in longer, wider rows when they were large or tall enough, though when small they would have been 'liners' in short-row beds. Rows of trees and most shrubs were kept weed free by a scuffler or broad-bladed horse-drawn implements, a boy often having to lead the horse for the man handler behind. A day's work covering several miles was wearying, and it was of course the same method as used in farming for root crops. Lifting orders from beds in autumn or spring began with a bunch of tags on which the plant name and quantity and order number were written. Each had its looped string with which to attach it to the plant. Back in the packing-shed sorting, wrapping and packing for despatch was also labour-intensive. Parcels over 5 kg weight had to go by rail and the larger stations had horse trolleys to collect packages.

My few months at Wallace's did not satisfy my yearning to handle plants intimately, especially to propagate them. One outlet for energy for a time was to help in lifting some large standard rhododendrons for the forthcoming Wembley Exhibition of 1924. The method was to dig a trench all around the tree and then to probe beneath what was a huge ball of soil matted with fibrous roots. Once the tree began to rock, as men on either side pulled with ropes, the soil was thrown back under the heaving ball, which weighed a tonne or so. It involved pulling, alternately with poking soil underneath, so that the tree slowly rose until it stood above ground. It was then moved on rollers to be taken to the railway yard on a timber jill.

Wallace's was famous for lilies and while I worked there dozens of cases of bulbs packed in sawdust arrived from Japan. Most of them were sorted out to fill orders, while others were taken away to be potted for display at shows to attract more orders.

There was strict discipline at such nurseries and clearly defined grades of status, from Mr Robert Wallace at the top to such as me at the bottom. One did not stop to chat with those working on other jobs, nor walk about at anything other than a smart pace. Hands, if free, must be neither in pockets nor clasped behind.

The rules were less rigid at the nursery of Arthur Charlton & Sons. An uncle who lived at Tunbridge Wells had put a word in for me and I was invited to take over a little stock of alpines as propagator at 30 shillings a week. All alpines were pot grown and plunged in ashes. The beds were sided by railway sleepers on edge. There were several greenhouses and the nursery was long and narrow, close to a railway embankment with a steep-sided stream enclosing it on the other side. Only indoor plants for the Pantiles shop and perennials in a long series of standard 1·8 m beds were grown there, apart from the alpines that I was thrilled to take over. There was no snobbery there and it was a bustling concern, everyone appearing to enjoy what he did. So did I, but I made some mistakes of which I can still feel ashamed, though at the time they were tolerantly overlooked by John Charlton, my boss, as he realised, with me, how scanty was my experience. Although it was a modern general nursery at the time, by present-day standards, it was primitive. It was modern in such things as having a steam lorry, which was used for landscape work and to fetch trees and shrubs from the hardwood nursery at Rotherfield; and there was a single flush lavatory for everyone, but hygiene was not at all in evidence and the skirting stream took away a fair amount of rubbish.

John Charlton was quite interested in perennials. One day he came to me with a catalogue he had received from Thomas Carlisle of Twyford, who was an up-and-coming specialist, and in heavy type the cover announced that within were 'The Thousand and One Best Plants'. From it John Charlton said he would like to extend his own range, but soon afterwards I decided to move again with an urge to go north. Eventually, in May 1925 I was taken on as propagator by R.V. Roger of Pickering at 32 shillings a week. This enabled me to save up to five shillings (25p) a week after paying my lodgings and the weekly ounce of tobacco.

Although here too hygiene and indoor working conditions were primitive, the nursery was well run and spacious. Mr Roger also had a shop in the town and landscape work was undertaken. At the time the nursery occupied some 40 acres and was kept clean and tidy with only horses to augment manpower. I was allocated a boy as assistant although, at 18, I was only three years Tom Fletcher's senior. Years later Tom became nursery manager. During that summer we had potted some 50,000 alpines and large quantities of cuttings were put in frames or in the 'prop' greenhouse. During a severe cold spell late in November and early December we made yards and yards of festoons with evergreens to adorn Rowntrees's store at Scarborough.

Disused railway sleepers and ashes were a boon for many nurseries. Sleepers cost about 2s. 6d. and ashes from railway yards or factories could often be had for the taking. Ashes were good for 'plunging' pots of both alpines and many dwarf shrubs. They kept down weeds and made for tidiness as well as reducing the need for watering. Ashes were equally valuable for paths and roadways until heavier mechanical transport took over from manpower and horsepower.

Clay pots were never an easy means of growing nursery stock but there were no alternatives where plants, or whatever, needed to be pot grown, rather than planted and dug up from open ground. Pots were heavy and fragile, with many sizes from 'thumbs' up to those as large as buckets. Sizes were known not by the diameter, but by numbers of the 'cast' used by the makers. Alpines were planted in 60s – of 8 cm diameter; larger sizes had smaller numbers – 48, 32, 24. There was no problem in using them, but keeping them separate to avoid breakages and transporting them, whether empty or full, and above all washing them before they were used again, was wearisome indeed. A barrowful of pots was too heavy and too dangerous a load for anyone to wheel.

Barrows for nursery work were made of wood, with mostly iron-shod wooden wheels, though rubber tyres were coming in. These barrows needed as much level floor space as possible on which to lay trays of plants, whether or not in pots. When fully loaded, they dragged heavily and with soil or bulk loads, were harder to lift, pick or tip than the metal type with the weight more on the wheel than the wheeler's arms. Traditional hand tools have scarcely changed but I regret the disappearance of the wheel hoe. This was a splendid tool for row work, with its blades of adjustable width behind a single wheel and twin handles. I knew of only one make – the American-made 'Planet' and although it is no longer available, I still possess one and much prefer it to a noisy, stinking petrol-driven cultivator for row work. It does a much better job for little or no extra muscular effort.

Horticultural peat was scarcely ever used in nurseries until the 1930s. Potting composts were based entirely on soil and for most nurseries the regular practice was to acquire an annual supply of turfy loam, piling it into a neat stack about 1·5 m high. There it remained for up to two years, to be sliced down and sieved as required, to have sand mixed in along with lime if needed and such fertilisers as bonemeal or other organic fertiliser added according to the requirements of what was to be potted. Leaf-mould was added for such plants as primulas, and this was often supplied by a local merchant, as was the turfy loam. Almost invariably pots were crocked from the usual ample supplies of breakages, crushed into small pieces with any tool that was handy. I had a hand-operated machine like a large meat mincer which was very effective.

Soil sterilisation was slow to become widely used. To save the time it took to weed potted alpines, I built a brick oven type for heating soil enough to kill weed seeds, but it did not last long for the heat burst the brickwork asunder. That was in the early 1930s, and after that failure I bought a steam steriliser. It was a portable tank beneath which was a space for water to be heated by the coal fire below, to produce steam which percolated the soil in the tank. It had to be carefully tended, as the right amount of time and steam were critical lest the soil was turned into hot mud. Two other methods have been used, one being a pressure boiler such as dairymen used and the other a flame thrower, but both these and a soil shredder have since become too labour-intensive and now sterilised loam is brought in.

Loam is no longer the basis for potting compost and nowadays most plant producers use up to 90 per cent sphagnum peat with perhaps some pulverised bark, to 10 per cent of soil. In my little department, about 35 per cent is soil and it is sterilised by a gas injected into a polythene-sealed mass.

There are three primary, but interdependent, factors that led to the vast changes that have taken place during my lifetime, especially over the past 50 years. Prior to 1939 there was a slow but steady rate of progress. Machines such as the rotary type were coming in for nursery cultivation. I had a Simar Rototiller by 1935 and later a Howard Rotavator, as I had never adopted the 1·8 m bed already described except for pot-grown alpines. I began with 18 m rows in what we called 'bays' for open-ground perennials. The ground was mechanically prepared in advance and then planted to a line with trowels on top, thus cutting out hand digging. We used two-wheel hand trucks rather than wheelbarrows and made broader paths to fit.

The trend towards labour-saving had therefore begun in the 1930s, but well in advance of any steep rise in wages. The basic rate rose only from 30 to 36 shillings during that ten-year period for a 48-hour week. It was of course the effects of war that set the inflation spiral in motion, concurrently with the necessity of inventions to offset steeply rising wages and increasing scarcity of labour. Of the 36 workers I employed in 1939, the majority had been in agriculture but made redundant by the advent of tractors during the previous 20-year depression. Only two were employed in the office at that time, though until 1935 I had coped alone with the office work. Incidentally, there were only two outdoor helpers when I took over the 15-acre holding at Oakington in 1931, so its growth to 36 acres of plants had called for a steady increase in labour also.

All but a few small postal parcels of plants went by rail from Oakington station. By passenger train consignments reached even long distances within 24 hours and even by the cheaper 'goods train' service it took only two or three days for deliveries to be made to places as far away as Aberdeen or Penzance. Prompt despatch, along with quality and variety were paramount in my estimation. When after moving to

Bressingham I finally set about restoring the nursery in 1950 to its pre-war state and beyond, I insisted that the same criteria prevailed; but it was uphill work all the way, as inflation set in with rising wages and rail services went into decline.

By the 1960s Beeching's cuts in rail services were only part of the problems. Another was a change in the pattern of demand by the gardening public. More people had gardens, but they were more mobile as cars became more affordable, and so the need for garden centres was created where buyers could pick out what appealed to them and take it away. Ordering from a catalogue for autumn or spring delivery took longer and was costly. New housing estates, and cars, led to impulse buying and the new plastic pots put a stop to the age-old use of clays.

As a revolution in both production and sale of nursery stock, it was slow to begin in the 1950s but gained momentum in the next decade to establish a completely new pattern. I was reluctant to change, preferring to grow alpines in pots and perennials in open ground as I had always done and to keep to wholesale only; but our retailing customers were calling for container-grown plants, and because I had made a large garden attracting visitors with proceeds to charities, it created a demand for plants in a wider variety, as visitors saw them and wanted them. I gave in in the mid-1960s. There was pressure also from my two sons. Robert was keen on greater mechanisation, Adrian on growing conifers, heather and shrubs and both believing that we should open the door to retailing as well as supplying wholesale customers with container-grown plants.

Most readers will be aware of the outcome of these decisions. The business expanded rapidly and I retired in 1972 to look after the five-acre garden, five acres or more of nursery for special subjects which objected to mechanisation and to setting up a live steam-engine museum. I need say no more about this aspect except that I and my little band of helpers work mainly on traditional lines with hand tools. At the nursery there are machines for planting, potting and weed control and computers in the office. Nothing now goes by rail, but lorries deliver the packages and pallets of plants to all parts, even to the Continent. Total annual sales now run into millions of plants, still mainly wholesale, but some 35,000 retail orders are despatched autumn and spring, and the four-acre Plant Centre of recent years does so well with its wide variety, quality and service that I now wish I had allowed it to begin 20 years ago.

I am, nevertheless, thankful not to be at the helm of such a demanding business. Instead I am able to be with plants intimately for mostly seven days a week. More often than not my work enables me to be alone with my thoughts. Reflections on the past, present and future bring in a kaleidoscope of pictures, patterns and people. There is something good to be remembered about the old ways and not all the changes I have witnessed appear to me as truly progressive in human terms. There is in general less zest in work now that living standards are so much higher and too much reliance is placed on modern machines and technology, with too little on human skills and conscientiousness. What I resent most is that although practical objective breeding and hybridising has not kept pace with the progress in other directions, propagation by tissue culture is tending to undermine basic human skill. It is taking plants away to a laboratory from the heart of a nursery, yet it cannot be wholly relied upon not to incur loss and confusion. Breeding by similar scientific process may come, but not, I hope, in my lifetime, for I fear it holds untold risks and perils.

I doubt if more than just a few hybridists in the past have been motivated entirely by the hope of profit. The majority were plant lovers first and foremost, who wished to enhance subjects which interested them most as a creative act stemming also from imagination and curiosity. The fears I have for the future are relative to the development of scientific methods of breeding and mass propagation by tissue culture. This is coupled with the modern tendency of exploitation purely for profit. Laboratory breeding and factory production is likely to open the door for those who have no other interest in plant life than the means to material reward. True creativeness comes only from the compulsive incentives of those who work for love rather than just for money. Yet for non-professional gardeners, there would be advantages in more plentiful and probably cheaper supplies of new or scarce plants. Material progress is ever a two-sided affair, of gain for some and loss for others.

# RECOLLECTIONS OF
# PLANT RAISERS

This section can scarcely be other than reminiscent. Also it would be as impossible to adopt a chronological order in this context as it would be to record introductions alphabetically. I would not dare to delve beyond the span of my own life for hybridists and their cultivars, and because some raisers did not always keep to one genus, the memories on which I must rely are unlikely to cover more than the most outstanding achievements of others.

Flowers were often a topic amongst grown-ups in the Fenland village of Over, where I was raised. This was because my father grew a wider variety than anyone else, not only to sell, but for love. Flower growing for market was on the increase and as a boy I often became an eavesdropper when others came to ask father's opinion or advice, since he was by way of a pioneer in trying out different kinds – away from gypsophila, marguerites, china asters, pyrethrums and gladioli. Once, tagging behind father and another grower named Khedalehoma Hines, conversation came round to marguerites – now dropped in favour of 'Chrys. max.' (for *Chrysanthemum maximum*).

'Whoever can breed,' one of the pair announced, 'a yellow marguerite will make a fortune.' That statement stuck in my twelve-year-old mind, calling for action on my part. Father told me the rudiments of breeding by cross-pollination and how two species must be related to produce a hybrid. He lent me one of his brushes which he kept for his hobby of painting flower pictures but I could find no yellow relative of marguerites. The tall *Doronicum* 'Harpur Crewe' would have been a possibility but it had finished flowering and even the then best marguerite 'Rentpayer' had almost finished. By the following year father had gently persuaded me that it was a forlorn hope on my part. 'I think some expert would have bred one by now if it were possible,' he said with an indulgent smile. Always ready to stimulate my interest, he told me how he was about to try out heucheras for cutting.

It was largely the sight of those heucheras a few years later which made me decide to become a nurseryman in the true sense of the word. Growing for the cut-flower market steadily lost all appeal for me. One grew a crop which in most cases made one completely dependent on what a commission agent could get for the flowers in some distant city market. It was a gamble. The salesmen supplied the empty flower boxes by rail, but when telegrams came giving the prices the flowers had realised, there were many disappointments. Perhaps Leeds or Manchester would have brought better results than Birmingham or Covent Garden in London. It took time to switch markets because empties came by goods train, although when full of flowers they reached distant markets within hours if loaded at Swavesey station at tea time. And so, having cut and sent away flowers just as they came to their best, months' or even a year's growing and tending brought no sure worthwhile reward.

By the time I left school at barely 16, I had veered away from market growing, and was in favour of perennials rather than annuals and biennials. Perennials came up year after year. You knew they were there waiting to flower again in season, even if all top growth had gone during the winter months. So, of course, did most bulbs, but the hardy ones, like daffodils, left the ground untidy or bare all summer. By this time, 1922, I had one or two books on perennials – B. Thomas and A.G. Macself were names I remembered, and gradually a new world of plants opened up for me. I pored over *Gardening Illustrated* but was always avid to know more about perennials. Writers such as William Robinson and Gertrude Jekyll were somewhat beyond my scope, and I found intense interest in studying the catalogues of a few leading specialists in perennials and alpines.

## Amos Perry

Father often spoke of Amos Perry, who called his Enfield Nursery a 'Hardy Plant Farm', and used the claim for advertising, indicating that the sun never set on his plants because they were so widely distributed over the world. From Perry's, father grew for cutting the double white *Achillea* 'Perry's Variety', the deep-yellow *Anthemis* 'Thora Perry' and, I believe, a *Coreopsis*. At least three varieties of *Papaver orientale* were Perry introductions and two of them, 'Marcus Perry', an upstanding scarlet red, and 'Perry's White' are still with us. As might be expected, the *Hemerocallis* raised and introduced by Perry's 60 years ago or more have been ousted by the influx of new American cultivars. A few perennial asters were also raised at the Enfield Nursery, and I think I have overlooked other examples of its owner's enthusiasm for breeding. Two which he raised but to my knowledge have been lost, are the tiny orange *Geum* 'Gladys Perry' and the 'Major' form of *Catananche caerulea*. I have to rely on memory, for almost all of those old catalogues did not come through the years with me. Mr Perry was an innovator as well as a collector. At one period he specialised in ferns and in the 1930s could list 2,000 species and variations. Another of his ventures was in aquatics which he grew in a long series of concrete tanks set on gentle slopes so that a constant stream of water ran from one tank to the next.

Relatively few of the cultivars which Amos Perry named and introduced have stayed the course. Some carried the name 'Perry's Variety'. Others had family names, but it was said that when these were used up, he began again by inventing the surname Perfield, made from Perry and Enfield. Nothing, so far as I know, was given the name Frances Perry, the daughter-in-law who became very well known as a plant woman and gardening author – still contributing to the *Observer*. As well as having a vast knowledge of plants, Mr Perry was an expert at showing them off to advantage, expecially those liking shade and moisture. These were the firm's speciality in later years, but now the nursery and those specialities are but a memory. To my regret I visited the Enfield nursery only once. By then, the late 1930s, it seemed that the ferns and aquatics had become more important than the border perennials.

The *Heuchera* that began our own family involvement was *H. brizoides* 'Gracillima'. It was purchased from Perry's, but those that were used for breeding were of the *H. sanguinea* type named 'Trevor Red', 'Trevor Pink' and 'Trevor White'. They came about 1920 from the nursery of G.W. Miller at Wisbech (where I worked first on leaving home in July 1922) but were raised before the First World War at Trevor, a garden in North Wales. Once during my brief stay at Clarkson Nursery, I paused to watch white-bearded Mr Miller dividing heucheras with a knife. In less than a minute he looked up with a scowl and told me to get on with my job – of weeding not far away.

# Edward Bowles

Not far from Perry's Hardy Plant Farm was the garden of a gentleman named Edward Augustus Bowles who gave his name to several subjects, possibly in advance of their being officially classified. He was a collector rather than a hybridist, always on the look-out for the unusual. Whether or not he raised the compact free-flowering blue *Vinca minor* 'Bowles' Variety', it remains one of the best of this somewhat despised genus. His *Pulmonaria officinalis* 'Bowles' Red' is also still around, but has been superseded by 'Redstart'. The short-lived little *Viola* 'Bowles' Black' is scarcely a good garden plant, having a propensity for self-seeding. *Milium effusum* 'Aureum' likewise is more often listed as 'Bowles' Golden Grass' and is also short-lived. It has, however, the capacity of renewing from self-sown seed within a narrow compass so that only occasional patching up a group is necessary. The Bowles name is also attached to a golden-leaved sedge, *Carex elata* 'Aurea'. It is surprising that Mr Bowles, having a scientific turn of mind and a stalwart of the Royal Horticultural Society, should have allowed his name to take apparent precedence over the correct botanical nomenclature of plants that he introduced.

## Thomas Bones

Thomas Bones of nearby Cheshunt was a small unpretentious nurseryman. Although I seem to remember he raised new delphiniums in the inter-war period, none come to mind that stood out in competition with those from specialists such as Blackmore and Langdon. Mr Bones's legacy to gardens rests mainly on *Aster amellus* varieties which at that time were rather scanty. The most popular blue was 'King George', which was in fact of German origin. It began to circulate in Britain just prior to the 1914–18 war, and in the upsurge of patriotism the name 'Kaiser Wilhelm' was not to be tolerated and the Kaiser's British cousin's name was given instead. The three cultivars raised by Mr Bones were, I believe, the fine pink 'Sonia', the deep-blue 'Bessie Chapman' and the large-flowering mid-blue 'Advance'. For all their high value in making a late summer and autumn display, some *Aster amellus* seem to lose vitality in the course of time. 'King George' remains a fairly strong grower with me, but 'Sonia' is less robust than it used to be, and I have lost 'Bessie Chapman'. 'Advance' still grows strongly, but I have not propagated it from cuttings to become sale plants and it might be that frequent tip cuttings is a cause for loss of vigour – a not unknown phenomenon in a few other instances.

## Vicary Gibbs

The Hon. Vicary Gibbs was an amateur specialist in asters of the michaelmas daisy tribe. He too was on the outskirts of London at Aldenham, but I have very little information available of what he raised for they emerged before my time. All I can say with confidence is that he bred from other than true Michaelmas Daisy, the species *A. novi-belgii* as well, and that few if any of his hybrids remain in circulation. Edwin Beckett was another of the pioneer hybridists of michaelmas daisies.

## Ernest Ballard

The man who carried on more or less where Vicary Gibbs left off – Ernest Ballard of Colwall, near Malvern, stands supreme in this particular field and was responsible for raising more improvements than anyone else. Many are still being grown in spite of their losing popularity in recent years, due largely to a virus wilt disease and mildew. The first of Ballard's introductions came during the 1914–18 war, if not before, with such names as 'Beauty of Colwall'. Many carried the Ballard name prefixed by Marie, Freda, Helen and others, but it was said that those with clerical names from The Rector and The Dean to The Bishop and one or two more, were due to Ernest Ballard's antipathy to churchmen. He was indeed a man of strong views and I was once told by a friend of the family that all demands for information or money from Government officials were returned marked with the word 'Bosh' writ large across the missive.

A very fine, but still rare hepatica raised by Ernest Ballard must be mentioned here. So far as I know it is the only other subject for which he was responsible and it goes by the name of *H.* × *ballardii*, larger in flower than any other, of a sky-blue shade. I have grown it for 25 years and still have insufficient to offer any for sale. It is possible that Ballard began working on helleborus before he died. Although the nursery was taken over by that fine plantsman Percy Picton, Helen Ballard has continued to breed the 'Lenten Rose' *H. orientalis* and others, to produce some charming hybrids in a wider range of colour, including some very close to yellow, long stemmed and vigorous. It is a very slow process to increase these plants by division in order to keep them true to name or colour.

# A.H. Harrison

To come back to michaelmas daisies, a few others made notable contributions to the range. A.H. Harrison set up the Gayborder Nursery at Melbourne, Derbyshire in the 1920s until the 1950s. Several carrying the Gayborder tag proved to be of garden value, some being neater in habit than the Ballard range. Lanky height was certainly a disability with some, and if not supported gave a very disappointing display. By the 1950s the dwarfs, now known as *Aster dumosus*, were becoming much more popular and Gayborder contributed a few excellent varieties such as 'Jenny Margaret Rose' and 'Alice Haslam'. The smaller flowered but deep-reddish shade of 'Winston Churchill' introduced in the early 1950s was,

I suspect, bred from one of the 'Beechwood' varieties, introduced by William Wood of Beechwood Nursery, Taplow, Bucks. These too were small flowered compared with Ballard's, but made up in numbers in a more stiffly branching habit.

It was another firm at Taplow, Barrs, who I believe were the first to introduce the dwarfs in the 1930s, though I doubt if they were the raisers. In my 1939 wholesale catalogue were listed no fewer than 16 varieties, which shows how rapidly they were gaining popularity following the original five or six introduced by Barrs. Only two or three of that list are now in circulation having been superseded by more modern varieties. Incidentally, that last pre-war catalogue of mine offers 27 cultivars of *Aster amellus* and no fewer than 82 named *Novi-belgii* cultivars, scarcely any of which are now grown commercially.

It is not surprising that others were lured into hybridising michaelmas daisies to take advantage of the then existing popularity. Deliberate crosses may well have been made, but seedlings selected from the best were easy to raise and if the majority had to be discarded, anything showing improvements could quickly be propagated. A single plant might produce a score or more basal cuttings in its first year of growth. When rooted, the tips would double the stock which, if planted out in May or even June, could grow well enough to offer several hundreds for sale, in just two years from choosing a single plant selected at flowering time as worth propagating and naming. A few older hybrid michaelmas daisies have stood the test of time and are even making something of a come-back. Notable amongst these is the single blue *Climax* which was raised over 80 years ago. It lacks nothing in colour, grace and vigour. 'Little Carlow' is of obscure origin and though 30 cm taller than *Climax* at 1·35 m, it is well worth growing. So too are variations on the *cordifolius* type – small flowered, but small in this case is beautiful. One such is named 'Photograph'.

I cannot leave asters without mentioning two of my favourites, which are still not fully appreciated for sheer garden value. One is A. × *thompsonii* 'Nanus' which makes a shapely, greyish-leaved bush only 50 cm high and is set with spode-blue, yellow-centred flowers from July to October. It needs full sun and well-drained soil as does A. *spectabilis*. This has even brighter blue flowers on branching stems to 36 cm high from August to November, above dark-green leathery leaves. Neither have any disabilities and both can be left undisturbed for several years, given the right position.

# Lupins

I cannot be certain that intensive propagation from cuttings is a contributory cause of virus attacks or if intensive breeding itself may be a major factor. Be that as it may, lupins as well as many michaelmas daisy hybrids have become susceptible and now practically none are grown from cuttings to name. Perhaps the introduction of named strains which come fairly true from seed have affected matters, for these are certainly less costly to produce than from cuttings. Nevertheless, it was the pioneer breeders who did the groundwork by continually selecting and isolating the best seedling of the original but variable species *L. polyphyllus*.

The first of these pioneers was a Mr Downer of Worthing, who probably began working on lupins before 1914. The original species was nothing special in bluish shades, but Downer might have used the yellow *L. arboreus* (tree lupin) or even an annual through which pink emerged. For a few years he championed his lupins with a phrase which ran, I believe, as 'Downer's usually silent Lupins are making a great noise in the world'. This was to herald his deep-pink 'Downer's Delight' and 'Pink Pearls' in the 1920s, followed later by several others. As usual, other nurserymen soon cottoned on to a growing market, as did one amateur who became famous – George Russell.

Amongst the 38 named varieties all grown from cuttings listed in my 1939 catalogue, the names C.M. Prichard and John Harkness are included. Certainly Maurice Prichard had other varieties to his credit, for one is 'Riverslea', the name of the then nursery at Christchurch, Hants. John Harkness was in business at Bedale, Yorks – a firm well known then, but the family name has since become famous elsewhere for roses. My collection of 38 named lupins would not have included all that were in cultivation in 1939, but it could well be that 20 years later the total number of varieties raised, named and introduced, was getting on for a hundred.

And I very much doubt if more than half a dozen of them are still in cultivation and then only in one or two nurseries.

# George Russell

The George Russell story is worth a brief mention here. During the 1920s he lived at York, working as a railwayman, with a liking for flowers and especially lupins. By raising from seed and meticulous selecting, he was able to stage a few exhibits at flower shows. As a strain of assorted colours they were quite outstanding, finer than some of the named varieties then being offered by nurserymen; these became Russell Lupins, not to name but as a mixture.

One of the nurserymen who had an eye for greater things was James Baker, who had a nursery at Codsall near Wolverhampton. He was likeable and very progressive indeed in marketing, even if he was not a plantsman in the strict sense. His flair was for spotting and exploiting plants for which a nation-wide demand could be created. He was already into delphiniums and michaelmas daisies during the 1930s, using publicity from flower shows and a colour catalogue. Incidentally, he created boom sales in posy baskets of dried flowers known as 'Bakerwork', which were sold all over England by appointment in leading drapery and millinery shops. 'Jimmy' Baker's greatest coup, however, was to persuade the ageing George Russell to pull up both his own roots and those of his lupins and move to Wolverhampton where a new nursery had been set up at nearby Boningale. Before long new Russell Lupins to name became an annual event. All were increased from basal cuttings in early spring and vast quantities were sold, as well as the mixed strain and packets of Russell Lupin seed. George Russell eventually died when well into his 90s, but when James Baker also died not many years later, the business he created faded out.

So many of the specialists in hardy plants who were flourishing in the period from 1920 to 1960 have now become but a memory. Almost all of them were my customers, for it suited them to replenish stocks from me, when I was purely a wholesale producer from 1934 to 1965. In several cases their catalogues, to some extent, were based on mine, which made it less essential to maintain their own stocks. This began to apply especially after the 1939–45 war, as a result of soaring production costs for those retailing nurserymen who found trees and shrubs more profitable to grow than perennials.

James Baker's other main speciality during the 1930s was delphiniums. He exploited several varieties raised by Mr Bishop of Wrexham, but not exclusively, but I lack information as to his sources for the many he acquired, exhibited and introduced. It is possible, if not probable, that his firm raised and named some; for all his own propensities as an entrepreneur he had a devoted plantsman on his staff, Mr Mills, who might well have done some breeding. In any case, the names Codsall and Boningale were used for some Baker introductions, which may or may not have been raised there.

## Blackmore and Langdon

I must come back to Baker's when dealing with phlox, but to continue with the present context of delphiniums, the names Blackmore and Langdon stand out. They were the leading specialists at least 70 years ago and still remain in that exalted position. Although named cultivars are grown less widely nowadays, they have not suffered from the problems that beset michaelmas daisies and lupins. Most other nurserymen have dropped named varieties raised from cuttings in favour of the much more cheaply produced strains raised from seed. Likewise, fewer amateur gardeners have the space, time or cash to grow the massive spikes of the 'Queen of the Border' kinds, for which Blackmore and Langdon became justly famous.

As a young nurseryman I saw prestige in growing and offering as wide a range of delphiniums as possible. Most of them were of Blackmore and Langdon origin and during the 1930s I acquired from them a small stock nucleus from which to produce, in due course, plants for sale. My 1939 catalogue had 60 varieties – all large flowered, apart from the twelve coming under *D. belladonna*. Some, by the way, were quite expensive if fairly new varieties, as much as 2s. 6d. (12·5p), but older ones were one shilling (5p) or £4 per 100 as the trade price. Well over half those listed were Blackmore and Langdon delphiniums, but a few bore the Bishop-raised stamp, or were of obvious Continental origin – such as 'Lize van Veen'. Some had interesting well-chosen names – like 'Smoke of War' and 'Dusky Monarch'. One, named 'Jenny Jones', reminds me that a Mr Jones was also a breeder of delphiniums during the inter-war period, with a nursery in Kent I believe. So popular were delphiniums at that time that even some amateurs were able to find an outlet for outstanding variations.

The *belladonna* type of delphiniums suffered from neglect whilst the large-flowered, majestic-spiked ones were much admired and so widely grown. There were not many variations of the latter grown abroad and British specialists reigned supreme with often truly splendid exhibits at all the principal flower shows. I grew about a dozen varieties of *belladonnas* in the belief that they were less demanding as garden plants. Being less tall and having a much more branching habit, the number and brilliance of their flowers compensated for lack of size, but even now, the number of varieties remains scanty compared with the large-flowered kinds, with only a very few new introductions since 1939. At least six of my twelve are still grown and I have added only one in recent years. This came from Germany as 'Volkefreiden', a name that I thought to be a disability for such a fine rich-blue variety and I anglicised and abbreviated the name to 'Peace'.

Some comment on other aspects of breeding should come here. In the 1930s the then leading Dutch firm of Ruys launched the first pink variety named 'Pink Sensation'. And sensation it was, with some kinship and resemblance to the *belladonna* habit with spikes 90–120 cm tall. I never knew what species had been used in the cross to produce a true warm pink, but suspected it was the reddish *D. cardinale*, a plant too tender and short-lived to flourish in British climates. Naturally I went all out to build up stocks, and by 1937 was offering it at £6 16s. per 100 for one-year-old plants. It grew strongly and sold well and continued to do so until a few years ago, when a slow relapse from vigour set in. Now, it is rather a struggle to keep enough for a garden group and is probably another case of weakness developing from intensive propagation. The post-war efforts of Dr Legro to breed red delphiniums is a sad story. For the last 25 years he has laboured and still has not found one, as far as I know, to survive more than about two-three years. Some we tried at Bressingham were of startling brilliance in red and salmon shades but failed to be perennial. This failing would be due to using such red species as *D. cardinale* as a parent. It is possible to produce new colours by this means, but at the same time it is likely to implant the short-lived element in its genetic make-up.

There has been a constant but unsatisfied demand in recent years for what was the newest and most expensive *Delphinium* in my 1939 catalogue. It is named 'Alice Artindale', an exquisite sky blue on rosette-type flowers for much of its 1·5 m spike. My selling price (wholesale) in 1939 was £3 per dozen, but if I had such plants available for sale now they would be snatched up if I asked £10 per plant! Twice I have been able to acquire a small plant in recent years, but the first one was too small even to survive. The second, as a favour from a nurseryman whose total stock was only about a dozen, was also tiny, but it was pot grown and may in time be large enough to tempt me once again to build up a stock. Almost all my named delphiniums (over 50,000) remained unsold in 1939–40 when demand ceased because of war. They were mostly ploughed under in order to grow food crops and although I began again to rebuild stocks on moving to Bressingham, the demand never made a worthwhile recovery against the upsurge of seed-raised 'Pacific' types, and those bred as the short-lived *Astolat* hybrids of the early 1950s. These bore names of the Arthurian legendary personalities. I still have just a few of the older large-flowered varieties. These include 'Etonian', a large-flowered mauvey blue, the relatively dwarf 'Cinderella', growing to less than 1·2 m and 'F.W. Smith', a very old gentian-blue variety with a white eye and one of the small number of good varieties that was not raised by Blackmore and Langdon. One not so old was given to me as the 'finest white delphinium ever raised'. It is 'Basil Clitheroe', raiser unknown, but the claim is probably beyond dispute. It is (1·8 m) with fine almost double pure-white flowers and a sturdy habit.

If I were to record all my experiences as a grower of delphiniums, much more than the above could be listed. What I can say here in conclusion is that I am pretty certain the net result in financial terms would be well on the debit side. 'Alice Artindale' was introduced and probably raised by Artindale's of Sheffield with a nursery at Boston, Lincs. It was an old-established firm having a wholesale cut-flower outlet at Sheffield, and the Boston nursery grew large quantities of cut flowers for this purpose. *Paeonias* were a great speciality with a range of well over 50 varieties. When I began to exhibit at flower shows in the later 1920s I was somewhat overawed by the magnificent displays put up by such firms as Artindale's, even though my aspirations and ambitions were lively. I used to drive a little solid-tyred, chain-driven Trojan van to Leeds, York or Harrogate shows crammed with mainly dug-up perennials in flower. This was a departure from the more usual method of showing cut flowers, in the belief that people could then see how plants grew for height and habit. Being hard up, I mostly slept in the empty van rather than pay hotel fees, but such frugality seemed to widen the gulf between me and the owners of such big firms as Artindale's.

John Artindale and John Harkness of Bedale became buddies at these big flower shows. Jokes were made about their lack of frugality, especially in the refreshment marquee where much of their time was spent. They left order-taking at their exhibits to underlings. Harkness was not so much of a specialist, but grew a wide range of perennials. Apart from at least one lupin already mentioned, he produced a dainty light-pink *Sidalcea*, 'Elsie Heugh', and at least one Oriental Poppy, 'Olive Harkness'. I fancy there were others and that the deep-mahogany-orange *Gaillardia* 'Mrs Lascelles' was his, with possibly a *Verbascum*, neither of which have remained in cultivation, nor some lupins including a fine yellow one bearing his wife's name. Lascelles is the family name of the Harewoods and Mrs Lascelle's husband, the Revd E. Lascelles, gave his name to one of the best of the pre-war delphiniums.

The brother-in-law of John Harkness was George Gibson, who had a nursery at nearby Leeming Bar and who, incidentally, put his name to *Potentillam* 'Gibson's Scarlet' rather naughtily, for it was – I am told on good authority – actually raised in Cornwall by Captain Pinwillis and originally named 'Pinwillis Scarlet'. The two nurseries with related ownership were said not to be friendly rivals. It was said that George had been a Harkness employee, and on marrying into the family, set up on his own. He did not grow a wide range of perennials and his speciality at flower shows was his 'Sunbeam Strain of Iceland Poppies', sold by packets of seed to the public.

# H.P. Read

I would credit the Harkness nursery with raising more new perennials than anyone else in the North. Although I have no reliable list of them, I do know that along with others up and down the country he produced at least one *Chrysanthemum maximum*, for it was named 'V.L. Harkness'. At that time marguerites were important for cut-flower growers, but although my boyhood interest in hybridising had been kindled by their potential, they were not amongst my favourite flowers. I even came to dislike them in a way because in helping my father, I handled so many. The cut stems gave off a rather stinking odour as one stripped the leaves or when taken out of water. I did not know until years later that breeders here and there were already working on marguerites. In a quiet way H.P. Read of Brundall near Norwich was making some progress, not on coloured marguerites so much as on producing a double-flowered variety. Nor would Mr Read have imagined that his 'Esther Read' which was the first truly double form ever raised, would become so well known that people dropped any reference to its parental specifics as it became the most popular florists' perennial plant 20 years later. Acres of it were grown countrywide, and by the simple use of dyes it was available in a variety of colours.

Spurred on by initial success, 'Horace Read', 'Pauline Read' and 'Jennifer Read' followed, but though double flowered, all had faults of one kind or another – stems or constitutional weakness. Then in the 1950s Horace Read collaborated with Lord Darnley in an effort to breed a yellow in its own right. His Lordship, by the way, had raised a selection of new monardas but in my judgement they showed very little improvement or variation on the varieties already in existence. Limited success came from the joint venture. 'Cobham Gold' went no more than half-way to being yellow. Only the centre of the double-petalled flower was any justification for the name. Much the same could be said of the next one, given the

1 This geranium was named 'Laurence Flatman' in appreciation of his 40 years devotion to the Nursery

2 *Potentilla* 'Blazeaway' enhances the range of colours in these already colourful plants

3 *Echinacea* 'Robert Bloom' was named after my eldest son in 1955; he is now Managing Director

4 *Achillea* 'Moonshine' has gained popularity far and wide, after being discarded for a time

5 The man who assisted greatly in raising new varieties chose this for his namesake as *Kniphofia* 'Percy's Pride'

name 'Moonlight', which had only a hint of overall light yellow. It proved, as did so many, to be weak stemmed and to have a less than vigorous basal growth.

During that period, my own interest in what the trade referred to as 'Chrys. max.' was minimal. The wider range of perennials appealed to me much more. So I took very little notice of new varieties coming out. A business friend, Colin McMullen of Wisbech, set up a new nursery near Chester as Burleydam Nurseries. He had faith in the profitability of launching new varieties, from flowers to fruits, and made contacts with breeders willing to have their successes launched under his banner. One of these was John Murray in Scotland, and the first of his semi-double, strong-growing Chrys. max. came out as 'Wirral Pride'. It was followed by the improved 'Wirral Supreme' and this is still widely grown – well short of fully double but taller and more robust than 'Esther Read'. For a few years Burleydam Nurseries flourished, but faded out with the death of the owner. It was not until the 1980s that I took the slightest interest in Chrys. max. again, in the belief that no one since had worked upon them. Cut-flower growing in Britain was becoming uneconomic and in rapid decline. Then there arrived from a well-wishing amateur a plant of one yet to be named which he invited me to try as the best double variety ever raised. Having grown it for three seasons I am strongly inclined to back his judgement, for it is not only a fully double pure white, but is a sturdy grower, as well as a modest 75 cm with reliable basal growth.

As a youthful nurseryman I was not greatly attracted to other types of chrysanthemum. Then, in 1936 my interest was suddenly and unexpectedly aroused by an offer from America. Bristol Nurseries, Connecticut (who introduced the double *Gypsophila paniculata* 'Bristol Fairy') were keen to launch both their 'Korean chrysanthemums' and a batch of dwarfs called fancifully 'Azaleamums. It was explained that a selection had been sent for trial to the specialist firm of Wells at Merstham, Surrey, at least two years before. This had not led to the hoped-for commitment to launch them in Britain and Bristol Nurseries were offering to let me do so. I readily agreed, partly because Ben Wells was a competitor with a wide range of hardy perennials. His slogan of 'If its's

Hardy Plants it's Wells' was to me at that time a challenge.

Along with the six Koreans, I also invested in five of the 'Cushion' or 'Azaleamum' varieties and set about propagating as swiftly as possible. Much credit went to my young propagator Len Smith who found that almost every leaf was a potential new plant. By the following year we had enough to justify a coloured leaflet with which to tempt my retailing customers. However, Ben Wells had at last decided to launch them himself and discovering that his tardiness had let me in, invited me to collaborate with him to avoid a clash. He received me cordially and gave me lunch, but we finally parted without agreement. The stumbling block for me was that having eight varieties to my six, he would not guarantee to supply the other two so that we could trade on equal terms. My advertising leaflet went out in the following spring. It brought a profit mounting to just about £1,600 and that was the figure I paid later that year for a poorly drained Fen farm of 200 acres at Burwell. At that time I was intending to extend plant production to compete with imports from Holland on similar peaty soil. In the event, what I grew there had to be ploughed under, as at Oakington, due to the advent of war. At least I survived the war and was able to begin again; not so Ben Wells, who lost his life at sea on his way to America in 1940, so it was said, and his wife gallantly tried to carry on the nursery but finally had to give up.

Although there was no financial compensation for wartime losses of nursery stock, I became absorbed in a venture far removed from growing hardy perennial plants due to a lucky strike with chrysanthemums. This was the opportunity to convert some very wild land for food production – having to tackle drainage problems and lots of bog oak, reed beds and bushes. By 1943 I was farming 540 acres with hardy plants as little more than a hobby. It was said to be one of the toughest wartime land jobs undertaken, but at the time I enjoyed it. Another spin-off came with the incentive to write my first book *The Farm in the Fen*, published by Faber and Faber in 1944.

The story of how I came to move from Oakington and then to Fordham to be nearer the farm at Burwell has been told in another book. It included the move to Bressingham in 1946 and a rather disastrous interlude with my family in Canada from 1948 to 1950. It was not until my return to Bressingham that I wholeheartedly became a nurseryman again and made contacts with others who were also interested in producing hybrids. For most of them, the war period had merely been a slack time, but now a new era had begun though I was largely unaware of it at the time. Of this more must be said later.

# Iris

Some of the plants I have mentioned were in fact introduced soon after the war as a continuance of breeders' efforts begun long before. Most of the relatively few people who were engaged on hybridising hardy plants had concentrated on already popular genera. It was perhaps irises that had appealed to both breeders and public more than any other subject in the late-nineteenth century and early years of the present century. Possible improvements in the large-flowered *Iris germanica* had captured widespread appeal in western Europe and America, though when the craze declined in Europe the latter took over. The results of intensive hybridising have already been documented elsewhere.

I grew just 50 varieties for sale – of the June-flowering *I. germanica*. Then names were truly international. French breeders were represented in such as 'Depute Nomblot' and 'Souvenir de Madame Gaudichau' and 'Pluie d'Or'. Germanic influence is seen in 'Flammenschwert' (Flaming Sword), 'Schwartz' and 'Neubrunner.' It is less easy to distinguish between American and British varieties, though I believe one of the most popular, 'Lord of June', along with 'Empress of India' and 'Shelford Chieftain' were British. During the 1920s and 1930s there must have been at least six nurseries in Britain that specialised in a large collection of *I. germanica* with a selection as large or larger than mine. It would not be fair to say that the American breeders virtually took control, as the British steadily lost interest; but the fact remains that it comes as a surprise to note how many varieties both old and new are listed in *The Plant Finder* as being still available from various British sources. Some stockists may be small or in a semi-professional way who maintain quantities of each more for love than for profit.

To complete my scanty knowledge and memories of *Iris*, the first improvements of the species *sibirica* were those of British growers, including Amos Perry, who was one of the first to improve the *sibiricas* and who raised and named three if not more apart from 'Perry's Favourite'. In this section too, a welter of new varieties has fairly recently come from America, along with the low-growing, early-flowering section formerly known under *I. pumila*, now specified as *I. chamaeiris*. In appearance they are somewhat like miniature *I. germanica* but lack the range of colour to be seen in these. That almost all *Iris* have such an appeal is not surprising and not for nothing were they termed the 'poor man's orchid'. Even so, I do not grow many in my garden for the simple but personal reason that their glory is so fleeting. In my experience the more highly bred they are, the less free they are to flower, and some of the oldest, along with such types as the ancient 'Fleur de Lys' or *I. florentina*, make a brave, reliable display.

What might be said to be the most sumptuous of all *Iris* is the Japanese *I. kaempferi*. It comes not only with large, fairly open flowers, but occurs in a variety of colours but mainly whites, blues and pinks. The Japanese began breeding them in the seventeenth century (as they did with chrysanthemums and paeonias) and improvements are still emerging. They are less easy to grow than most other iris, needing as they do enough but not too much moisture and a somewhat acid soil. From time to time British specialist firms have offered a range, but their inherent lack of adaptability has limited demand even for the very fine mixed Higo Strain.

# James Kelway

The old established firm of Kelway has produced a notable range of easy-to-grow iris, intermediate between the various types of iris, akin to *I. germanica*. All have the prefix name Langport attached to the 14 named varieties. This first reference to the Kelway nursery brings in two other genera for the record of breeders and the hybrids they produced. Perhaps it is strictly incorrect to use the term hybrid. Breeding by selection from a species which held an inherent tendency for variation from seed is not truly a hybrid – a term which usually indicates that differing parents are used to make a cross. James Kelway was a leading professional in the first 25 years of this century. His venture into paeonias began earlier, for these are amongst the slowest hardy plants to propagate. Seedlings take up to five years to produce flowers and if crossing or selecting from a batch of seedlings, as I did with heucheras, in hopes of an improvement or interesting variation, then several more years would be needed to have sufficient stock for sale; to propagate them by division is a skilled art. James Kelway probably worked upon what were the best of those already in existence, many of which were of French origin raised during the middle 1800s.

The Americans were also old-time breeders but such as 'Duke of Wellington', 'Lord Kitchener', 'Lady Duff', along with 'James Kelway', were doubtless English. I grew about 30 varieties for sale in 1939, but Kelway's, Artindale's and one or two other firms offered many more, as well as those grown in quantity in permanent beds for the cut-flower market. Kelway's continued breeding for several years after James Kelway died leaving no heir to carry on, but the tradition as paeony specialists has carried on under the present ownership of John Lloyd, even if most new varieties seen in Britain are of American origin. One leading French specialist in paeony breeding was the firm of Lemoine.

Another Kelway speciality was the pyrethrum now classified for no practical reason as *Chrysanthemum coccineum*. It was not difficult to breed these nor so long a process as in the case of paeonias. They had inherent variability and indeed will in no way come true to the variety or colour from which the seed is collected. Plants from seed will, if well tended, flower within a year and propagate freely from basal cuttings or division in early spring. With a brisk demand in the then expanding outlets for cut-flower growers, James Kelway concentrated mainly on single-flowered pyrethrums. One of his first reds took his name, followed by the pink 'Agnes Mary Kelway'. There may have been others, but inevitably as I was not concerned with other than growing them for sale in the early days, I had no reason to trace the origin of all 40 or so varieties I stocked. Kelway's 'Glorious' was a latecomer, but it became the most popular crimson red after its first appearance in the late 1930s. By then competition was hotting up.

# Herbert Robinson

Herbert Robinson of Hinckley began breeding pyrethrums soon after the First World War. He too concentrated on the market potential for cutting which demanded strong stems and large flowers. His first, 'Eileen May Robinson', *circa* 1925, was a winner in every sense, and with its clear pink flowers became more widely grown than any other. 'Harold Robinson' and 'Scarlet Glow', the first a darker shade of red than the second, followed and 'Sam Robinson' came later as a deeper pink than 'Eileen May'. Last of all was 'Crimson Emperor', but for some reason it never became widely grown in spite of its very large flower and very deep colour. I suspect two probable reasons, one being that during the 1950s when it was launched, flower growing for market was on the decline and secondly, there appeared a disease which affected some stocks, making them lose vigour in growth and flowering capacity – which decimated those I had bred in the 1950s.

The French nursery of M. Cayeaux had, like Kelway's, bred pyrethrums as well as paeonias. The name is represented in 'Yvonne Cayeaux', the only double I knew having a hint of creamy yellow. 'La Vestalle' was also double, shell pink, whilst 'Triomphe de Paris' was a carmine-red double. The largest double red was and still remains 'J.N. Twerdy' and although I tried to trace its origin, it remained obscure. Here I can confess that the single-flowered 'Bressingham Red' was so named at the request of the man who raised it – Mr R.O. Walker of Leeming Bar, Yorkshire. To trace the origin of cultivar names along with the people many of them commemorate would be a very tedious task. Those nursery-raised plants bearing a family name were naturally a useful means of publicity which I also have adopted. Unlike some such as Perry and Kelway perhaps, I have restricted such names to real people and have not indulged in Latinising a name for a cultivar as if it were a species. Kelway's did so with *Anthemis* 'Kelwayi' and *Campanula* 'Hallii' was the name chosen by its raiser Alva Hall in the 1920s.

The most inept such name occurred when an improved *Scabiosa caucasica* was distributed under the name 'Goldingensis'. It originated in the village of Fordham, between Newmarket and Ely, where both my parents were raised.

A Mr Golding was one of many flower growers there and having worked up a stock of a seedling he had selected, the time came when he had no more planting space and a surplus stock. Having jealously and zealously kept it to himself for years, he was in a quandary. Not trusting any other growers he went to the village schoolmaster for advice and Mr Mallinson obliged. By suggesting it should bear a Latin name based on Golding, plants could be sold far and wide and so obviate local competition. And so it was, but Mr Mallinson was probably not aware that a cultivar should not pretend to be a species, though he should have known as a schoolmaster that 'ensis' is the Latin suffix for a place, not for a person.

## Isaac House

*Scabiosa* 'Goldingensis' made some impact amongst cut-flower growers but not for long, because the first results of a specialist breeder were about to emerge. Isaac House of Westbury on Trym was a true plantsman and very deliberately set out to improve his favourite flower now that its value for cutting was being appreciated, as did Herbert Robinson with pyrethrums a little earlier. Just as 'Eileen May Robinson' came first and remained a star variety, so too did *Scabiosa caucasica* 'Clive Greaves'. Both are still standards for both have a robust constitution. Many other scabiosas followed, some from Isaac House including his own namesake, but very few have stood the test of time. I listed eleven in my 1939 catalogue but 40 years later there are only two in good supply – the blue 'Clive Greaves' and the white 'Miss Willmott'. I can but surmise that this lady, who at one time employed 90 gardeners on her private estate, was the actual raiser. If this was so, then it pre-dates even S. 'Goldingensis'. At a guess I would say that at least 30 selected scabious bore cultivar names, hailed at the time of their emergence as distinct or improved. Now I have but three or four others as garden groups and none so thrifty as 'Clive Greaves'. That only ten named hybrids are listed in the *Plant Finder* confirms the belief that despite popularity as garden plants, the eclipse of the cut-flower industry has a considerable bearing on scarcity, plus some weakness due to over-breeding, because the oldest introductions retain more vigour than the more recent ones. Much has yet to be learned in the field of plant genetics and pathology.

Isaac House was also credited with breeding *Dianthus* of the 'Garden Pinks' types. He introduced 'White Ladies' as an improvement on the old 'Mrs Sinkins' raised in 1868. It certainly had longer stems and was purer white, but although it is still around, Mrs Sinkins is still a favourite due to its strong perfume. There are scores of named pinks still in existence, some having been introduced generations ago. In recent years there has been an upsurge of interest in them and thanks to such collectors and producers as Sophie Hughes of Monmouthshire, plants are now available in great variety from her and one or two other specialists. The pre-eminent specialist in dianthus of the pink or carnation type was the firm of Allwood's. Montague Allwood made a cross between the two and 'Allwoodii' has become justly famous. The marriage brought longer stems to garden pinks and a longer flowering period as well as larger flowers and more colour variety on to *Dianthus plumarius* – the 'pink' species. This legacy of the latter was a neater growth and more sturdy constitution. The first 'Allwoodii' came out about 1920 if not before and almost ever since occasional new ones have appeared. Most, if not all, carry girls' names and the rich double-pink 'Doris', raised I believe in the 1950s, has sold in its thousands every year. A favourite of mine is 'Susan' which I first saw and grew in 1923. It is pink with a crimson centre. The firm Douglas of Bookham, Surrey are top specialists and it could be said that the family, excluding the smaller, alpine types, has been a favourite subject for breeders for at least 250 years, and several are still in cultivation somewhere. The doubles were generally favourite, but some singles such as 'Brympton Red' and the speckled 'Constance Finnis' (raised by that fine plantswoman Valerie Finnis) are very good garden plants. It comes as some surprise to find that the up-to-date edition of the *Plant Finder* lists nearly 700 dianthus in existence and these are known to be still available from growers who now cater for those who love them.

The alpine types of dianthus must come under a different heading, where breeders have worked much more recently than is the case with many border perennials. But sweet williams (*D. barbatus*) are neither alpine nor true perennials. What we know as sweet williams were bred about 1740 and were named after William, Duke of Cumberland, who brutally crushed the Jacobite Rebellion headed by Bonnie Prince Charlie. Other green-leaved dianthus hybrids are more perennial though needing frequent rejuvenation by cuttings. I have had and lost more than once 'Flandria', 'Prince Bismarck' and 'Napoleon III' – both the latter names indicate that they were bred a long time ago.

Of the two nations represented by these names, the Germans have been much more active over the past 100 years or so in breeding perennial plants. Karl Foerster and Georg Arends stand out as the leading German breeders but before recording what I know of their achievements, I must insert two non-climbing clematis raised in France. 'Crépescule' and 'Cote d'Azur' are cultivars of *C. davidiana*, itself a sub-species and possibly a hybrid of *C. heracleifolia*. Both have bright-blue hyancinth-like flowers on deep-rooting bushy plants. They were introduced about 1900.

## George Arends

Georg Arends set up a nursery at Ronsdorf, high up in the Ruhr district of Germany in the 1880s. Twenty years or so later he came out with a range of hybrids, astilbes under the name *A. × arendsii*. It was the result of crossing not just two species, but four, *A. davidii*, *A. japonica*, *A. astiboides* and *A. thunbergii*. As could be expected, their progeny were very varied in height, habit and colour, from white to pink and deep red. Many of the original batch are still grown, but since they emerged in 1907 there have been several more and the dwarf *A. simplicifolia* has also been used as a parent. I first went to see the Ronsdorf nursery in 1952 when it had passed to his equally talented son. Herr Arends told me that many a bomb had caused vast damage during the war but he bore no grudges. He was in fact an Anglophile, having spent some years on the Reuthe nursery at Keston, Kent before returning to Germany.

I was greatly impressed by the man and the work he was still practising in a none too hospitable climate 800 feet above sea level. He did me the honour of asking me to introduce to

Britain three first-rate plants which he had raised and that had barely survived the bombing. *Sedum* 'Autumn Joy' (translated from Herbstfreude), *Sedum* 'Ruby Glow' and *Hydrangea* 'Preziosa'. Of the 37 *Astilbe* cultivars in the present Arends catalogue 33 were raised at Ronsdorf. My third visit was in 1987. Herr Arends had died some years before, but after a long struggle to save the nursery his daughter and grand-daughter had fully made good a period of unavoidable neglect. New hybrids are again emerging. I would say that no other continental hardy-plant nursery has developed and distributed so many hybrids of value in so wide a range. This range includes five bergenias – two of which, 'Abendglut' and 'Silberlicht' gained the RHS Award of Merit. Two of the others, the cherry-pink 'Morgonrote' and the white 'Abend-glocken' are still listed by some nurseries though 'Purpur-glocken' seems to have vanished.

Herr Arends also raised many other good hardy plants. There were the hardy chrysanthemums 'Citrus', 'Goldbronze' and 'Sioux' and at least one erigeron, 'Wuppertal', all are now gone. Also five eryngiums, *E. alpinum* 'Amethyst' and 'Opal' and under what is now called *E. × zabellii* were 'Jewel', 'Robusta' and 'Violetta'. 'Opal' and 'Robusta, seem to have gone.

As well as introducing two standard phlox, 'Leo Schlageter' and 'Paul Hoffman', now gone, Arends crossed *P. divaricata* with *P. paniculata* and produced 'Anja' (reddish purple), 'Hilde' (lavender with a pink eye) and 'Susanne' (white with a red eye), all long flowering and very dwarf. These have all but died out in Britain but are again being used for hybrid-ising on the Continent.

Other good plants from Georg Arends included *Geum* 'Werner Arends', *Hosta sieboldiana* 'Elegans', *Kniphofia* 'Express', *Trollius* 'Alabaster', three *Primula denticulata* in different shades, alpine phlox, five different *Saxifraga × arendsii*, alpine and border sedums, as well as the well-known *Campanula poscharskyana* 'Stella'. Even this list is incomplete.

## Karl Foerster

Karl Foerster has become somewhat legendary as a plants-man, yet his range of hybrids was less wide than that of Georg

Arends. His nursery was at Dahlem, near Berlin and was established after the First World War. Being situated behind the Iron Curtain made for remoteness and many of his cultivars came to Britain via West German and Dutch nurserymen. Whereas most of Arends's introductions came and stayed to grace British gardens, Karl Foerster was so prolific that relatively few of his did so. I invested in several of his heleniums and heliopsis, but so many proved to be so much alike that one tended to be sceptical. He introduced for example about eight new heliopsis, but one species *H. scabra* produced only one colour and so many yellow varieties were rather superfluous. Asters, delphiniums, chrysanthemums, phlox and veronicas, as well as some ferns and grasses, were Foerster's main subjects for hybridising, but he was an undoubted authority revered and admired. To my regret I did not meet him personally and since his death at the age of 95 his work still lives on to a large extent.

Some very good garden plants had their origin in Germany and many have become standard varieties in Britain. That perennials are widely popular is proved by the number of specialist nurseries with a very wide range. It is I believe true to say that more new and varied cultivars have been raised in Germany over the past 30 years than in Britain or elsewhere. Some of them in my opinion have been named and introduced with too little discrimination, and have been from already popular genera such as asters, phlox, heleniums. On the credit side several new forms of grasses have shown improvements, notably *Stipa*, *Miscanthus* and *Deschampsea* as well as a few *Polystichum* ferns. Some of these were bred by Karl Foerster but a few other names are outstanding. In this context their names must be restricted, but the catalogues of Arends, Klose, Pagels, Kayser and Seibert and the very full one of Countess von Zeppelin von Stein are worth studying. Heinze Hagemann of Hannover is another specialist in perennials who has produced hybrids. I doubt, however, whether one of his most outstanding introductions is in this category. The fully double *Doronicum* 'Spring Beauty' (Fruhlingspracht) is a sport – a spontaneous break. All other doronicums are single flowered.

Although this diversion to include German hybridists is scantily dealt with, there would have been a gap had I kept strictly to British sources of hardy perennials. It would be a large gap indeed to have mentioned only British raisers of *Phlox paniculata* when probably more than half of those grown in Britain were introductions from continental Europe. German, Dutch and French have all contributed. Since 1945 those of British origin have been predominant in British gardens. The *Plant Finder* lists a mere 89 names of those available from various British sources and most of them are of British or American origin. My 1939 catalogue offers 91 and the 1958 edition 94. These statistics need to be explained more fully, for the 1989 catalogue contains but 21 cultivar names. I am quite sure that if a complete list of phlox which have been on offer in Britain over the past 60 years or so appeared it would amount to around 400. I am equally sure that I could pick out from such a list 300 at least that I have grown at one period or another. Over the years there has been a decline in the proportion of foreign-raised plants not entirely due to home-bred kinds being superior or to patriotism, but to clever advertising. I can but briefly and inadequately mention the early breeders, but it is fairly certain that the French began to develop *P. paniculata* (then known as *P. decussata*) at least a century ago. Early in the 1900s the firm of Fairbairn from near Carlisle came out with a range, including the still popular violet-purple 'Border Gem'. H.J. Jones, who also raised some new delphiniums, worked on phlox in the 1920s, but it was again James Baker of Wolverhampton who blazened a whole new range called the Symons-Jeune Phlox. Captain B. Symons-Jeune was a landscape gardener, but claimed to have put new blood into the race by deliberate hybridising. Larger trusses of flowers and sturdier growth were the attributes, but as a mere grower I could see very little sign that they were such a breakthrough, and I certainly had ample variety for comparison. But with a colour catalogue and massive displays at shows, they sold in great numbers over a period of several years after the Second World War.

Here I must go back a little to 1944 when Mr Fred Simpson of Otley, Yorks, invited me to see what he had bred, firstly in Korean Chrysanthemums and secondly his selection of new phlox he was raising. He had hoped that I would launch them for him as soon as stocks were large enough. The Otley

Korean Chrysanthemums were thereabouts ready in sufficient quantities, but I was still up to the neck in my wartime job of land reclamation and farming so I had to decline and they too came under the Baker banner. I am not sure who launched the phlox for it took place during my interlude in Canada. Incidentally, Fred Simpson was in no position to launch either himself due to the limitations imposed by age and space.

He gave the phlox names of famous, mostly Royal residences – 'Windsor', 'Balmoral', 'Sandringham', 'Barnwell', 'Glamis', 'Holyrood', 'Hampton Court', 'Harewood' and 'Marlborough', and most of them are still around, as well as 'Otley Choice' and 'Otley Purple'. So it is that the overall list has proliferated, and in addition there have been several introduced from abroad. One which is still outstanding is 'Spitfire', but it first came from Germany in the late 1930s as 'Frau Alfred von Malthner'.

Here I should explain why I used to grow so many phlox and other cultivars of popular genera. It was largely because as a wholesale-only producer many of my retailing customers listed what they considered the best. Whether they bought from me to replenish their own stocks, or to meet their own particular demand, my list had to cover all possible requirements as well as new varieties which I grew and offered in order to keep up to date. Deletions from my range could only be made if orders for certain varieties fell and it became uneconomic to continue growing them. Nowadays, at Bressingham we grow as many or more acres of phlox than 30 years ago, but in far less variety. It is worth noting, however, that a few very old ones have gone back into production because they and not some of the more modern ones have not only stood the test of time but still stand out for colour. Two, for example, the suffused pink 'Jules Sandeau' and the clear pink 'Rijnstroon' were amongst the first I ever grew 65 years ago.

The dwindling popularity over the past 25 years of what were the most popular hybrids, i.e. michaelmas daisies, delphiniums, lupins and phlox has been offset not only by a greater interest in other genera, but by a resurgent demand for previously neglected species. Here again my 1939 catalogue highlights the change-over in what could be called the fashion in plants. The three genera in question are hemerocallis, hostas and hardy geraniums. Very few of the latter have come in recent years as hybrids, but whereas I listed but three in 1939 including the hybrid 'Russell Prichard', now there are over 30 and the *Plant Finder* lists well over 100, though this includes alpine types. The species still predominate but several good hybrids or improvements on a species have been introduced in recent years. I doubt if more than a very few have been deliberate crosses, but I do know of one such. It was the Revd Folkard, vicar of a Fenland village who invited me to see his work, but the one named 'Ann Folkard' was the most interesting. It was a cross between the trailing *G. procurrens* and the bushy *G. armenum* (*G. psilostemon*), and though it makes a wide summer spread with an abundance of golden-green foliage, the base plant is clumpy. The colour of the cup-shaped flowers is vivid purple red – a telling contrast for many weeks.

The cultivar 'Russell Prichard' was also a deliberate cross and it reminds me of Russell Prichard's father, one of the foremost plantsmen in the first half of this century. Maurice Prichard of Riverslea Nursery, Christchurch, had a very wide knowledge of both hardy perennials and alpines and his talents as a hybridist covered many genera from border perennials to the choice *Kabschia* and *Engleria Saxifragas*. He was a kindly, generous man but sadly none of his three sons took to the business and the nursery went to ruin a few years after its founder's death in the early 1950s. Incidentally, it was Prichard's who supplied me with twelve hybrid potentillas for ten shillings in 1922 when at 16 my urge to collect plants had just begun.

Here again mention should be made of early French ventures into hybridising which for some reason lapsed after a few years. I still possess some of those richly coloured cultivars and the names 'Arc en Ciel', 'Mons. Rouillard', 'Glorie de Nancy' and 'Flambeau' are indicative of their origin. It must have been a Frenchman who raised *Nepeta grandiflora* 'Souvenir d'Andre Chaudron' and indeed I acquired it from Barbier et Cie of Orleans in 1927. It grew rapidly but I lost it during the war period for it does best if replanted frequently. In 1950 I saw what I believed to be a new one of this type in an American catalogue, but discovered on growing it that the name had been changed to 'Blue Beauty' for simplicity's sake.

For the two other genera to enjoy belated popularity, hemerocallis and hostas, the Americans are largely responsible. In 1934 I listed only eight of the 'Day Lilies' and only two hostas – then under the old name of *Funkia*. Such is the demand now that nearly two pages are taken up with them in our illustrated retail catalogue. With recent trials of new ones we topped 200 kinds – practically all of them hybrids raised in America by both amateurs and professionals. Scores of new ones are registered every year by the American Hosta Society. The first hybrid however was raised over a century ago in England and is still in demand. Its name is 'Thomas Hogg', and the Surrey nursery under that name is still in existence.

I would like to think that the late Eric Smith was ahead of the Americans as a hybridist. Whilst working for Hilliers of Winchester and later as a partner in the short-lived firm of The Plantsmen in Dorset, he was hybridising both hostas and helleborus and kindly sent me some for trial in the early 1960s. With such a subject as hostas in which the leaves are if anything more important than the flowers, Eric Smith's aim was to develop bluish-leaved hybrids as well as pleasing variations. I have no knowledge of what parents he may have used, but of the dozen or so cultivars he raised and named few have been surpassed and 'Halcyon' is particularly popular; and I am fairly certain that the American enthusiasts used them for further development. Perhaps they are raising so many new ones that they also vie with one another to give them outlandish names; and such names as 'High Fat Cream', 'Big Daddy' and 'Fringe Benefit' stamp their place of origin. One professional breeder called Paul Aden tends to boast over such names, which he has chosen for some queer reason of his own.

Much the same story applies to hemerocallis which name is less used in America than 'Day Lily'. The first breeders were Europeans and in England Amos Perry and George Yeld were pioneers, working on relatively few of the 15 or so species which make up the genus. Although adaptability and reliability are a great asset, as with most hostas, hemerocallis also have excellent foliage to complement the flowers. The hybridists have expanded the colour range and combination enormously, and it is no wonder that they have become so well known and established as good garden plants. One wonders, however, whether with so much breeding taking place in both these subjects they will become vulnerable to the attacks of some unexpected virus, as happened with lupins and some michaelmas daisies. So far, there is little sign of any infection, but meddling with the natural processes of evolution – trying to beat Mother Nature at her own game – is often in a sense provocation leading to adversity.

## Achillea

My memory runs dry on the raisers of some perennials but a few lesser-known people must be included along with at least some of the plants they introduced, mainly from genera not so far mentioned. For this the alphabetical order of plants is adopted beginning with *Achilleas*. Some have been mentioned already, but not 'Coronation Gold'. It was raised by Miss Pole of Lye End near Woking, named to mark the Coronation in 1953. This too as a bushier, less tall form of *A. filipendulina* is still widely available. Not so Miss Pole's *A.* 'Lye End Lemon', a hybrid of *A. millefolium*. Although quite distinct it fell short of being lemon yellow, but is more of a creamy primrose shade in its flattish heads. One other of this devoted lady's hybrids was a deep-pink *Aster novae angliae*, also with the Lye End name. I may have overlooked one or two more of her introductions but I must not fail to mention her successful endeavours to keep the Hardy Plant Society alive. She followed me as Chairman, which position I had held since initiating its formation in 1957. By about 1960 I felt its amateur members should play a more active part in running the Society – as eventually they did.

## Aconitum

Next comes the *Aconitum*. The name 'Newry Blue' applies to a cultivar of *A. napellus* raised by Tom Smith of Daisy Hill Nursery, Newry, Northern Ireland. It reminds me of the wide range of plants he grew and listed 50 years or more ago. 'Newry Blue' is still a more or less standard variety but the trollius to which his name was given seems to have gone. It was a good clear yellow, but as with heliopsis, a large number of introductions all having the same basic colour inevitably led to some being put aside. Reverting to aconitums, a Mr Barker of Kelmscott, near Ipswich, worked on the tall late-flowering *A. autumnale*. He probably made crosses also with *A. carmichaelii*, though 'Barker's Variety' and 'Kelmscott' lack the vigour of that species. They have rich violet-blue hooded flowers on 1·5–1·8 m spikes. I prefer Georg Arends's *A.* × *arendsii* with its massed display of amethyst-blue flowers at 1·05 m for September-October.

## Agapanthus

The present popularity of *Agapanthus* is in great measure due to Lewis Palmer of Headbourne, Hampshire. For many years he tried out various forms and species for hardiness, as well as making crosses. The Headbourne Hybrids as a mixed strain came as a most valuable addition to the range of hardy plants, which scarcely existed before. No one that I knew of grew agapanthus prior to 1940 except as specimen patio plants in tubs to be taken indoors over winter. At first I used to cover open-ground plants with litter, but some were missed out in the harsh 1963 winter when soil froze deeply. They survived as well as those that had been protected. Several new varieties have been named, but as with those I have introduced they are not the result of more hybridising but selected Headbourne seedlings.

## Bergenia

Bergenias were considered 50 years ago as not worth growing except where little else would survive. My 1939 wholesale catalogues listed none, for there was no demand; but by degrees they came in a few years later during the 'ground cover, trouble free' period. It was then found that some, given a fair chance would fit in as both flowering and foliage. New freer-flowering hybrids were raised both in Britain and abroad. One of the first was 'Delbees', a cross between *B. delavayi* and *B. purpurascens*. It was raised by whoever ran the Ballawley Garden near Dublin and although a tall, untidy grower (later named 'Ballawley') it has near red flowers.

Mr. H.G. Pugsley an amateur hybridist introduced several new ones in the 1960s, samples of which he sent to me for trial and one of which he named 'Bressingham Bountiful'. Another was named in honour of Margery Fish and his own name went to 'Pugsley's Pink', but none of them were outstanding. Several others, some of British origin but mainly from Germany, have come to give a wide selection. At Bressingham we grow about 20 but the Klose catalogue lists over 30.

# Erigeron

As with so many popular genera, the erigerons have attracted breeders in various countries. I wish I knew who raised 'Quakeress' for it is one of the oldest hybrids and is still one of the most reliable as well as being a pleasing shade of lilac-pink. The name of one I no longer grow, 'Mrs F.H. Beale', reminds me of Maxwell and Beale in Dorset, whose great speciality was heathers, and I dimly remember Mr Beale as a portly, jovial partner in another firm which no longer exists. Another to close down was that of Ladham's of Shirley, near Southampton. *Erigeron* 'B. Ladham's' was one of the most popular and distinctive 60 years ago, very free flowering, which was rare at the time. Though I still listed it in 1939, it seems to have disappeared entirely. In 1925 when I was propagator for R.V. Roger of Pickering, I remember lining-out over 7,000 rooted pieces in a frame to meet the brisk demand. *E.* 'Merstham Glory' was one of the few cultivars raised and named by the then leading firm of Wells, already mentioned in connection with Korean Chrysanthemums.

Ernest Ladham broke away from the parent firm to set up a nursery at Elstead, Surrey. He was a clever grower as well as a breeder and came out not only with the dwarf *Erigeron* 'Elstead Pink' but the tall, late-flowering *Cimicifuga* 'Elstead White' and I fancy one or two other hybrids that escape my memory. As a youngster I was warned that I needed to be very alert if dealing with this Mr Ladham. Many post-war improvements have been made to hybrid erigerons, but some of them including the near double pink 'Foerster's Liebling', are now suffering from what appears to be a virus.

# Eryngium

That fine plantsman Leslie Stringer of Donard, Co. Down, raised a very charming form of *Eryngium alpinum* which has not been surpassed. In very recent years a new range bred mainly from *E. alpinum* and *E. tripartitum* has come from abroad. One from the continent, named 'Calypso', has variegated leaves but because neither root cuttings nor seed will perpetuate this feature, it has to be produced from tissue culture.

# Helianthus

In helianthus, like heliopsis, the species are all in yellows. *H. multiflorus* have produced the best by far, making stout bushes up to 1·5 m with a long profusion of single, semidouble and fully double flowers. The most popular of the doubles is 'Loddon Gold' and I must assume that Thomas Carlisle raised it at about the same time as his tall pinkish *Campanula lactiflora* 'Loddon Anna'. This would be in the 1930s and it was then that two very different *Helianthus* were first launched. The flowers were single but large and of a rich yellow, but the roots were inclined to wander invasively, as with one with even larger flowers, 'Monarch'. Those I saw for the first time on an exhibit from Bees of Chester were close on 15 cm in diameter, but not so when the plants I acquired flowered on my nursery with a disappointingly, ungainly habit. It was puzzling, until I learned that for shows, Bees disbudded the flowers to make them remain large. As for its tendency to run below ground, this was such a nuisance that after a few years I threw it out, having done so previously in the case of the old *H. regidus* 'Miss Mellish', for the same reason. Such invasiveness, I felt, was not fair to pass on to unsuspecting customers. Two other good cultivars of the more worthy *Helianthus multiflorus* bear the names 'Capernock Star' and 'Supreme', as anemone-centred and semidouble to go with the full double of 'Loddon Gold'.

# Papaver

Unlike peonias, most papavers, the Oriental Poppies that were popular 50 years ago, seem to have been replaced by a new range of cultivars. Of the 20 cultivars I listed in 1939, only one is in the 1989 catalogue. This is 'Beauty of Livermere', but over that period I had in fact been growing it under a different name. Having lost nearly all during the war period, I did not set about restocking with full endeavour till 1950 on my return from Canada. With only four papavers, one named 'Goliath' was included in several more I purchased for stock. It was a fine, upstanding blood red, and became a favourite. Years later a gardening correspondent suggested sending me a plant for trial of 'Beauty of Livermere' as the very best of all reds. I had forgotten its appearance, but having accepted a trial plant, it proved to be identical to 'Goliath'. Papavers call for no special skills in breeding and this no doubt is responsible for a dozen or more new introductions in recent years, several hailing from America.

## Pulmonaria

Pulmonarias have come in for more attention in recent years. Margery Fish was one of their champions but likely as not, one of her many friends and admirers named a new variety with silvery mottled leaves in memory of her. Another was named 'Highdown' from the garden of the author of *The Chalk Garden*, Mr F.C. Stern. Mr Mawson, once expert rock and landscape gardener, also raised one which is the excellent but rarely seen 'Mawson's Variety'. Incidentally, he was responsible also for a very good salmon-pink papaver named 'Jenny Mawson'.

## Schizostylis

*Schizostylis*, the Kaffir Lily, consists of one species only, but the *Plant Finder* lists 13 variations of it. I doubt very much if any are other than sports or natural breaks in which seed has played no part. Two that I introduced occurred by this means – a different colour appearing singly, or here and there in a batch at flowering time. I named a large-flowered red 'Major' and the pink was 'November Cheer'.

## Sidalcea

Sidalceas are in somewhat the same category as papavers, for having a brief stay on earth. Of the 16 cultivars listed in *The Plant Finder* only six were in my 1939 range of 15. One of the oldest hybrids still in existence, a favourite light pink, is named after a famous gardening cleric who lived near Diss, the Revd Page Roberts, but 'Sussex Beauty' appears to be lost. As a genus, seedlings from existing cultivars need no cross-pollination to produce variations.

## Solidago

True hybridising certainly took place when a Mr Walkden brought out a range of new *Solidago* hybrids in the 1940s. He used as one parent what had been known as *Solidago missouriensis*, but is now *Solidaster lutens*. The new name indicates that it is itself a by-generic hybrid. For the other parent Mr Walkden may well have used existing cultivars, but his aim was to reduce height which was the fault of several 'Golden Rods'. He succeeded in this and in addition produced larger flower heads, and one of the first was an instant success – 'Golden Mosa'. This was followed by 'Golden Shower', 'Golden Falls', 'Golden Gates' and then he switched to names all beginning with Le – 'Leraft', 'Lemore' and 'Lena'. As a nurseryman Mr Walkden had been one of my customers – as were most other professionals mentioned already, but having retired from business whilst still breeding solidagos, he distributed his new varieties without charge. As a result of Walkden's work and of some different short-growing solidagos from Germany, the older ungainly and often invasive types such as 'Golden Wings' have been eclipsed.

## Alpines

My notes on hardy perennials and those concerned with raising new cultivars have been somewhat sketchy and far from complete. Although what we know as alpines are themselves hardy perennials, it would have been an even less orderly record had I included them. For one thing, I myself was less intimate with alpines and those who brought out new ones, even though in 1939 I grew about 200,000 in pots in a fairly wide range. Another reason for separating the two in this book is that a considerable number of true alpines were raised by keen amateurs. As a wholesale producer I did not exhibit at flower shows and my preference for perennials kept me rather out of touch with happenings in the realm of alpines. As with most specialist nurseries, many of the pre-war names are now but a memory. My acquaintance with them was scanty and with amateur hybridists it was virtually non-existent.

To record what I know or remember about alpines must be mainly alphabetical since it has proved somewhat impractical to base it on the personalities involved. One of the best-ever selling alpines goes to the credit of Miss Ellen Willmott. *Aethionema* 'Warley Rose' has been a best seller since the early 1920s and is one of several distinct hybrids which take her name in a broad spectrum or that of her vast garden at Warley Place. *Campanula* 'Warleyensis', *Epimedium* × *warleyense*, a *Potentilla* and a *Campanula* 'Miss Willmott' with a similarly named *Parahebe*, along with *Ceratostigma willmottianum* are still well known.

It is with a peculiar though slight sense of shame that I have to record that my 1939 catalogue contained no less than 39 cultivars of *Aubrieta* to name. And as a matter of interest, the cost of a collection of 100 plants in ten varieties, carriage paid, was 28 shillings (£1.40). Several are still in cultivation as the *Plant Finder* with its 63 varieties indicates.

Maurice Prichard is one of the few names of professionals to name new varieties, but the once famous alpine specialist Clarence Elliott of Six Hills Nursery, Stevenage, raised 'Carnival' and 'Vindictive'. His nursery was swallowed up by Stevenage New Town, but his son Joe carried on for several years at Broadwell, Glos. To the Elliotts, credit goes for *Armeria* 'Vindictive', *Penstemon* 'Six Hills', some choice primulas and saxifragas to mention just those which come readily to mind. Clarence was a man of forthright opinions, autocratic to those not privileged to know his very different real personality.

Mr Barker of Kelmscott who bred some tall, late aconitums was also the first to produce a double-flowered *Aubrieta* named 'Barker's Double', a violet purple. It came out as a novelty in the late 1930s and was followed by others with the

Kelmscott name. Since then, doubtless from seed of the Barker Varieties, more doubles have appeared – including two that I named – but they lack the vigour of the single flowered. One of the latter, 'Dr Mules', of remote and unknown origin, is a good deep blue and remains as vigorous and popular as ever. The deepest red shades such as 'Russell Vincent' (Prichard) and 'Mrs Rodewald' have also languished and I believe died out.

Campanulas, ranging in height as they do from 1·5 m to 5 cm have yielded a fair number of hybrids. One of the dwarfest species, *C. cochlearifolia* (formerly *C. pusilla*) has provided about eight named cultivars, one or two of which are true hybrids from the crossing with other species. One came out under the invalid name of 'Hallii', a white raised by Alva Hall of Harrogate. He advertised it quite widely as a startling new break 60 years or so ago, but it was still close to *C. pusilla* and the name of the other parent was not disclosed if I remember rightly. The pale-blue 'Miranda' I fancy was raised by the famous alpine specialist and author Reginald Farrer. *C. carpatica* also has many named cultivars, but as a variable species it is unlikely that any deliberate crossing was involved. This applies also to the taller *C. persicifolia*. The prolific flowering but invasive *C. poscharskyana* was introduced some 50 years ago and a few hybrids have emerged which are much more to be desired. It was Georg Arends who raised *C.* × 'Stella' by using *C. garganica* for the other parent. 'Stella' is clump forming with long sprays of starry blue flowers. It has the added virtue of flowering a second time if cut hard back when fading, and I have tempted it to flower under glass in winter by potting it in September. Other cultivars of somewhat similar habit but paler in colour have come under the names 'Glandore' and 'Lisduggan', pointing to an Irish source.

The very well-known alpine specialist Will Ingwersen, one of my oldest friends, produced a different type, but using the very reliable *C. portenschlagiana* (*muralis*) instead of *C. garganica*. It is named 'Birch Hybrid' but little of the *C. poscharskyana* is noticeable in its neat habit and long display of violet blue flowers. Where two species are crossed, it is taxonomically correct or at least permissible to marry their botanic names as well. Jokingly perhaps, Will Ingwersen told me that he had considered naming it *C.* × 'portenscharskyana'.

Only a few alpine dianthus can be mentioned out of the many raised this century. The rich-red form of the green-leaved *D. alpinus* hybrid raised by Joe Elliott is named 'Joan's Blood', presumably with his wife's permission. But Joe has always had a sense of humour to go with his love for alpines. One of the best and brightest, 'Inshriach Dazzler' came from John Lawson, who took over Jack Drake's alpine nursery in Scotland. From there too came the best and deepest pink variation of *Geranium sanguineum* named 'Shepherd's Warning'. Dianthus of all types have intrigued both specialists and dabblers for a very long time – much longer than some of the hybrids have survived. Those of *alpinus* or *neglectus* parentage are amongst the latter, but one such raised by the short-lived Cambridge nursery of Bedford and Page about 1937 named 'Crossways' is still available from one source according to the *Plant Finder*.

It would be an impossible task to trace the origins of the hundreds of hybrid dianthus still in existence. So it would in the case of helianthemums, although probably no more than 100 have been named. Some have been selected from seedlings, but self-sown appearances are not unknown. One such recently named 'Annabel' is a double clear pink sent to me from an amateur who kindly agreed to the name of a baby, lost through cot-death syndrome, who I had been asked to commemorate by a correspondent. 'Marigold' which I raised and named 50 years ago is inexplicably no longer in cultivation. A new range came from Scotland in the 1930s all named after mountains with the prefix Ben. These 14, with a wide range of colour, tended to dominate for several years. All were single flowered and all are still in production.

Lamiums have become popular as good ground coverers and named hybrids of the *L. maculatum* include some with silvery foliage such as 'Beacon Silver'. Another is a good form of the original species named 'Chequers' to be seen in both British and German catalogues and has the distinction of being the only plant emanating from Bressingham that I did not name. It was spotted by our late herbaceous foreman, Bill Green (after whom I named a phlox) in the hedgerow of the lane in which he lived. It is known as Chequers Lane because it adjoins a pub which was formerly known as The Chequers.

Compared with taller kinds of potentillas, very few cultivars of alpine character have been raised. One of the best, *P.* x *tonguei* is itself a hybrid but of obscure origin. This makes lateral sprays of shoots close to the ground with orange, dark-centred flowers. E.B.Anderson once wrote in an RHS booklet that it ought to be classed as a weed but although I find it vigorous, it is not weedy. *P. nitida* however was improved by Sir Jocelyn Gore-Booth of Lissadell in the west of Ireland. Neither 'Alannah' nor 'Lissadell' are startling improvements and mention is made because prior to about 1930 'Lissadell' was almost a place of pilgrimage for alpine enthusiasts. Amongst its attractions were a large rock garden and a wide collection of plants in a natural setting. Several other subjects were developed which all became popular in Britain. They included the Asthore strain of primulas and I believe *P.* 'Red Hugh'. However, when I called there in 1958 the owners had long since gone and the place had become sadly derelict.

Some primulas readily respond to hybridising – none more so than primroses and polyanthus, although the latter have been developed more as strains for bedding rather than colour produced from seed. Occasionally, however, a sterile one appears which if worth while has to be increased by division. Such a one was 'Barrowby Gem', a pure yellow which was introduced by R.V. Roger of Pickering about 1926. It was quite a sensation when exhibited at Chelsea for the first time and became a best seller for other nurseries also. For me, it did not survive the war period and when I was able to stock it again, I found it lacking in vigour and there was never enough to sell. Now it is very rare and the *Plant Finder* gives only one source. That source is David Chalmers of Stonehaven, Scotland, whose firm has raised over a long period a wide variety of primulas, especially of the primrose type in both double and single flowered.

Hundreds of cultivars exist of primroses and auriculas, some of ancient origin. Most of the plant breeders I have mentioned have included primulas of one type or another which they have raised and named, but so have many others including amateurs. A Mr Dalrymple brought out the Bartley strain of 'Candelabra' type. The name 'Bees' crops up in *P. beesiana*, and the founder of the firm, A.K. Bulley is seen in *P. bulleyana*. Both are, I believe, collected species but they were crossed to become the Bullesiana Strain. At the bottom of the height scale is the intriguing little *P.* 'Johanna'. This was a cross by the alpine specialist in Gothenburg Botanic Garden a few years ago. He used as parents two species which I had failed to grow for long in my garden, *P. warshenewskiana* and *clarkei*, but 'Johanna' flourishes and is a joy with its new growth set with 3 cm high flowers of brightest pink in March.

What I have written about primulas is to do little more than touch the surface. Much the same must be the approach to saxifragas, for the range of primulas listed in the *Plant Finder* is above 800 species and cultivars with saxifragas about 500 – all ostensibly still in cultivation in Britain. Some of the choicest saxifragas are scarcely for outdoor culture, but for safety and display are best confined to an alpine house. These are mostly slow growing and silvery leaved, which have yielded hybrids as much if not more by amateurs than by professionals. A few inter-species hybrids have been achieved, a notable case being that of Maurice Prichard's 'Primulaize'. *S. primuloides* is like a small 'London Pride' (*S.* × *urbium*) and the prostrate *S. aizoides*. The result was more appealing than either parent, tiny sprays of deep pink in one form and salmon in another, coming on close green rosettes after most saxifragas have finished.

One of the best dwarf yellow sedums is also a cross between two species. It is 'Weihenstephaner Gold' with *S. kamtschaticum* and *S. middendorfianum* as parents and was raised by Dr Hansen at Weihenstephan. This establishment is a large garden, government backed, designed to stimulate public interest in horticulture in Germany. The majority of hybrid or improved sedums are amongst the late-flowering kinds and in pink or reddish shades. Joe Elliott introduced 'Vera Jameson' while Jim Archibald's 'Sunset Glow' is a neat grower reaching about 30 cm with glistening crimson flowers. A very dwarf one with purplish foliage and prostrate heads of near-crimson flowers is 'Bertram Anderson'. If it was not raised by its namesake, it at least commemorates a very fine amateur plantsman, E.B. Anderson.

As long as I can remember there has always been more than enough sempervivums to make an adequate collection, with hybrids outnumbering the species. Of late there has been another influx of hybrids, mostly from America, to boost the number to over 600. Some may be deliberate crosses but grown together they are promiscuous enough to need no persuasion. Though they have a charm of their own, the selection now is quite bewildering and I must dismiss them from this context with mention of only one. It is S. × *laggeri*, a small cobwebby silver which was the first I acquired as a gift in 1929 – and it is still in my opinion unsurpassed.

Of the 600 or so violas in existence, the vast majority are hybrids. Some resurgence of popularity is to be welcomed and even 'Maggie Mott', so popular 60–70 years ago and so scarce in the 1970s has come back into favour. Only one other entices my comment. The *cornuta-gracilis* type, smaller in growth and flower has produced what I believe is the first really black of good constitution. It is 'Molly Sanderson', which the lady of that name raised in Northern Ireland a few years ago.

# A-Z OF PLANTS RAISED
# BY THE AUTHOR

To be successful in raising and introducing new cultivars of hardy plants the first essential is, in my opinion, to possess a fair knowledge of what are already in existence. Such foreknowledge applies also to the species of any given genus. This is not difficult to acquire if one is, or wishes to become, a specialist in just one or two genera, and given time and continued interest, one's knowledge can widen to cover several. In the course of over 60 years as a specialist nurseryman, I have been able to raise new cultivars from about 40 different genera of perennials and alpines, and the reason why it is vital to have a fairly intimate knowledge of what are already in existence is how to be selective. Anyone can raise from seed subjects likely to show variations, but there would be no point whatever in going on with selections unless they showed distinct improvements in one way or another – e.g. quality of flower and a new break in colour.

It is only through collecting, growing and knowing a wide range of plants that I have become familiar enough with some of them to attempt hybridising. I have no knowledge of modern techniques in which botanical factors such as chromosomes are employed. Many of my introductions have arisen simply by raising seedlings from subjects known or likely to be variable, or in hopes that bees would do the work of cross-pollination. One learns from experience what will never vary from seed, or what may need manipulation in order to encourage a species to do so. Generally, however, true species will breed true, and seed from cultivars will seldom do so, although some have been 'fixed' as in the case for example of *Geums* 'Mrs Bradshaw' and 'Lady Stratheden'.

Hitherto those interested in breeding have concentrated largely on a relatively few genera which happened to respond to improvements or variations. The result has been that in total, thousands of cultivars have emerged. Fashions have changed somewhat and attention in the past few decades has switched from delphiniums, iris, michaelmas daisies and phlox to hemerocallis and hostas. With the exception of phlox, I have always felt urged to work away from these front-line subjects in the belief that some less favoured genera would yield garden-worthy new cultivars.

As a nurseryman it has been difficult to cope with the welter of new varieties coming from already popular subjects such as those above. By the time trials have been made in order to propagate only the best for sale, a fresh batch of 'novelties' is introduced by the hybridist so that it is virtually impossible to keep up to date. In recent years some hundreds of new varieties of hemerocallis and hostas have emerged annually from American enthusiasts, making a final selection for those wishing to distribute the most worthy quite bewildering. This factor has strengthened my long-standing resolve to concentrate on subjects which have not been so exploited.

## ACHILLEA

In recording alphabetically the genera which have yielded new cultivars for me, the first is one on which I have never set out to hybridise. Yet *Achillea* 'Moonshine' has proved to be one of the most popular introductions over the past 30 years and it came about almost by default. In the early 1950s when I was keen to build up a wide collection of perennials, I imported a hybrid from a Swiss nursery with a German name meaning sunshine or sunray. It flowered with a deep-yellow head at about 60 cm, but the habit was straggly. Seed was saved, luckily, because the plants died during the first winter. From the seed, which included some from the compact, silver-leaved *A. taygetea*, about 40 young plants grew, but having flowered most of them also died. One to survive was at the end of the row close to an old apple tree and because it had good silvery foliage but had not flowered, I let it stay. It appeared to be very close in form to A. *taygetea* and it stayed for two more years; but still it did not flower and but for having a bare space in one of my island beds, it would have been thrown away. Having divided it into about six pieces, the effect of it now being in full sun was remarkable. Within weeks of planting in March it was in flower with its light-yellow heads shining in the sunlight against its silvery filigree leaves. It was obviously of *taygetea* origin, but was sufficiently different in being more rounded in habit and freer to flower to warrant naming after a further year's trial.

From that one, almost discarded plant, hundreds of thousands of *Achillea* 'Moonshine' have been reared and used in gardens both in Britain and overseas, yet for several years I made no attempt to breed from it. Finally, another cross was made with the species A. *clypeolata*, because in my experience 'Moonshine' tended to become somewhat twiggy if left alone for three or four years, thereby losing some of its evergreen silvery foilage and flowering less freely. This was its only fault, but A. *clypeolata*, though of clumpy habit with a compact base, tended to damp off and die out in wet winters. Its flat heads were a little larger and of a much deeper yellow, and with hopes not very high that something good would come from the cross, a batch of about 20 seedlings was raised.

Having flowered for two years, only one appeared to be worth keeping. It had the erect habit of *clypeolata* and a slightly paler colour than 'Moonshine', at about 50 cm high, but to make quite sure it was reliably perennial, I allowed it to stay undivided for two more years. Then, in 1985, I divided it into five pieces. All lived, and confirmed my belief that it had considerable merit. One quite outstanding feature was the way in which secondary side heads flowered freely as the terminal one began to fade; and that fading did not detract from the overall charm. Its long serrated silvery leaves are not quite evergreen, but are soft and complement the whole. It is now named 'Anthea' after my daughter and stocks are being sufficiently increased to meet the expected demand. Incidentally, 'Anthea' has potential as a cut flower, as has a recently introduced German variety named 'Schwellenberg'. This is an improvement on A. *clypeolata* which it resembles in colour, but is freer to flower at about 45 cm and is reliably perennial. However, all these dwarfer types need to be in full sun and well-drained soil.

## ACONITUM

The aconitums ('Monkshoods') have suffered from neglect, partly I suppose because of their poisonous roots. This stigma applies only if the roots are eaten, and there is no likelihood of this happening inadvertently or otherwise. Not all species produce the little fleshy crowns below ground that are toxic. Some species have quite fibrous roots and this applies to the creamy-white species *A. septentrionale*. It is the earliest to flower, with hooded flowers on 90 cm spikes above abundant greenery. The flowers are, however, rather small and not very effective, but from a batch of seedlings I spotted one with clearer ivory-white flowers and a more upright habit. It gained an Award of Merit when shown at the RHS Hall in the late 1950s, under my name for it, 'Ivorine'.

About the same time two others appeared amongst seed-lings from the cultivar 'Newry Blue' crossed with *A. napellus* 'Bicolor'. The latter has flowers as the name suggests of both blue and white, suffused and very effective. Both parents had the fault of being somewhat lanky, at about 1.2 m. The need I saw was of a stiffer habit, and luckily two seedlings obliged out of a batch of over 100 raised. One which I named 'Bressingham Spire' was much sturdier than 'Newry Blue', with stiffly erect, tapering 1·05 m spikes of violet blue, clothed below with dark glossy-green, fingered leaves. It flowers in August and September and the numerous secondary spikes, although smaller, make for long flowering. It is a splendid subject to complement the many yellow-flowered plants that tend to dominate the late summer scene.

The other selection, which I named 'Blue Sceptre', is at its best in July and August and grows to a very modest 60–75 cm. It has the same stiff habit of 'Bressingham Spire', but the flowers are blue, merging to white on spikes less tapering and very different from the rather loose-branching spikes of 'Bicolor'. The rootstock is a little less vigorous than of most aconitums, but like others responds to fertile soil, not too dry, and all do well in partial shade.

6 I chose 'Gloaming' for this cultivar of *Campanula latifolia*. Its unusual colour keeps it always in demand

7 *Agapanthus* 'Bressingham Blue' was selected as the deepest colour from over 2000 seedlings on trial

8 *Pyrethrum* 'Bressingham Red' was the name suggested by a Yorkshire grower who wished me to launch it

9 *Helenium* 'Coppelia' is not too tall and just the right colour for blending with other colours

## AGAPANTHUS

The popularity of agapanthus has increased enormously since the introduction of Lewis Palmer's 'Headbourne Hybrids' in the 1950s. These South African natives were previously thought to be short of fully hardy and were often in patio tubs to be taken under cover over winter. Mr Palmer raised seedlings from some he had grown in open ground and found those having fairly narrow leaves were hardy, whereas broad-leaved types were less so. This was my experience also, for by 1955 I was already growing a few species in ordinary outdoor conditions. One had been acquired under the name *weillighii*, but a visiting taxonomist told me that it was an invalid name and was in fact a hybrid which needed to have a cultivar name. Being a fairly deep blue I called it 'Isis', and so it has remained. From it, seed was saved to raise large quantities for sale, along with the then new 'Headbourne Hybrids', which it resembled in height and habit. All were fairly consistent in this respect – at 75–90 cm tall – though 'Isis' was a somewhat deeper blue than most of the Head-bournes. These, Lewis Palmer told me, were the result of a long process of selecting seed from species such as *A. mooreanus* having fairly narrow leaves, because they had proved to be the most hardy. The broad-leaved kinds were less able to withstand severe winters when the soil became frozen solid to a depth that damaged their dormant crowns. Although many shades of blue were included in this strain, none were deeper than my 'Isis'.

About 1967 I looked over a bed of 2,000 or so seedlings, row by row, with the intention of marking any that I considered outstanding. Marker sticks were placed in nine plants that were of a deeper blue than any I had ever seen. All appeared to be exactly alike, but the following spring I lifted them to plant undivided, close to my house for further observation, but on flowering a second year they were still all identical to one another.

One has to be patient, and knowing from experience that agapanthus divide more readily when they grow into sizeable clumps, I decided to leave them alone for one more season. It so happened in that summer of 1969 a lady visiting from South Africa asked me if I would be interested in some very deep-blue agapanthus she had, offering to send seed when she returned. Thanking her for the offer, I invited her to see mine, then in full flower. Her eyes widened and with a wry smile she told me that mine were distinctly deeper blue than hers, and naturally the news came as a fillip to me. It took nearly ten years to work up these nine plants to over 1,000 so as to make it a feature, pictured in colour in our catalogue as 'Bressingham Blue'. During the period when stocks were being increased, a Trial of *Agapanthus* cultivars took place at the RHS Wisley Gardens. I decided not to include 'Bressingham Blue' but one of the judges who saw it at Bressingham was quite firm in his opinion that it was a deeper blue than any in the Trial.

The only white-flowered *Agapanthus* I grew at that time (apart from the rather poor *A. umbellatus albus*) was 'White Giant' which I had obtained from the Continent. At 1·2 m it was quite a giant, but I found it rather shy to flower profusely as well as being ungainly. There were, however, a few whites in the large batch from which 'Bressingham Blue' was selected, and one of these was less tall and freer to flower than 'White Giant'. In due course this was introduced as 'Bressingham White'. It is still on the tall side at 90–105 cm, but lacks nothing in vigour and freedom to flower.

Somewhat spasmodically, further batches of seedlings still known as 'Headbourne Hybrids' have been raised. The seed included more recent forms from Lewis Palmer which tended to have larger heads and broader leaves. They proved to be a little less hardy than his earlier selection, at least when young plants, but as they grew into larger clumps they seemed to be more frost resistant. I selected one of the finest, from which to save seed, and three years later picked out one plant outstanding for colour and size of flower head. It was 23–25 cm across and of a glistening rich-blue shade. At the time of writing stocks are still insufficient to launch, keeping to my policy of lifting for division only after two years' growth in one place. All being well, it should be ready for distribution in 1992, and will bear the name 'Bressingham Bounty'. It grows to about 90 cm and is comparatively late flowering.

For several years seed of the late Roland Jackman's 'Liliput' have been raised in hopes of a more vigorous miniature. A. 'Liliput', which might be classified as A. *mooreanus* minus flowers at little more than 30 cm. Its flowers are of a deepish blue dangling from small terminal heads, but it is slow to increase and seems never to make up into a clump large enough to freely divide. Successive seed sowings have yielded only a small proportion of miniatures, the rest being up to twice the height or more and much inferior to such as 'Isis'. Perseverance to produce one with more vigour, or better still a range of miniatures in different shades, may eventually be rewarded and there is little doubt that there would be an eager demand.

## ANEMONE

One of my regrets is that I have never made a serious attempt to hybridise anemones in existence as herbaceous perennials. Someone, I know not who, made a cross to produce A. × *lesseri*. Its upstanding rosy-red flowers on 38 cm stems in early summer suggest the white A. *sylvestris* to be one parent, but a red species for the other exists only in a variant of the related *Pulsatilla*. Be that as it may, I merely set out to produce as near red as possible in the later flowering A. *japonica* or *hupehensis* which grace the August-October period with white and pink flowers on wiry stems. Only a modest reward emerged, for 'Bressingham Glow' is well short of being red. It has, however, full-petalled flowers and is a shade deeper rose-magenta than any I have had or seen. It also has vigour and more basal foliage than most, with flowers on upstanding 60 cm stems. A second, later, selection with somewhat lacy and crinkled foliage was never propagated or named because there was virtually no difference in the flowers. Had they appeared together in the first place I think the latter would have been the one to introduce. In the event it has remained as a clump only a few yards from the back door of my house, but I can see no way of using it as one parent of a ruby-red hybrid.

## ASTER

The most prolific source of hybrid asters has been and still is the *Novi-belgii* group of Michaelmas Daisies. The first came, I believe, from the Hon. Vicary Gibbs at the turn of the century. Later, the most successful breeder was Ernest

Ballard of Colwall, but after 50–60 years of intensive raising and vegetative propagating, a wilting disease took hold, adding to the widespread attacks of mildew. In addition, many new varieties were excessively tall, and the larger flowers were more prone to flop unless supported. It was the need for shorter-stemmed varieties that prompted me to enter this already rather saturated area – to bridge the gap between dwarf *dumosa* types and the 90–120 cm high types. Some success came, but not until michaelmas daisies were losing popularity as a whole for their inherent faults. The first of my selections was named 'Royal Velvet', a violet-purple semi-double growing to barely 60 cm, and the second was a deep red called 'Royal Ruby', of about the same height. It is so vigorous that a group of single-rooted pieces planted in March will produce a rounded head of some double, golden-centred flowers 3 cm or more in diameter. Neither have appeared to inherit wilt and though 'Royal Velvet' is not quite immune to mildew, a fair demand for both remains.

One of the most valuable inter-specific crosses ever made came from Herr Frikart, a Swiss nurseryman. He crossed the shapely *Aster thomsonii* with an *A. amellus*. Both were blue, ray-petalled, yellow-centred flowers and the result was *Aster × frikartii*, 'Wonda von Stafa', which has become one of the top 20 border perennials. Three others from the same breeder were named after the well-known Bernese Oberland mountains, 'Jungfrau', 'Eiger' and 'Monch'. Only the latter is still in good supply and it differs from the original *frikartii* only in being less branched and more upright. Both have fine blue flowers over a long period at about 90 cm from early July, from clumpy disease-free plants. It was in hopes of widening the colour range that we repeated Herr Frikart's cross in 1954, but to achieve it, the dwarf form of *A. thompsonii* was used together with the pink *A. amellus* 'Sonia'. Very few seedlings emerged, and only one of these other than blue. It was left as usual to flower a second year and thereby proved its height of no more than 60 cm, and the colour was a pleasing lilac shade. It occurred to me to name it after my wife but she was the first to point out that 'Flora Bloom' would be rather inept, and so it had to be 'Flora's Delight'. As a plant it is rather less vigorous as well as being shorter than the Frikart hybrids and needs very well-drained soil to avoid loss from winter wet. As with all *amellus* it is not safe to divide and plant in autumn, although pot-grown stock is safe enough. I also introduced a selection of *Aster amellus*, 'Nocturne', with deep-lilac flowers on plants reaching about 75 cm.

# ASTILBE

Until a few years ago almost all astilbe hybrids were of German or Dutch origin. Georg Arends brought out a new range by crossing species, to which the group name *arendsii* was given. In my time I have acquired and grown over 40 cultivars of continental origin. The first I introduced was 'Snowdrift', in 1975, a sport from the white 'Erlicht' with a fuller spike. It was my son Adrian who saw a group in the garden and encouraged me to build up a stock. Other efforts to raise did not begin until praise of that fine pink 'Bressingham Beauty' gave further encouragement. This was simply a seedling I picked out in 1967. As might be expected, having a wide range already in my garden varying in height from 15 cm to 1·8 m, scope was not lacking. By 1978, a splendid variation on the low-growing species A. *simplicifolia* had appeared. It had dark-green, deeply dissected bushy foliage and 25 cm sprays of pearl-pink flowers. It also had vigour and unlike some astilbes, remained effective for several weeks – July to September. I gave it the name 'Sprite', and it has proved to be a consistent best seller. Indeed, one garden centre owner told me that he reared and sold a regular 5,000 annually.

Astilbes possess overall attraction with complementary foliage at flowering time and of value throughout the growing season; but where soil is lacking moisture or richness they fall far short of the ideal. And it must be said that they do not improve with age. Their natural tendency is for the hard crowns to rise to above ground level after two to three years and thereby lose vitality for lack of fibrous roots. The easy remedy is to mulch in early spring to encourage fibrous roots near the surface. An alternative is to replant more deeply in enriched soil but cut back first the old rather woody stock from underneath the plant. The build-up of this old, outworn material is a deterrent to an abundance of flower and foliage.

To return to 'Bressingham Beauty', I am reminded that the

manager of Bees Nursery gave the opinion that this was the best pure pink variety ever raised, and was equally excellent for forcing, being a metre tall. During the 1980s it has been my pleasure to watch and assess the performance of another batch of seedlings. They are a very assorted lot, but though two are about to be launched, others are coming along which may well be worthy of naming and introducing. To be going on with 'Elizabeth Bloom' is again a fulsome pink, but less tall at 75 cm than 'Bressingham Beauty'. It flowers abundantly with a rich background of greenery in July and August. 'Sheila Haxton' is later and shorter at 45–50 cm. A link with one parent A. *sinensis pumila* is obvious, not only for its darker widespread foliage and its tendency to spread somewhat below ground, but in its stumpy, pyramidal spikes. It is a deeper pink than 'Elizabeth' but a clearer shade than *sinensis pumila* – and it flowers for a long time. On the stocks there is one with the habit of 'Sprite', but having a tinge of pink, and a dwarf red which so far appears to be rather better than the well-known A. 'Fanal'. A diminutive shell-pink *simplicifolia* type is also being studied – distinctive for being only 10 cm high, but I must keep to my policy of not naming and introducing a new variety until it has been thoroughly tested over a period of several years in varying conditions.

## Astrantia

The species is quite popular for all its lack of colour, and indeed its greenish-white heads are favoured by flower arrangers. Mine, I suspect, is a natural hybrid between A. *major* and A. *rubra*. The latter is a dull deep-red on a not very vigorous plant, but the offspring is strong growing at 75 cm and decidedly colourful as astrantias go. It will be named 'Ruby Glow'. It could be said to lack the glistening pink flowers of A. *maxima*, but is of compact clumpy growth, whereas *maxima* spreads quickly below ground and needs curbing – as well as having leaves not unlike the pernicious 'Ground Elder'.

## Aubrieta

These invariably come readily from seed and beyond an awareness of what named cultivars exist, require no special skill to pick out an improvement. Seedlings are usually a mixture unless raised from well-isolated plants, but even so will vary somewhat in form and colour. That some named cultivars lose vitality after a few years of being propagated from cuttings is doubtless due to this cause, and aubrietas are not the only hybrids to suffer. The double-flowered varieties are especially prone to this inherent consitutional weakness. It was in hopes of replacing such as 'Barker's Double' that I raised a batch of seedlings to include the then best single red, 'Mrs Rodewald', and from my earlier double pink, 'Mary Poppins' which was losing vitality. From about 250 seedlings not one double appeared to resemble the mauve-purple 'Barker's Double', but one was an exceptionally good double pink which I named 'Bressingham Pink'. After nearly 20 years it is still quite vigorous and this applies also to 'Red Carpet', which was another from the same batch though it is single flowered.

In my experience the richest, deepest colours – furthest removed from the original species, pale-blue A. *gracea* – are generally less strong or durable than the paler shades. Amongst the latter, 'Lilac Time' and 'Oakington Lavender', two vigorous cultivars which I selected and named in the early 1930s, are still going strong. At that time the first doubles raised by Mr Barker of Kelmscott, near Ipswich, had not appeared as far as I can remember.

Incidentally, aubrietas grow and survive in well-drained limy soil and have no liking for richness.

## Bergenia

These are amongst the most adaptable subjects, and increased popularity in recent years has brought a flush of new cultivars. Some of the best have come from the Continent with deeper pinks and greater flowering freedom. Amongst them was a white, raised by Georg Arends of Ronsdorf, named 'Silber-licht' – 'Silver Light'. In my garden, however, it took on a rather ragged, untidy appearance after a year or two, with the woody above-ground rhizomes becoming bare of leaves. The slightly off-white flowers also indicated the need for a purer colour as well as a more compact leafy plant. Seed was saved from 'Silberlicht' to make a mixture with one or two of the best pink shades and several hundred were planted out in the mid-1970s.

This batch was allowed to flower twice, but only two were selected for further trial. One, which proved to be the hoped-for improvement on 'Silberlicht' was named 'Bressingham White' and it has since become widely known and accepted. The other selected seedling was slower to increase, but its colour, salmon pink, was a welcome break and has become distributed as 'Bressingham Salmon'.

Relying on bees for cross-pollination, a further batch was raised in 1982. One, named 'Bressingham Ruby' has the most colourful leaves I have ever seen in a bergenia – a glossy reddish-purple for much of the year, though naturally the colour is suffused with green especially when young. In addition, the habit is compact and the flower spikes of a bright pink are full and abundant.

## CAMPANULA

My interest in campanulas, especially the alpine types, began when I was barely out of my teens. By about 1928 my collection had topped a hundred species and cultivars of all types; but then came the realisation that this was out of keeping with my ambition to become a successful nursery-man, starting almost from scratch. I had noticed, however, that bees crept in and out of the fragile bells and so I collected seed from some of the smallest kinds, including what was then known as *C. pusilla* – now *cochlearifolia*. At that time the best-known cultivars were 'Miss Willmott' and 'Miranda', as well as the white that Alva Hall of Harrogate had recently introduced as *hallii*.

Amongst the resultant seedlings were three that differed from these. One had larger flowers than the mid-blue 'Miss Willmott', which I named 'Oakington Blue' after the village where my budding nursery was situated. It was only four miles from Cambridge and so the name for a clearer light blue came to mind as 'Cambridge Blue'. The third selection differed in having a small cluster of deep-blue bells on each stem as opposed to single stems for each on other *pusillas*. It had the same habit of spreading below ground, however, and I named it 'Blue Tit'. To my knowledge all three are still in cultivation apart from the original stocks I still have, but only one new cultivar has been raised since and this is the double-flowered 'Elizabeth Oliver'.

Many years later *C. wockei*, a tiny but clumpy late-flowering campanula yielded a deeper-lavender flowered variant which I named 'Puck'. It makes a low 8–10 cm mound when flowering with thin deep-green foliage almost hidden. Having no tendency to spread, it retains compactness for many years. I also found a seedling with deeper-blue flowers than that splendid hybrid 'Stella', which took the name 'Constellation'. This type I can but guess comes from a cross between *C. garganica* and *C. poscharskyana*. The latter is invasive, but the hybrids from it are clumpy and send out 45 cm sprays in great profusion with lavender-blue, paler-eyed starry flowers, not bell-shaped.

Whilst still at Oakington I raised seedlings of *Campanula lactiflora* 'Prichard's Variety'. Though I knew it would not come true – the species itself being variable, I wished to offer a good strain as well as the uniform Prichard's, which was the deepest colour at the modest height of about 90 cm. Some reach up to 1·8 m but amongst those seedlings I found one which was little more than 15–20 cm in height. Its habit was leafy and mounded, set with lavender-blue trumpets almost as large as the taller ones. As with 'Prichards Variety', it had to be increased only from cuttings or division and in due course, about 1937, I introduced it as 'Pouffe'. Many years later a white one of similar form has appeared, rather oddly. A new customer wrote ordering 'Pouffe' to go with the dwarf white one she had, in the belief that it was a recent novelty, she having grown 'White Pouffe' for a long time. A swop was of course the natural outcome, but though the white makes a wider mound of soft greenery at about 30 cm high, the flowering is less free and less attractive as a whole than my light-blue form.

*Campanula carpatica* and its variants are dual-purpose plants – to grace a bed as border frontal positions or amongst alpines. Scarcely any reach 30 cm and have upstanding cups of blue or white from June onwards. The sub-species *turbinata* is dwarfer with flowers just as large, but having a limited range of colour. I set out to remedy this by crossing back to *C. carpatica pelviformis*, a good blue with saucer-shaped flowers. The result was 'Blue Moonlight' with much the same flower shapes but of a glistening azure blue. It has been consistently free flowering, only 10 cm high, and remains one of my favourites. The name 'Bressingham White' was given to an improvement on the old variety 'White Star' – larger flowered and a purer white. Another hybrid with a *turbinata* link is on its way as a seedling from that charming later-flowering light-blue 'Chewton Joy'. It has large bowl-shaped flowers so profuse that scarcely any foliage is visible, hidden for several weeks by the 12 cm dome of ethereal blue, shining enough to name it 'Blue Sheen'.

*Campanual glomerata* is another variable species and has the named forms *superba*, *dahurica* and *acaulis*. The latter indicates a short or even stemless flower spike, but those I have grown as *acaulis* have been white flowered from 15–30 cm tall. The others in violet blue are 60–90 cm, except for the early-flowering 'Joan Elliott'. A seedling that I named 'Purple Pixie' is quite different from any of the above. Unlike most, it does not spread quickly below ground but keeps to a compact rootstock. It flowers from early July for several weeks – later than any other, and the dark leafy stems 45–50 cm high have violet-blue flowers clustered along their slender upper length. Except for being clustered it does not appear to be a *glomerata* type and it remains something of a mystery how it appeared in my garden. I can but conclude it came self-sown as a natural hybrid, and I can claim no credit – as with one or two other plants, for having raised it.

The cultivars I named of the species *C. latifolia* 'White Ladies' and 'Gloaming' were also self-sown seedlings. All of this type grow to 1·2 m or more in rich soil, especially if in some shade. They have strong stems which terminate in a cluster of quite large flowers held obliquely. Both violet blue and white are consistent with the species and from seed an occasional in-between shade will appear. One of the latter appealed to me greatly on first sight for it was an unusual smoky-blue shade. In due course I named it 'Gloaming', and in the 20 years since first being offered there has never been sufficient numbers produced to satisfy the demand. I have tried to meet this by seed-raised plants but not a single one of its unique colour has appeared, and it makes no rapid growth for division. Even white seedlings are somewhat variable and I once spotted in with a group of *C. latifolia macrantha* 'Alba', one that stood out for the purity of its white bells. This, under the name of 'White Ladies' has proved even more difficult to increase and for the past few years it has been omitted from our catalogue in order to build up a reliable, adequate stock.

Campanulas were among Percy Piper's favourites also, and with no prompting from me he crossed the well-known *C. persicifolia* – of which several cultivars, both blue and white, double and single, exist – with *C. latiloba*. This used to be *C. grandis* and 'Highcliffe' was the best form with rich deep-blue flowers along much of its 90 cm stems. In general, *C. latiloba* is stronger growing and more reliably perennial than *C. persicifolia* (i.e.peach-leaved) with more rosetted, light-green basal foliage. From the cross, which carried Percy Piper's own name, the majority of seedlings were almost all consistent with one parent or the other. Percy's namesake was, we decided, an improvement on 'Highcliffe' and larger flowered, and a sufficient improvement to delete it. This was a mistake for it eliminated further comparison when seeing it elsewhere and I had some doubts whether Percy's plant was distinct enough after all.

## CHRYSANTHEMUM

Five cultivars I have named are included with some diffidence because they appeared from seedlings raised with no intention of any being selected and introduced. One in fact was self-sown – a dwarf *C. maximum* or 'Shasta Daisy'. I allowed it to stay undisturbed to flower a second year in case it grew taller. But again it made a wide dome shape only 38 cm or so high, so thickly covered in white daisy flowers that the obvious name for it was 'Snowcap'. It has since become popular in America as well as in Britain.

The other four are autumn-flowering spray chrysanthemums. 'Peter Sare', named after my garden foreman, has pure-pink, yellow-centred single flowers on a neat sturdy habit, at 60 cm tall. 'Autumn Melody' is a double deep rose with an orange centre flush, 60–75 cm. 'Pink Progression' has masses of smallish single pink flowers in October, November, at 90 cm. All are safe to leave plants *in situ* over winter where well drained. The fourth makes a large stocky clump, even some spread, for it is from 'Bronze Elegance'. The colour is coppery orange on its double button or pom-pom-type flowers above dense bushy growth, 50–60 cm, with the name 'Peter Pan'.

## CROCOSMIA

Perhaps the most spectacular hybrids to begin life at Bressingham are the *Crocosmias*. The choice of using this name collectively has been quite arbitrary, but so little authoritative information as to the correct generic names has emerged to be sure. The group of closely related genera includes *Antholyza*, *Curtonus*, *Montbretia* and *Tritonia* as well as *Crocosmia*. Some are of course synonymous, but which has to remain an open question. *Antholyza* and *Curtonus* probably are, and so far as I know, only one species exists – *paniculata*. It stands for a strong-growing, corm-based subject with sword-like leaves up to 90 cm. The flowers on somewhat arching wiry stems are rather small, of a dull burnt-orange colour. Because it had proved to be extremely hardy with a fairly steady increase of its corms, it was used as a parent with *Crocosmia masonorum*. This had the reputation prior to 1963 of not being fully hardy, but its fiery orange flowers of open-petalled, up-facing trumpets were vastly more spectacular than *Antholyza* and the habit much more refined.

It acted as a spur to cross these two subjects when the *Crocosmia* withstood the severe frosts of 1963, when with no snow cover the ground froze solid to below the level of the corms. Rather haphazardly a more slender-growing *Montbretia* was also 'fiddled' as Percy Piper used to say. The result was a batch of several hundred seedlings and two years later the process of selection and elimination began. First it was whittled down to about 25, and the next year to six as the final choice. They ranged from barely 60 cm to 1·2 m in height, and there was ample evidence that cross-pollination had brought some new and exciting variations. Some had closer kinship than others with one or the other of the three parents. Those nearest to the *Montbretia* had the characteristic spread by sending slender new shoots out from the corm, others had larger corms with less spread, but the ability to make new ones attached to old ones that had previously flowered. These were of *Crocosmia-Antholyza* marriage and the first to be named was 'Lucifer' – infinitely superior to *Antholyza paniculata*. The deep orange-red flowers come on graceful sprays up to 1·2 m high in early July to give a spectacular display until well into August. Next come those indications of a half-way parentage between *C. masonorum* and *Montbretia*. 'Vulcan', and the slightly paler, 'Emberglow' were both fairly dwarf, late flowering and vigorous, deep orange-crimson mahogany differing just enough to keep separate. 'Vulcan' grows to about 60 cm and is about 30 cm shorter than 'Emberglow'. 'Bressingham Blaze' and 'Spitfire' were taller and brighter, one brilliant flame orange and the other with more of an orange-yellow colour. Both flowered from mid July onwards, and are very free.

The last to make up into sufficient stock was an improvement on *Crocosmia masonorum*, which I named 'Firebird', and it has been everyone's favourite ever since. Its arching wiry stems amid its lush green blades up to 75–90 cm reach up and out to show its large opened petals to the sun and to the human eye. Sadly, as I write, stocks are low due partly to the flood of August 1987 and even more to a disastrous attempt to meet the demand by means of tissue culture. But 'Firebird' will be back on offer.

A later cross has given two more cultivars now in sufficient supply to catalogue. 'Jenny Bloom' is a pure, warm butter-yellow, vigorous and prolific in growth. It is closer to *Montbretia* than to *Crocosmia*, but at 75 cm at least it is a potential cutting variety. It flowers from mid-July for several weeks and is due to become a favourite, as it is of my youngest daughter after whom it was named. The other recent introduction is 'Bressingham Beacon'. This is taller than most montbretia types, but has the same habit with a steady spread from rhizomes which, as with others, become flowering corms. The colour is orange flame and this too has cut-flower potential. The range of new cultivars is likely to be enhanced still more over the next few years for there are others raised in Ireland coming along after the stringent trials they have to undergo before they are released. Our attempts to breed from the pink flowers of what is mostly called *Montbretia rosea* (now known as *Tritonia rubrolucens*) have met with no success. Nor can I imagine pink in any other shade to merge at all well with the orange and flame colours which predominate those now in existence.

A fairly safe guide to degrees of hardiness in crocosmias is to go by the size of the corm. The larger the corm, the hardier it will be, but those with more of the montbretia habit have not only smaller corms but more lateral shoots coming from them. This indicates the preferred planting depth and whereas the latter need be no more than 8 cm deep, the larger and more robust are best at 10 cm. It follows that the shallow-rooting ones are more susceptible to soil-penetrating frost and in cold districts a litter covering is advisable for 12–14 weeks of winter. Some crocosmias have old corms attached, up to three or four, one above the other. I fancy this is a form of food storage and to detach the top one tends to inhibit flowering. All are best in a sunny position and well-drained soil.

## Dianthus

Including carnations and pinks, these have been interbred for at least two centuries and some of the oldest hybrids are still to be seen. Indeed, there has been quite a resurgence in them and a few specialists have built up quite a large collection. Hybridisation has never ceased, but only on one occasion did I attempt to do so. That was in the late 1920s when Montague Allwood was producing hybrids as the then new 'Allwoodii'. One, named 'Susan', appealed to me for its crimson-centred, double pink flowers, but it was rather tall to be used as a rock garden plant. From a batch of seedlings saved from the semi-double 10 cm tall 'Prichard's Variety', I was able to pick out one of that height, but with much the same colouring as 'Susan'. I named it 'Dubarry' – having recently read of that lady's charms, but another selection has over the years proved to be more popular. This, to which the name 'Oakington' was also given, is a warm pink almost double, barely 10 cm high. It has a carpeting spread and flowers very reliably in June-July. Since then there has been no lack of new cultivars from breeders year by year, and it seemed pointless for me to continue when so many other genera were being virtually ignored.

## Dicentra

Very careful emasculation would be required by anyone attempting to cross-pollinate dicentras. It must have been done, however, because some years ago a strain of seedlings under the name 'Rokuju Hybrids' appeared. They received no fanfare and so far as I know were raised by a scientist rather than a plantsman, and the name suggests a Far Eastern location. Distribution was limited to only a few nurseries and gardens. Those I received were a nameless mixture mostly quite dwarf, but one grew away from the rest with pearl-white lockets on arching stems about 30 cm high, above lots of pretty glaucous foliage. Discarding all as worthless but this one, I found it increased rapidly and when young flowered for months rather than weeks. It had to be given a name before any could be offered and 'Pearl Drops' appealed as suitable for what I believed would be a great demand. So it proved, but whilst I was not the raiser, it never occurred to me that anyone else would introduce it so long afterwards; however, after having it on sale for about five years, the identical plant turned up from elsewhere under the name 'Langtrees'.

I contend that 'Pearl Drops', which does not pin it down to a supposed place of origin, is the more valid name. It has obvious kinship with *D. formosa* or its close relative *D. eximea*, and from the latter I can claim to have raised a new hybrid which I named 'Adrian Bloom'. The parentage was the American cultivar 'Bountiful', which has a much larger pink flower than the species. 'Adrian Bloom' is close to being red and has a long flowering season from May to July, at least when in good soil. It appeared about 1968, but ten years later an American variety named 'Luxuriant' appeared which Adrian himself took a fancy to. We have argued over their respective merits and although we agree that there is very little to choose between them, Adrian now admits that his name is carried by a very good plant.

All dicentras are longer living in very well-drained soil. In my garden the soil tends to congeal and form a pan below. Although the *eximia* and *formosa* types have no deeply penetrating fleshy roots as does the well-known *D. spectabilis*, their roots are somewhat fleshy with an outward rather than downward spread. This is the probable reason why the hybrids tend to rot in my garden, remaining lively only in their outer parts. Young plants grow and flower splendidly, but I find replanting those outer parts every year after digging deeply is the only way to maintain the vigour.

## ECHINACEA

This is another genus that needs good drainage. So far as I know only one species, *E. purpurea* exists with the folk name of 'Purple Cone Flower'. The centre cone, almost black, stands well above the rayed petals on terminal branches about 90 cm tall in late summer. Until recent years 'The King' was the most popular but it had the fault of being less than erect, and the petals drooped excessively, spoiling the effect. A German cultivar named 'Abendsonne' did not have this fault and was a warmer shade – with less purple magenta; but this had a weak constitution and in hopes of finding one with none of these disabilities, a large batch was raised from seed in 1954. Several were selected for colour, size and substance of flower, and finally one was chosen and given my elder son's name – 'Robert Bloom', although several years elapsed before stocks were adequate. A dozen of the best of the rest, slightly variable, were also grown on, to become 'Bressingham Hybrids', and these have been re-selected since to become indistinguishable from 'Robert Bloom'. One other is on the way and is destined for being shorter at 75 cm, but it seems variable. Like the rest, stems are strong but the colour is nearer to purple-lilac, lacking only the rosy hue, but with these improvements I saw no virtue in keeping 'The King' which has been deposed, in my garden at least.

## ERIGERON

Our efforts to breed new erigerons at Bressingham were in the long run less successful than early hopes appeared to foretell; but the story is worth recording if only to indicate how a lack of botanical knowledge and scientific application can lead to errors and disappointments.

The story begins in the late 1940s when almost as a hobby I tried to make improvements to the uniquely coloured, but short-lived *E. aurantiacus*. It came readily from seed but varied from pale to very deep orange shades in its ray-petalled flowers, and in height from 23–36 cm. Always hopeful that one or more of the most vigorous and colourful seedlings would retain vitality for more than the usual two years, I asked Percy Piper to cross-pollinate from the fully perennial *E. macrantha* kinds such as 'Mesa Grande', 'Merstham Glory' and 'Quakeress'. The latter was a pale-lilac shade, but most reliable cultivars then grown were lavender and violet blue, all about 60–75 cm tall.

By June 1952 a bed of some 250 seedlings was coming into flower. Some had far more vigorous growth than others which were obviously of the compact habit of *E. aurantiacus*. These, in fact, proved to be no different either in form or colour to the selections I had previously made, and being the first to flower, tended to sharpen interest in those still to open, with every indication that they would prove to be fully perennial – but as they opened almost all were in shades of pink, lilac and lavender. Some were inclined to be floppy in habit, from 50–75 cm in height, but several were sufficiently different from any existing cultivars to encourage me to begin selecting and growing them on as new introductions.

About 15 were staked and given a number. When lifted and divided the following March, some made up to a dozen rooted pieces and these grew to produce flowers by June. It was then that I decided to restrict the final selection to six and give them names which would link them as a new range, using the terminal 'ity' to each choice. In hopes of having them judged by others, three plants of each were sent to Wisley Gardens for Trial by the Standing Committee. Rather than rely entirely on my own opinion, it seemed best to name those to which the committee gave Commendation or Award in the belief that this would enhance sales and since my own stock could be relied upon to flower fully in 1953, the final named selection could be launched in 1954.

It was when I learned that the Wisley judges had decided to defer making their decisions until 1954 that I was put under considerable embarrassment. I could not afford to propagate all 15 still under number, because of the time and space it would take, knowing that about half would have to be dumped in order to name only six of them. So the final selection was up to me, in hopes that the Wisley judges would come to the same conclusions. By way of a little insurance I decided after all to name eleven, though with much reluctance. This, then, is how so many 'itys' made their debut and how the Wisley Trial became irrelevant:

'CHARITY',
Slight pink, 60 cm, loose habit

'DIGNITY',
violet mauve, 50 cm

'FELICITY',
large flowered pink, 50 cm

'FESTIVITY',
lilac pink, 60 cm, fairly upright

'FRIVOLITY',
rosy lavender, 60 cm, loose habit

'GAIETY',
free flowering, bright pink, 60 cm

'PROSPERITY',
mauve blue, almost double, 45 cm, erect

'SERENITY',
violet mauve, 75 cm, rather lax

'SINCERITY',
mauve blue, 75 cm

'UNITY',
bright pink, 50 cm, compact

'VANITY',
a taller pink, 75 cm

All the above are June-August flowering.

Not all have survived the test of time and garden worthiness, but I do believe that had they been restricted to six, and had I not been strictly wholesale only at the time, they would have been much more widely distributed. Many of my retailing customers were inclined to scoff at new varieties and stick to what they termed 'bread-and-butter' plants, and at that period perennials did not enjoy the popularity they have achieved in the past few years. I still have most of the 'ity' erigerons in my garden. In the end, 'Dignity' received an Award of Merit while 'Charity', 'Felicity', 'Frivolity', 'Prosperity' and 'Serenity' were all Highly Commended.

A few export orders came from both America and the

Continent, but when it was reported that some varieties had not survived the first winter abroad, it confirmed my belief that it would be expedient to discard some. In any case, some were rather alike, so 'Felicity', 'Frivolity', 'Sincerity' and 'Unity' were dropped, but two others appeared from a later attempt and were named for being quite distinct. 'Amity' was and still is a good upstanding lilac pink at 75 cm, but 'Dimity' is totally different in habit. It makes mounded clumpy growth and the pink, finely rayed flowers, having orange centres come on thereabouts lateral sprays, so that 23 cm is about the maximum height. I have often puzzled how it appeared amongst others – and how to keep it going, because twice my whole stock has dwindled to almost nothing. It appears to have a kind of death wish after about two years of profuse flowering and not even the effect of cutting-back as flowers fade restores vitality. It is curious because when having to buy in fresh stock, the sellers have said they found it reliable enough if divided and replanted every other year. It is, however, the closest in habit and colour to *E. aurantiacus*, but the original aim to induce the latter to become a reliable perennial remains as elusive as ever.

It is worth remembering that the hybrid 'B. Ladham's' had orange-tinted buds like 'Dimity', though it was taller at 60 cm and quite erect. Although it was in widespread cultivation during the 1920s and 30s, it seems to be now entirely lost to cultivation. This must be the result of some inherent weakness which in time reduced its capacity for survival. By contrast the old variety 'Quakeress', a pale lilac pink raised before 1914, remains strong growing and I am currently working up a sale stock after the 40-year relegation to merely a garden group.

## EUPHORBIA

This genus with its widely varying species has not so far received much attention from hybridists. The hardy species have become far more popular than anyone would have imagined 50 years ago, when scarcely any were available to the gardening public. Their recent popularity has promoted some species to be raised from seed and here and there improvements have occurred to be given cultivar names. The

species *E. griffithii* was one of these. It began to be distributed
in the early 1950s, but I found it to be a rather untidy grower,
apt to romp below ground and to flop above with lax stems up
to 90 cm, tipped with orange flower bracts in early summer.
To hasten a build-up of stock, I raised some from seed and just
one stood out from the rest with sturdier stems and deep
fiery-orange 'flowers'. It was certainly worthy of the name
I gave it of 'Fireglow', and as stock and sales expanded it
superseded the original species. Incidentally, the species was
at first recommended as a shade-loving subject, but I found
that both it and 'Fireglow' were much more effective in full
sun.

## GAILLARDIA

These colourful perennials are not the most reliable. They
need light soil and sun and are apt to flower themselves
to death. The one perennial species in cultivation is *G.
grandiflora*, but those raised from seed are described as
hybrids. A question I cannot answer is that of parentage,
from which hybrids were produced, and the answer may
well be that it is inherently variable. Some have in the past
been named but few have retained perennial vigour. The
zoned colours of yellow and browny red are most typical
of the species, but one introduced about 1948 was the deep
brownish orange-red colour overall. To me this 'Wirral Flame'
was rather lacking brilliance and when I raised some from
seed, growing next to the bicolour 'Ipswich Beauty', one plant
had the flame colour I had hoped for, to be given the name
'Mandarin'. To keep selections true to name and colour they
must be propagated from their fibrous roots.

## GERANIUM

It is quite extraordinary how the 'hardy geraniums' have come
into their own in recent years – at least among the more
discerning gardeners. Some people still do not realise that
what have been known, and to an extent still are known, as
non-hardy geraniums are in fact pelargoniums. With just one
or two exceptions, all true geraniums are fully hardy, and well
over 100 species and cultivars are in existence – including
true alpines as well as bold perennials.

One of my regrets is that we made only one deliberate effort to produce hybrids, and from only two species. These were both alpines – the robust, magenta-flowed G. *subcaulescens* and the more delicate, grey-leaved G. *cinerium*. Both are tufty growing, deep-rooting species and the cross was made with the notion that a less fierce colour would enhance the appeal of G. *subcaulescens*, as more colour would do the same for G. *cinereum*. Not many progeny came, but two appealed greatly. One was close to G. *cinereum* in habit, flowering more widely from its silver-green hummocks, of a light-pink shade. 'Apple Blossom' was the name I chose but its delicate charm, more closely linked as it was to G. *cinereum*, was not so appealing as the other more vigorous seedling. This had less silvery leaves, but the little bowl-shaped flowers on low-reaching sprays were entrancing, with crimson markings on a lilac-pink base. And it flowered on and on all summer.

This, under the name 'Ballerina' has now become widely accepted as probably the best hybrid alpine geranium. An ailing connoisseur in Victoria, British Columbia, with a very large collection, once cheered me by saying that if he had to part with his collection of geraniums, 'Ballerina' would be the last to go – and this before he knew I had raised it. Since its debut another was raised which had flowers and growth a little larger, but of deeper colour. I named it after Lawrence Flatman whose long service to my firm was of great value, but a few complaints came from customers who did not consider it sufficiently different from 'Ballerina'. As a result a further selection was made and the name transferred to a new stock.

At the time of writing we have a wide variety of geraniums, both species and cultivars on trial. Only the above are, to my regret, our own hybrids, but one tall species produced a variation which has been in demand for several years. It was picked out from seedlings of G. *armenum (psilostemon)* which has intense magenta flowers on robust 90 cm bushy growth. At first or distant glance 'Bressingham Flair' might not appear very different from the species, but when closer examination and comparison are made the colour is less vivid, with a hint of pink in the magenta. This was once dropped from our catalogue because a trade customer had complained of its being not sufficiently different. Unbeknown to me, the stock was run down and sold as *G. armenum* until only my garden group remained. It was from this that I had to propagate and restore for sale again when enquiries continued for 'Bressingham Flair' by those more discerning than the complainant had been.

## GEUM

It might well be that some hybrid geums have an inherent weakness which causes progressive loss of vigour after a period of years. The seed-raised hybrids, 'Mrs Bradshaw' and 'Lady Stratheden' are short-lived but at least they breed true, but 'Fire Opal', 'Princess Juliana', 'Rubin' and 'Dolly North', which grew well enough 40 years ago, appear now to be thereabouts exhausted, and renewal from seed is rather unlikely. Their flame and orange colours are missed.

All I have succeeded in doing is to raise a much dwarfer one, smaller even than the old but sturdy hybrid × *borisii*. This had *G. montanum* as one parent, but my 'Baby Tangerine' has flowers at 15 cm and could be described as a miniature *borisii*. It is the same shade of bright orange but has a much longer flowering period. Judging by its tufty, easily divided growth, it should have no constitutional disabilities.

## HELENIUM

Almost all heleniums in cultivation are hybrids and the true species from which they originated are likely to be seen only in the 'Order Beds' of botanic gardens. One must surmise that this propensity for crossing was inherited, needing little but proximity and insects to do the rest. The only true species I have encountered are yellow, which raises the questions to how the deep-brownish shades were introduced. Perhaps they came from *H. autumnale* of which there is a 'rubrum' form in nature. I can find no likely reason, however, for a few hybrids being less than half the height of *H. autumnale*, which grows to 1.5 m in gardens. The cultivar 'Crimson Beauty' is barely 60 cm and 'Wyndley' is not much taller. Both were raised and introduced long ago and because 'Crimson Beauty' is a rather dull mahogany brown, I have tried to breed into it and 'Wyndley' the richer colourings seen in the taller hybrids. Most of these are much too tall and although 'Wyndley' is neat and a bright orange-brown bi-colour, the need was and still is for a new range under 90 cm.

Several new varieties came from the Continent in the 1930s and later. All were well over 90 cm, and though some were fiery coloured, 'Moerheim Beauty' was the most outstanding and remains popular still for its warm reddish-brown-orange, but our efforts to breed such colours on to the shorter 'Wyndley' and 'Crimson Beauty' which were raised a lifetime ago, have proved disappointing. Indeed 'Wyndley' has never produced any seed, straight or otherwise, which yielded other than taller progeny. Because Percy Piper kept no detailed records of crossings, I could not know the source of a batch of seedlings raised about 1960. All I can record is that amongst them was a pure deep yellow which I named 'Butterpat' and an unblotched, rich brown-red 'Bruno'. They were both rather tall to be very excited about, at 1.2 m, but another with large flowers, suffused coppery orange, was a sturdy growing 90 cm, which took the name 'Coppelia' and held first place in my estimation. It flowers in the July-September period whereas 'Bruno' and 'Butterpat' are later. One of my dislikes of the taller heleniums is their tendency for their stem leaves to fade, often before they come into flower. It occurs regularly when plants become old and with too many stems and too little nutriment in dry weather or poor soil.

# HELIOPSIS

All heliopsis in cultivation are improvements on the species *scabra* and considering all are in shades of yellow, it is quite surprising how many have been raised and introduced. Dubious credit is due to that famous German hybridist Karl Foerster, who named at least a dozen, for so many are much alike. One I introduced, 'Incomparabilis', gained an RHS Award of Merit in 1932, and it is still popular for being semi-double. I did not raise it, having obtained it a few years before from Orleans, but I have dabbled spasmodically since then in hopes of raising a fully double one. They are in my view very good garden plants with a long season of rayed or semi-double flowers with no fads, all in the 90–120 cm range of height.

As recently as 1987 I selected one from a batch of seedlings that had a distinctive habit, sturdily erect, with branching terminal heads of chrome-yellow flowers. Individually these were small, but they were virtually double. But they, and many other plants, were under water for over a week as a result of flooding in August 1987. In the hopes of its survival I lifted it with a few other selections I had staked, once the flood receded. Sadly though the new break was not amongst those that made new growth the following spring. Of the few that did, I marked one or two that appeared to be better than either the best semi-double 'Golden Plume' and the largest orange single 'Desert King', but one hesitates to name others when so many, so much alike, have already been introduced, albeit that only three or four are to be found in British nurseries.

# HELLEBORUS

For anyone interested in plant breeding, patience is a very needful virtue, and this certainly applies to helleborus. Seed is slow to germinate and if after three or four years' nurturing a promising selection of a break is seen on first flowering, one is likely to have to wait a further two or three years before a single plant can be divided for a modest increase. This applies to the slow clump-forming group of species of which *H. orientalis* is best known, rather than to the even better known 'Christmas Rose' – *H. niger*. The latter has yielded variants, but white remains inviolate and scarcely any improvements have stayed the course. Seedlings fill 95 per cent of the constant demand.

The ratio is less pronounced in the *H. orientalis* ('Lenten Rose') group, and it was to meet the demand for specific colours that I named two selected seedlings over 30 years ago. It took half that period to work up an adequate stock from division before naming and listing them.

The fascination we all have for helleborus is largely due to their being harbingers of spring, coupled with their longevity once settled in the semi-shade they prefer. Because winter is often still with us in February when the first flowers usually open. I named one 'Winter Cheer'. It is close to pink with golden stamens and a tracery of crimson markings within the bowl-shaped flowers. The other name – more inspired than some I have chosen – is 'Heartsease'. This is of a purplish-maroon shade which is also highlighted by its yellow stamens. Perhaps the choice of names has helped, but the demand ever since has always been greater than the supply. It is only in quite recent years that further selections have been made which include more variety of colour and larger flowers, but none of them are far along the slow process of stock building and I quite think others of my family will have the privilege of giving names to the final selection. None of this group, which includes other species I know as *H. cyclophyllus*, *guttatus*, *antiquorum*, *kochii*, *olympicus* as well as *orientalis*, can be relied upon to breed true from seed. They are indeed so promiscuous that some true species have become obscure.

# HEUCHERA

My involvement with this genus goes back in time more than any other. But for one or two breaks, through war and a spell in Canada, it has continued up to the present time; a period of almost 70 years. My father was a market grower of flowers and fruit rather than a nurseryman and was always on the look-out for plants that might have cut-flower potential. So it was that about 1919 he obtained a stock of two heucheras that had appealed to him when visiting nurseries at Wisbech.

One of these was the 'Gracillima' form of *H. brizoides*, with tiny pink flowers on graceful wiry sprays in early summer, about 75 cm tall, above a mound of rounded evergreen foliage. Growth is vigorous, and as with all heucheras, below the leaves are crowns, as tips to somewhat hard fleshy shoots which lengthen with age. The same hardness, though fairly brittle growth, extended below ground with very little fibrous roots to be seen except when young, as planted divisions.

As a schoolboy I was not often asked to help pick or pack flowers for market – none being cut on Saturdays and Sundays. But I was sufficiently interested not only to help some evenings in season, but to make comparisons between different kinds of plants, perennials especially, as opposed to china asters, stocks, statice and gypsophila. The difference between *Heuchera brizoides* 'Gracillima' and the 'Trevor Red' variety of *H. sanguinea* was that the latter had larger flowers, shorter stems and fewer coral-red bells on each 45 cm spray, and I preferred it for brilliance. Father's judgement was that it was less profitable to grow because of it being less profuse. In addition, salesmen at distant city markets had reported that it was not a good traveller. Even *H. brizoides* was, however, tedious to pick and bunch, needing 20 or more slender stems to make a bunch presentable.

I cannot claim that it was my suggestion that a cross between the two might produce a hybrid to put more colour into *H. brizoides* – perhaps a red. The interest of hybridising had been implanted in me a year or two before as I related on page 12. Heucheras, however, appeared to need no human agency for they are irresistible to bees. So much so that when picking their flowers one had to respect them or risk a sting. By 1922 father had a batch of seedlings as a result of planting his two varieties close together. It was late in that year that I left school because I wanted to be a nurseryman, not to grow flowers for market, but to grow plants for sale. Market flower growing did not appeal. One had to cut them just as they were coming up to their best and then in a rush, not knowing in advance whether or not returns would be profitable and then wait for another year before their flowers were seen, briefly, again.

Most of father's seedling heucheras flowered in 1923 and were of the *brizoides* type, small flowered and long stemmed. In their second year two were selected out of about 200 as being distinct improvements, and propagating began. One was coral red with slightly larger flowers and the other a clearer pink than 'gracillima'. Father decided to put his surname to the red one and in due course its flowers were sent to Covent Garden. The price it made was encouraging and when by 1930 the stock had increased to 20,000, he decided to release some to the trade. At the RHS Hall it gained an Award of Merit as 'Bloom's Variety'. The pink, to which the name 'Pink Spray' was given, was less successful, being less free to flower. It was deleted from my catalogue on this account and although several were sold during the later 1930s, I lost sight of it until 1988, when I saw it in a garden at Ambleside and was given a nucleus stock for old times' sake.

Flowering freedom was all important from every angle, but the lurking enemy of spring frost was an annual anxiety. The unfurling stems are soft and tender and in the year that we hoped the new heucheras would bring much needed cash, a frost in early May decimated the crop which would have been ready for cutting three weeks later.

In 1931 my parents, unselfishly, decided to move and took on a near-derelict glasshouse nursery at Mildenhall, leaving me to carry on at Oakington. Over the next three years cut-flower growing gave way to alpines and perennials in ever-increasing variety and quantity, but my interest in heucheras remained, not as cut flowers but as border plants of merit. Only a very few named varieties were in cultivation or in nursery catalogues and these were of the *sanguinea* type such as the French raised 'Pluie de Feu', which was very similar to 'Trevor Red'. It was, I believed, a genus to be highly rated for garden value and I decided it was up to me to widen the choice. As a young nurseryman starting from scratch, yet very conscious of the opportunity that my father had given me to forge ahead, the only handicap was lack of capital, but it required no outlay to raise more heucheras from seed. All I needed to do was to plant a selection of the best so far in close proximity, knowing that the bees would do the cross-pollination for me. These included a new variety named 'Huntsman' which was advertised as the best red heuchera of the *sanguinea* type. It was a slight improvement on 'Trevor Red' and 'Pluie de Feu', but like them was none too free to flower. I believed this factor was if anything more important than colour and size of flower. The boost from the Award of Merit for 'Bloom's Variety', with its free-flowering quality stemming from the *brizoides* parentage being dominant, seemed to point the way ahead.

When the first batch of 1932 seedlings flowered, however, only two of the *brizoides* types appeared to be worth selecting as improvements. The rest were about as mixed as could be – including a few with more clustered sprays coming doubt-less from the old variety 'Edge Hall', a plant of which had been in the segregated block for pollination. I never knew the origin of this, but suspect that it was a variation on another species – possibly *H. cylindrica*, of which more later. It had clustered spikes of dull-pink flowers. By 1935 I had the pleasant task of naming and propagating eight new varieties as follows:

'CORAL CLOUD'
A true *brizoides* type with 75 cm sprays above shiny crinkly-leaved foliage. Individual flowers of coral red, much larger than *H. brizoides* 'Gracillima'.

'CRIMSON CASCADE'
Much the same as 'Coral Cloud' except a deeper red. It was, however, dropped after a few years as being not sufficiently different and somewhat less reliable in growth and freedom.

'APPLE BLOSSOM'
This reasonably large-flowered selection was a rather pale pink growing to 60 cm. It was deleted after a few years for lacking freedom in flower and for lack of brilliance.

'CORALLION'
An invented name for what I considered an outstanding large-flowered variety. Warm coral-rose, large flowered and very free, 50–60 cm. Sadly my stock had disappeared by 1945 and I have never come across it since.

'FREEDOM'
This and the following were nearer to the *sanguinea* type but all except one in particular were much more prolific, hence the name. The bells are quite large but dangle from a fairly compact spray, only 50 cm tall. The colour is a soft pink, leaves light green.

'GAIETY'
A little taller than 'Freedom', sprays erectly held at about 50 cm, large flowered, carmine rose.

'JUBILEE'
Named for that of King George V in 1935, this has large flowers of a clearer pink than the old cluster-sprayed variety 'Edge Hall'. Compact and reliable at 50 cm.

'MARY ROSE'
Near to *brizoides* but less tall at 50 cm with erect sprays and somewhat larger flowers of a clear pink. It may still exist but I no longer have it.

'OAKINGTON JEWEL'
A fairly large-flowered crimson at 60 cm with dark-green shiny leaves having a hint of purple.

I should mention that in 1934 I staged an exhibit at Chelsea Show entirely of heucheras. Sales were not spectacular and I decided to become a wholesale-only producer of perennials and alpines. No more flower shows were attended from 1934 to 1965. Being strictly wholesale only was not conducive to distributing widely new cultivars or, for that matter, any uncommon species of perennials. My trade customers were shy of investing in any but 'bread-and-butter' kinds and an annual catalogue with no illustrations was my only means of advertising new varieties. It was the lack of interest on the part of the majority of my retailing customers that finally and belatedly drove me to appeal direct to the gardening public.

One means of displaying the post-war batch of new heucheras came when the RHS staged an official Trial at Wisley Gardens. By that time I had been at Bressingham long enough to select several more from a batch of 2,000 raised from seed sown in 1948 before I went to Canada. When I returned in 1950 they were ready to flower, and making selection was a soothing antidote to the ill-fated Canadian venture. Percy Piper and I spent many an evening walking slowly up and down the rows with thrill and bewilderment at the fascinating variety, in company with legions of bees. It was bewildering because not only were there so many of merit, but some new shades including orange scarlet, brownish red and other combinations not seen before, in heights ranging from 30 cm to 75 cm or more. Because Percy had faithfully cared for the plants in my absence, he had a right to stake some that appealed to him more than to me. He was much more appreciative than I of these having cut-flower potential. So it was that between us we tagged over 50 and then began to throw out some poor or nondescript plants in order to prevent seed being taken from them. At this stage I had decided for the first time to market heucheras as a seed-raised mixture under the name of 'Bressingham Hybrids', which now are known and sold world-wide.

The 50 staked plants were dug up in August and planted by themselves after being divided carefully to make two or more of each. This was done not only to increase stocks which might eventually be named, but to observe rates of growth and to test the flowering propensities of each. Each June, for the next three years, the process of re-selection and elimination went on until the final choice fell in a further twelve to be named:

'BRESSINGHAM BLAZE'
This fiery red with marbled leaves was spectacular enough for its name, but after a few years it lost vigour and stocks were seldom good. When in good form it was about 60 cm with large open bells, but sprays were short branched.

'CARMEN'
Intense carmine-pink erect sprays, medium-sized flowers freely borne above dark foliage, 60 cm.

'FIREBIRD'
Glowing crimson-scarlet, erect and free, 60 cm.

'GLORIANA'.
A mistake was made over naming, so that for a time it was also labelled 'Captivation'. A very deep pink, but eventually dropped in favour of 'Carmen'.

'LADY ROMNEY'
Selected by her ladyship on a visit, this small flowered pale pink was another to be later dropped.

'PEARL DROPS'
Also small flowered, but very dainty with arching sprays of *brizoides* form. White with just a hint of pink at 60 cm.

'PRETTY POLLY'
The dwarfest of them all and one of the freest to flower. Dangling soft-pink flowers no more than 30 cm.

'RED SPANGLES'
The ultimate blood red and so far as I know unsurpassed. Large flowered on 50 cm sprays above abundant greenery for a long time.

'SCINTILLATION'
Outstanding for its coral rimmed, deep-pink bells on 60 cm stems. This remains a firm favourite.

'SPARKLER'
Slender sprays, medium-sized flowers of a carmine-scarlet colour, lush dark-green foliage, 60 cm, and reliably free to flower.

'SPLENDOUR'
Unique for colour, deep salmon-scarlet, medium-sized flowers. From the first it has been of poor constitution and has almost vanished from my garden.

'SNOWflakes'
A true *sanguinea* type in habit with quite large bells on 50–60 cm stems. I have not seen a better white than this.

'SUNSET'
This too is proving difficult to entice vigour, but the colour is not lacking. Large, coral red, 50 cm.

Of the above, several were given Awards and Commendations at the Wisley Trials. Although we have not grown them in vast quantities in the nursery, there has been a fairly steady demand. Mishaps have occurred in propagation, however, due to those concerned attempting to increase them from immature cuttings rather than straight division. Stocks are low at the present time for this reason. I must not omit to mention also that some heucheras may be infected with gall as they become old and less thrifty. This has an obscure origin and may be a virus. It takes the form of a tightly congested nub of incipient shoots near the soil surface. If noticed – and it inhibits normal growth above ground as well as flowering – plants are best destroyed since divisions of healthy pieces may carry on the infection. We find, however, that tissue culture is a sure means of being rid of it.

Having so long-standing an affection and interest in heucheras, it was natural that I collected some other species as well as cultivars raised by others. Few of the latter were acquired because very few had been raised and introduced. Two or three came from Germany but did not appeal as sufficiently outstanding either to propagate for sale or for breeding. One named 'June Bride' came from America. It is a modest lady, a mid-pink, and when later told it had been selected from a batch of seedlings raised as 'Bressingham Hybrids', I could not give it undeserved extra marks on that account.

Of the acquired plants, I suspect that one named 'Bakeri' is in fact a hybrid. It is not startling but appears to flower freely. Others, including two or three dwarfs only a few centimetres tall are not only shy to flower but lacking in colour. *H. americana* is a variable species with very small brown-green flowers in later summer. The foliage, however, is distinctive with purplish zones and the variety 'Palace Purple' is really outstanding, the large leaves being almost beetroot red and showers of minute greenish-cream flowers come in July-August. I first heard of this plant in 1981, from Dr Wherry of the New York Botanic Garden. But before stock from him finally arrived at Bressingham in 1984, stock of a similar plant was offered by Kew. This was built up from a seedling spotted by Brian Halliwell in the Queen's Garden behind the Kew Palace and it was this stock that we finally introduced as 'Palace Purple'. I still have a group of Dr Wherry's plant in the garden and both plants seem to be the same. One other late-flowering species must be mentioned which, although only recently acquired, has much distinction. It is *H. villosa*, and if the foliage is a uniform light green, the masses of tiny white flowers on 60–70 cm airy sprays make it very worthy of a place.

The species *H. cylindrica* has been grown in my garden for many years but until some flower-arranging ladies asked for plants, I did not bother to work up a stock. Its greenish flowers on a pokery spike at 75 cm did not appeal to me so I decided to breed from it. The result was 'Green Ivory' and 'Green Marble', both with green-white flowers, but the latter had marbled light-green leaves as well. Both are vigorous and free with a more spreading habit than any other heucheras and the cylindrical spike of the species is retained.

A third one of this type is 'Hyperion' from the same batch, but its flowers are pink with only a hint of green, whilst the growth is more compact. The demand for all three has surprised me.

At the time of writing I have about a score of the most recent selections on trial. Having raised so many in the past, it is now imperative to be rigorous in allowing them to stay undisturbed long enough to fully prove themselves. Only the very best, showing decided improvements or distinction, will be named and introduced at some future date.

**10** The tapering leafy spikes of *Aconitum* 'Bressingham Spire' are symmetrical and erect

**11** From the original batch of *Dicentra* Rokuju hybrids this selection—'Pearl Drops'—has proved to be by far the best

**12** In 1952 several *Erigerons* were raised from a deliberate cross—this one is 'Festivity'

13 *Heuchera* 'Red Spangles' was amongst those which gained ⁚ ʌemier awards in the Wisley Trials

14 Till this *Bergenia* appeared a pure white was needed and 'Bressingham White' filled that need

15 Named after my youngest daughter 'Jenny' this *Crocosmia* was her choice from a dozen selections

## HEUCHERELLA

It is the practice in nomenclature to marry the generic names where species belonging to separate genera produce a hybrid. The above name therefore stands for a cross between *Heuchera* and *Tiarella*. I suggested the cross as a possibility to Percy Piper in 1950 and one of the first uses he made of the camel-hair brush I gave him was to take the pollen from *Heuchera* 'Freedom' and *Tiarella wherryi*. It may have been vice versa or a two-way cross, since Percy kept no written records. Very little seed was set from whichever it was, and more disappointingly only one seed germinated. This was nurtured with great care and it flowered for the first time later the next year, 1951. There was no doubt it was a bigeneric hybrid, with somewhat ivy-shaped leaves close to the ground, having a hint of gold. The flower sprays stood erectly to about 30 cm in which pink dominated the open bell shape, but lit up with almost a sparkle of white within. As stock increased from division – being a 'mule' it did not make seed – I found that it grew best in a little shade, as do tiarellas, and good light soil. I named it 'Bridget Bloom' after my eldest daughter and since it was first introduced in 1955, it has been consistently in good demand. This is due not only to its dainty charm but to its long season in flower. In favourable seasons it is seldom out of flower from May to October, but it is not for heavy or highly alkaline soils. It thrives best in sandy, humus-rich, half-shady conditions.

## KNIPHOFIA

Some people still express surprise to see what they have always regarded as 'Red Hot Pokers' in many shades other than red. Although almost every shade of yellow through to ivory-white exist, the salmon or pink tints have failed to appear amongst the thousands of seedlings I have raised over the years. Prior to 1939 I was content to let such breeders as Watkin Samuel, Maurice Prichard and Mr Richards of Bees Ltd produce new varieties without attempting to compete with them. During the 1950s, however, the influx had virtually ceased, giving me incentive to begin. My aim at first, as with many other subjects, was to produce shorter stems as well as to widen the range of colour.

The shortest species in existence was the latest to flower, *K. galpinii*. Its orange-yellow spikes, 38–45 cm tall, were at their best in October, by which time all but one or two very tall ones had finished. By chance some mixed seedlings as yearling plants were flowering out of their normal season, and Percy Piper acted promptly on my suggestion to use the dwarfest of these to cross with *K. galpinii*. It was chancy because *galpinii* was not fully winter hardy – and incidentally the winter of 1962–3 killed off practically my whole stock of nearly 2,000. However, by 1963 selections had already been made from Percy's 1959 cross and had come through the winter's frost which had penetrated several inches deep into the soil.

The cross had yielded several hundred seedlings, but though the majority were around 90 cm in height, a few were under 60 cm with unmistakeable signs of *galpinii* parentage. This was indicated by thinly rounded grassy foliage, rather than bladed, and slender flower spikes carrying somewhat drooping tubular flowers. Overall they were as graceful as they were distinctive, and finally four were picked out for propagation and naming as soon as stocks were large enough to offer. This took several years, but by 1968 one of them, 'Bressingham Torch' was ready. Some losses had occurred through being too hasty and it was the period when I found it risky to divide kniphofias every spring. The other three also were given the Bressingham prefix – 'Flame', 'Comet' and 'Beacon', but by the time these came up to the required quantity the stock and that of other varieties had come under a threat. Losses were occurring more widely, newly divided and planted pieces were dying and examination showed a rot which was a smelly mushiness. Cambridge plant pathologists diagnosed it as violet root rot, for which there was no known cure. It also decimated Beth Chatto's stocks of the cultivars raised and it has taken some years for them to be made available again. It also attacks asparagus.

This set-back occurred at the same time as Trials were invited by the RHS at Wisley. I sent several cultivars, including the new dwarfs, which incidentally all flower in September as well as October, but in the spring of the year in which judging was to take place, the announcement came that the Trials were to be abandoned and all plants therein destroyed because the virus had become widespread. They included a number from other sources than Bressingham and indications were that some of those sent by others had also been responsible for the spread of the infection.

At Bressingham it was rife and began to affect old plants as well as young, freshly planted stock. It seemed pointless to do the usual division and planting and over the next few years a large proportion of the score or so of 'standard' varieties grown for sale in the nursery had to be deleted. Some died out completely, and with very few exceptions the only remaining healthy stocks were those that had remained undisturbed in my garden. Sadly 'Bressingham Beacon' and 'Flame' had all died. Three small plants of 'Comet' and one of 'Torch' were all that remained and these I carefully dusted with Captan with more hope than conviction that this would save them from extinction.

Naturally such severe losses made me ponder very objectively. Indications were that the virus attacked first those plants that had been cut up for division, and that when left alone in some isolation they escaped its ravages; also that once a plant became infected in the slightest degree it was doomed. I deduced, therefore, that if the knife were used it must never cut into fleshy growth to leave a wound open to the virus. Only after at least two years' growth was it possible to separate mature pieces using a knife just to sever, as it were, the umbilical cord – the now hard, thin connecting root which had enabled a side-shoot to grow away from a central crown. Without much assurance that such a compound as Captan or Benlate would act as a safeguard, I nevertheless dusted the roots when at last 'Comet' and 'Torch' were large enough to divide.

It took ten more years to grow sufficient 'Comet' to sell again with 'Torch' lagging behind. The latter flowers at 45–50 cm and is a fiery orange red at its best in early autumn. 'Comet' is 8 cm or so shorter and is the more vigorous of the two, flowering at the same time – well into October. It is all the brighter for being two-toned, each little tubular flower on stumpy but slender spikes being yellow based and red tipped.

By taking care over dividing and planting on fresh ground, the virus now appears to have been eliminated. Another helpful means has been to delay division until May, by which time the new growth is strong enough and young plants quickly make fresh roots. This applies to all types of kniphofia and generally the latest to flower are the last to be divided. A few such as *K. primulina praecox* will sometimes begin flowering in May. So does 'Atlanta', but although this gained an Award as a cultivar, I am pretty certain that it is none other than what I used to grow as *K. tuckii*.

Be that as it may, the virus decimation of the 1960s was incentive enough to raise many more from seed, knowing that the bees were our friends in helping to widen the range of form and colour. Over the years more selections have been named and distributed and although most of these are taller, the colour range has been widened a litte. One was a 1.2 m canary yellow which held a hint of green. It also held a special appeal to Percy Piper who had been responsible for seed collecting and raising seed, hence the name 'Percy's Pride'. One appealed to my youngest daughter Jenny so was named 'Jenny Bloom'. It was distinct for being faintly tinted salmon at the tip of its flowers. This grew to 1.05 m and flowered as did 'Percy's Pride' in July-August, but it lacked vigour and regretfully had to be deleted from the catalogue on that account.

Along with 'Percy's Pride' were two others of merit. One, which I named 'Shining Sceptre', was a stately 1.2 m, orange gold, July–August flowering, which lacks nothing in vigour and has a wide poker head. Much more demure and with narrow grassy leaves is 'Candlelight'. It is amongst my top favourites, not only because of its graceful spikes of pure lemon yellow, but for its long flowering property – on stems no more than about 60 cm. Another taller one about to be released has a more decided green tinge in its primrose-ivory coloured 1.2 m spikes. The name, provisionally, is 'Ice Queen', but I am not entirely satisfied with this. A name has also to be chosen for one as near-white as can probably be. 'Ivory Pinnacle' might be suitable but as with heucheras and crocosmias, any more of the many new selections under Trial will have to be very distinctive before being named and distributed. There must be 20 of the dwarf grassy-leaved ones, but if one or two prove to be earlier to flower, apart from considerations of colour, then it would be sensible to go ahead with them. Apart from the tall white, one or two others are quite spectacular in the flame-red colour range with huge pokers standing 1.8 m tall. It seems fair to conclude therefore that with due care and devotion future prospects of more cultivars of real garden value are bright.

# LIGULARIA

The two cultivars I have named have not come from a deliberate crossing, but from a purely fortuitous occurrence to enhance the range of the genus. As a genus the ligularias have been somewhat neglected. Most of them not only take up space, some being rather coarse, but tend to droop on hot sunny days and fall short of being worthy in dry or poor soils. Until fairly recent years the name *Senecio* covered what we now refer to as *Ligularia*, but I have never discovered where the takeover ends. The species *L. clivorum* is, or has been, probably the best known in spite of its huge outspreading leaves, so demanding of space. Much less known is *L. veitchiana*, with smaller leaves and a more upright habit at 1.35 m. Both have deep-yellow daisy-type flowers on terminally branching stems and both make massive clumps.

I have only raised seedlings from the purplish-leaved, orange-flowered *L. clivorum* 'Desdemona', which has come true. I could not, therefore, account for a seedling, obviously self-sown, which appeared between the garden group of 'Desdemona' and that of *L. veitchiana* not far away. When eventually it flowered it had more resemblance to the latter, but the colour was orange-gold. The habit was erect and leafy stemmed to 1.5 m and produced such an abundance of flowers 8 cm across that it was very well worth propagating – and I named it 'Sungold'.

The other ligularia came in much the same way, but from two very different species, *L. przewalskii* and *L. stenocephala*. The difference between the two is mainly in the leaf formation, one less deeply jagged than the other, but both having tall slender stems, almost black in *przewalskii*, up to 1.8 m. Flowers along the upper, slimly branched spikes are both yellow. Somehow a natural hybrid occurred between the two which at first I did not rate at all highly, even though it was more spectacular than either. Neither the parents nor the seedling made a mass of basal foliage, but roots were more compact than its parents. The new seedling brought very favourable comment, however, when it was increased to make a garden group. Its dark-green stems and handsome jagged leaves were indeed complementary to the bold 1.8 m spikes, especially against an evergreen background. The name 'Rocket' seemed to fit and since being distributed has been acclaimed and much sought after even in the United States, as well as becoming a 'standard' cultivar in Europe.

## MERTENSIA

So far as I know, no cultivar has ever been produced from any species. Not that many species exist, and few are at all widely grown, but they have charm, especially the spring-flowering *M. virginica* with its dangling azure, pink-tinged bells along arching glaucous-leaved stems from fleshy roots. Having tried with only partial success to grow a few other species, I was charmed by one, *M. pterocarpa*. This too was intensely blue, summer flowering, but less tall at under 30 cm. It had a low summer spread of glaucous foliage but made scarcely any size of rootstock. Nor did it set seed, as did a somewhat sturdier but small-flowered species *M. ciliata*. This produced a little seed, whereas *pterocarpa* did not, but by planting in close proximity I hoped, somewhat in vain, for a cross that would marry the best features of both. All but one seedling came up as *M. ciliata* – seed having been collected from both. The one stranger seemed to be at first hopes fulfilled, but although it grew quite vigorously for a year or two, it set no seed and made but little dividable growth from its fleshy rootstock. Having chosen the name 'Blue Drops' for its dangling sapphire bells on a glaucous-leaved 30 cm mound, I kept hopes alive by trying it in different soils and situations. No success came and indeed as the stocks of never more than 50 plants gradually dwindled and languished, after about seven years of cosseting it gave up altogether to become but a memory I would have preferred to forget.

## MIMULUS

No skill whatever is required to raise cultivars of this colourful genus. The species have interbred and strains, marketed by seedsmen, have come in a variety of vivid colours, whilst a few come true from seed. The latter are the dwarf kinds such as 'Wisley Red' and 'Whitecroft Scarlet', but they are usually short-lived. The taller ones with larger often multi-coloured flowers are perennial, but in need of frequent replanting. This is because they are shallow rooting and mat forming and as they spread the centre, or older parts, are apt to die out, presumably from exhaustion. Amongst the brightest and most reliable have been the orange and reddish-brown 'A.T. Johnson'. From seedlings of this and one or two others I picked out two that were not only bright with an orange-flame base to the large-lipped flowers, but enhanced with intriguing deeper-reddish spots and markings. The first to be named was 'Firedragon' a basically flame colour on large flowers above 30–38 cm stems, but with red spots within. June-July is when these mimulus make the bravest display given rich or moist soil, and they sometimes flower again if cut back and given a little feed or a replant. This applies to the other selection which I named 'Mandarin'. It differs by having a more orange base colour which is profusely spotted with flame-red spots and blotches.

Although even more variations could no doubt be induced by re-selection of seedlings, I have no intention of doing so. What I would like to do is to introduce pink as another colour into these robust, taller, large-flowered ones. The discovery a few years ago of what is temporarily named 'Andean Nymph', which is a very dwarf but small-flowered, long-living pink species, might prove to be a co-operative parent.

## OMPHALODES

This small genus of dwarf leafy plants, partial to shade, has small flower sprays in spring, which show its kinship with 'Forget-me-nots'. Of the few species in cultivation, *O. cappadocica* is much slower to grow and more refined than *O. verna*, which tends to romp and have a brief flowering season. Both are under 15 cm in height, but whereas *O. verna* has an albino form, I have never heard of a white in *O. cappadocica*. It is however slightly variable, both in height and colour, though I was not aware of this until I raised some from my own saved seed in an effort to keep pace with the demand. Not that it produces much seed, and like its relative

*Mertensia* is apt to be already shed at the time one expects it to be ripe – a case of there today and gone tomorrow and nestling as it does almost hidden by its dense, evergreen, narrowly oval leafage.

Less than 100 seedlings came from that first sowing and all but three appeared to be uniformly consistent with the parental stock – delicate sprays of small almost gentian blue, open flowers. The minority of three were of an intense sky blue, 8–10 cm, amongst shorter but slightly broader leaves. It needed more than a casual, overall glance to see the difference. Increasing slowly as this species does from division, I kept the three as a separate stock for about three seasons, unsure whether there was enough justification for giving it a cultivar name. It was a visit from my old friend Will Ingwersen that tipped the balance. In his opinion it was sufficiently different and it became 'Anthea Bloom' after my second daughter. Because it does not come true from seed and vegetatively it is even slower than straight *cappadocica* to propagate, it has not often been catalogued for lack of stock. Now I have it, as with some other slow subjects, on a two-year basis – which entails two beds to be propagated on alternate years as a means of keeping up a regular if limited supply.

## PENSTEMON

Some 30 years ago an American visitor kindled my interest in the wide range of *Penstemon* species native to his homeland. In due course, after he had become a member of the American Penstemon Society, he sent a packet which contained over 20 species new to me, with notes as to where they were collected in the wild. My interest was not so much in the very dwarf alpine types, but in adding to the limited range of hardy 'border' kinds.

Most of them grew well enough in the first season, though few flowered until the following one. But although none were startling and some were suspect for hardiness, it was not until the toll taken by the 1963 winter that I realised why so few of the taller species flourished in Britain. Nor, until told later, had I known that species native to the west side of America do not take to the eastern American climate.

Hopes of using any for breeding with the few reliable in

Britain vanished along with the majority of newcomers. Only one with a question mark for a name remained and proved to be hardy. It was not especially attractive, but its pinkish-purple flowers of tubular shape, above somewhat twiggy, narrow leaves at 38 cm high, continued for several weeks. The little group stayed for several years. On a visit, Valerie Finnis brought me, as usual, a few various plants and amongst them was this same Penstemon – still without a name. However, some seed from both produced variations, some paler, some deeper in colour. I selected only one, naming it 'Amethyst' because it was almost that colour, but did not consider it worthy of a sales boost. Since it appeared others have been raised along with hopes of something better. As for a specific name, Kew, on being asked to identify, said it was nearest to *P. campanulatus*, but what I had already as *P. campanulatus* in the pink cultivar 'Evelyn' was much taller and less bushy and much less hardy.

## PEROVSKIA

These are amongst the few shrubs that fit in well with border perennials and are of real value for a late display of slender spikes of small blue flowers. If cut back to about 30 cm in spring, the young growth, with small greyish leaves, soon renews its spikes for late summer flowering up to 1.2 m. The best-known species is *P. atriplicifolia*, but not far away in my garden was another, *P. abrotanifolia*, which I preferred for its prettier leaves and slightly larger, lighter-blue flowers. Seed of the latter was saved and one variation when seedlings flowered two years later appeared to be a cross. It too had thumb-nail sized leaves, larger than *P. atriplicifolia*, but like the latter were ash grey and serrated. As a cross it had the best qualities of both and flowered so profusely that the name 'Blue Haze' seemed to fit.

The original group has prospered ever since it was first planted in 1964. Its slow expansion below ground is easily rbed with a spade every two years and for the little trouble either of these 'Russian Sages' entail, they are very rewarding.

# PHLOX

If I were to list all the named varieties of herbaceous phlox that I have grown over the past 65 years, it would not be far short of 300. Unlike some subjects where new introductions inevitably replace the old, amongst phlox it is not unusual to bring an old cultivar back into circulation because colour and constitution have not been surpassed. In recent years I have done this with two that were in the original collection of ten which began my affair with phlox in 1924. They are the pure pink 'Rijnstroon' and the soft salmon-pink 'Elizabeth Campbell', but it was not until I noticed the absence of a very light pink amongst the 80 varieties I was growing about 1960 that seed was collected and sown in hopes of remedying the deficiency. When the seedlings flowered, none were exactly what I was looking for – an overall shell pink. The nearest to it was both ivory white and pink, with a deeper eye, and it appealed for being distinctive and took the name 'Mother of Pearl'.

Another seedling in this batch had stood out even before it flowered, for it had prettily variegated leaves. These were less showy than those of 'Nora Leigh' but the latter was scarcely an appealing colour in flower. Before long the newcomer held a decided advantage by producing a head of violet purple which harmonised well with the foliage. Stocks were rather slow to increase because the usual fast method of root cuttings does not perpetuate leaf variegation. Tip cuttings in spring will do so, but one must not weaken the mother plants by taking more than a few each year. I gave it the name 'Harlequin' when the supply was adequate. Sadly in recent years some deterioration in vigour set in. Perhaps, after all, propagation was overdone, but I was pleased to see it still flourishing at Threave in south-west Scotland not long ago.

In with that batch of seedlings were a few of the *Phlox maculata* type which Percy had slyly included as seed, because the cylindrical flowering 'Alpha' was one of his favourites. The species is about the average height of the more usual *paniculata* species, but the roots are more fibrous, shallow and outspreading, whilst the flowering period is longer given light, but not dry, soil. The colour range, however, is very limited and 'Alpha', a soft but telling pink at

75–90 cm tall, was thereabouts the only one in circulation. Scarcely any *maculata* type germinated but one that did, and flourished, was pure white with a crimson centre and it had a firm head. As a worthy companion for 'Alpha', I named it 'Omega'. Since then only one other *maculata* has been introduced, named 'Anya', a magenta pink. Incidentally, Anya herself is the grand-daughter of that famous German hybridist, the late Georg Arends of Ronsdorf, who, with her mother, is carrying on the family tradition.

The majority of new introductions of phlox have come from Germany and Holland – and are continuing still. In England there was a spate of new cultivars about 40 years ago, with the 'Symons-Jeune' collection, and some from Fred Simpson of Otley who named his after Royal residences from Windsor to Balmoral. The Symons-Jeune plants were distributed with the claim that they had been specially bred for vigour and other improvements, but on growing all of them I could see no trace of new blood. It was mainly because new British introductions had virtually ceased that I decided to make a modest attempt to do so.

In making selections from successive batches of seedlings, constitution, as well as colour, had to be the criterion. And yet, although the first to be named was not only strong growing with a fine head of warm salmon-pink unlike any other, ten years later it was found to be rather susceptible to eelworm. I had named it 'Mary Fox' as a tribute to the lady who was in charge of the nursery office from 1951 until she retired in 1984. The next was 'Eva Cullum', whose namesake headed the retail department from 1965 until retirement. This fine bright deep pink, so free to flower and with such abundant foliage, is still going strong. Not so the one in memory of a long-standing nursery foreman who died prematurely, 'Bill Green'. This too is pink but quite distinct, and sadly this too has languished, though hopefully not beyond recovery.

The fourth and last to be named was in honour of my most favourite composer, 'Franz Schubert'. Its colour is near to parma violet, with just a tinge of pink, enough to say it is a lilac shade. When seen by a visiting American nurseryman who knew his phlox, an order was given for 500 on the strength of its merits; later he reported all were sold through his catalogue within a month, one reason given was that members of the American Schubert Musical Society had pounced on it because of its name. A curious twist, but I am pretty sure that those people will not be disappointed in its performance.

There is only one alpine phlox to which I gave a name and that was 60 years ago. At the time *P. subulata* 'G.F. Wilson' was the nearest to blue in this mat-forming evergreen group. What I raised and named from it, 'Oakington Blue Eyes', has held its place as being brighter, but the place name has been dropped.

## POLYGONUM

This is another genus which has a large and diverse range of species to include some decidedly choice and a few pernicious weeds – such as the tall *P. cuspidatum* which defies most chemical killers. My special favourites lie naturally in the choice ones, mentioned elsewhere, but very few and perhaps only three species have shown the propensity for variation. They are *P. bistortum*, *P. affine* and *P. amplexicaule*. The first is the native bistort and in spite of its being a surface romper in most soils, the hoped-for deep-pink poker spikes have never appeared from seedlings. *P. affine* already had the cultivars 'Darjeeling Red' and 'Donald Lowndes', as improvements in colour and size of pokery spikes above its spreading leafy mats which make good ground cover. My 'Dimity' has proved more reliable as a perennial than either of these. It is more compact and therefore more densely leaved and is less liable to die out in patches after a year or two – which is the main fault of 'Donald Lowndes'. The broad fingery leaves of 'Dimity' also take on attractive autumn colouring and the stubby light-pink pokers are only 10 cm high. All are shallow rooted.

In contrast *P. amplexicaule* is deep rooted and although plants become quite massive in time, they may be left without fear of spreading invasively. Until about 25 years ago the only variations were a dull red, a pale pink and a not very pure white in the thin pokery spikes topping a rounded leafy bush, 1.2–1.5 m tall. None were spectacular because of lack of colour, but from seed of the red *P. a. atrosanguineum* appeared one that was much brighter – nearer to scarlet. By regular division of the very tough rootstock it eventually was introduced under the name 'Firetail', for the little terminal spikes are rather tail-like and stick out from the big leafy bush at all angles.

In good soil these polygonums will bush up to about 1.5 m, and when I learned that Edinburgh Royal Botanic Garden had a much dwarfer one, I became interested. Having made many exchanges with ERBG in the past I did not have to wait long for a sizeable piece of what had been named 'Inverleith' to arrive. From the first it romped away, producing a wealth of summer growth and a long season in flower at no more than 60 cm high. The little spikes were crimson, short of being brilliant, but a welcome addition none the less. It was, I believe, a chance seedling and a few years later I came across one a few metres from my garden group. As it grew it was noticeably different with larger leaves and when it flowered at about 75 cm it was pleasing to note that it also had fuller spikes of a richer red colour. As with others of its ilk it makes a dense bushy spread above ground, dying back to an expanding rootstock, and should have increased sufficiently to launch it under 'Taurus' by 1991.

## POTENTILLA

In considering this genus in the present context, some wistful thoughts and feelings occur to me. They stem from the fact that although I began to collect them when still a schoolboy because they appealed, yet only once in my lifetime did I attempt breeding. Perhaps it was because I was still adding to my collection over the past 30 years that with over 50 species and cultivars this process took first place. Several cultivars of the herbaceous type in the 30–60 cm height range had been bred in the past century, and it was from an assortment of these that finally some seed was sown and raised in the early 1960s. The result was rather disappointing for these were nearly all single flowered, whereas I had hoped for some doubles of such quality and brilliance as the intense orange 'William Rollison' or the rich crimson-brown 'Gloire de Nancy'.

Only one of these seedlings came as a colour break worth

propagating and naming. It was a single on 38 cm sprays of a very bright-orange base, flecked and suffused with scarlet. The strawberry-like foliage, which most of these herbaceous potentillas possess, was inclined to be silvery and I named it 'Blazeaway'. These plants are of course sun lovers and are otherwise easy to grow and so showy for frontal positions from June to August inclusive. I must try to remedy my own shortcomings.

I can take no credit for another I named 'Flamenco', for it was a self-sown seedling. It belongs to the taller, earlier flowering *argyrophylla* species. This has smaller flowers on longer, more branching sprays, 50–60 cm, and includes red and yellow forms, some with silvery leaves. The foundling is green leaved and very robust. Its blood-red flowers begin to open in May, and fade as that well known but less tall bright-red 'Gibson's Scarlet' appear. Many years ago I obtained one from Holland with the name 'Congo', but had no information on its provenance. It stayed as a group in my garden for several years and each year came the thought that it was very similar to 'Gibson's Scarlet'. Finally I placed one of each together and found no difference between them whatever.

## PULMONARIA

This spring-flowering genus has come in for much deserved popularity in recent years. Its adaptability to sun or shade and the attractive foliage so many possess to give ground cover when flowering ends, has at last been appreciated. I doubt, however, if many, or any, have been the subject of deliberate breeding. Early foraging bees, I imagine, have been responsible, and seedlings are not only easy to raise but sometimes self-sown plants appear. One of the brightest for foliage, following the sprays of blue which turn pink with age, is 'Margery Fish'. The memory of that redoubtable lady rests firmly not only on her generosity and knowledge, but also is perpetuated by those to whom she was a dear person, by giving her name to plants which she had introduced, after her death. I believe her form of *Pulmonaria saccharata* was one of them. Its large tongue-shaped, overlapping leaves are almost entirely silvered and the only one I have named came as a self-sown seedling from it. 'Green Marble' is its name, and the only difference is that it has broad silver blotches on a basically light-green leaf. Incidentally, I find all variegated pulmonarias more effective as foliage plants in sun, despite their being recommended as shade-loving subjects.

# PYRETHRUM

Rather obstinately, I prefer to keep to the old generic name rather than use *Tanacetum coccineum*, which is now said to be correct. These colourful daisy-type flowers of early summer are distinct enough to classify separately from the already overcrowded chrysanthemum generic compartment. As perennials they have been almost lifelong familiars for me. My father grew them as market cut flowers before I was born, and even after I gave up growing them for that purpose, the demand from cut-flower growers as well as from amateur gardeners continued. At one time I had about 50 named varieties and produced up to 100,000 plants for sale.

Pyrethrums were still enjoying wide popularity in 1953 when I learned that a new colour break had been evolved in Denmark. It was a salmon pink, single flowered, and wishing to keep ahead in a competitive market I made another busman's holiday, and on seeing it bought all the available stock of 2,000. Translating the name 'Abenglut' into English it was offered as 'Evenglow', but its one fault of being weak stemmed was a little more pronounced on our heavier soil at Bressingham. This fault made it less attractive to the cut-flower growers and with some determination I decided to attempt to breed from it.

Percy Piper took readily to the idea and although I suggested which varieties already in stock should be used for the purpose, he kept no record of them when crossing took place in 1954. Size of flower and strength of stem was the aim, combined with the colour of 'Evenglow'. Several hundred resultant seedlings were planted out the following year and they caused some excitement when they began to flower. What amazed me was the variety of not only colour but doubles and semi-doubles as well. Percy smiled slyly when I put it to him that he had gone well beyond my suggestions, saying that he thought it best to have a wide choice.

Marker sticks and labels were placed against the first selections and the following spring there were five to ten divisions to grow on of the seven best. Sales to the trade of existing varieties were beginning to fall off as stocks of the new ones slowly built up, due partly no doubt to flower growing for market becoming steadily uneconomic. Our new ones, therefore, would be a timely introduction as good garden plants. In order to make a splash with them in 1965 when we decided to open a retail side, and show at Chelsea, it seemed to make sense to wait until sufficient of all seven were available to meet the hoped-for demand.

It was not to be, for in 1966 only one or two were sufficiently open to include in our Chelsea exhibit. All were of course named by then. Sadly some are no longer in circulation, but the list below includes all that might have been had not a somewhat mysterious disease attacked them over the next few years. It was not an outright, swift killer, but something that inhibited vigorous growth, making plants, as it were, sulk. Leaves were fewer and shorter, flowers sparse and short stemmed. On examination the rootstock was lacking in fibrous roots and hardened to become quite woody. On enquiry I learned that other growers were also affected with the same trouble, and with neither diagnosis nor cure being offered by pathologists other than the usual 'burn all affected plants', we were in a rather hopeless situation.

On the nursery, stocks fell year by year until only a remnant was left. The new varieties were amongst them and although some were listed in the 1968/9 catalogue, few were sold because of losses and only those that appeared to be healthy could be sent out. For a time I took a rather fatalistic attitude – to hide some bitter disappointment. When faint hopes of recovery had almost gone as the majority of varieties were in danger of extinction, I decided to attempt to save them by experimenting with soil treatment in my own garden area. I used various chemical dustings and soil additives such as lime, soot, ash, sand and old pig manure. Some response came in the first year, but two of the best new ones – of which only a handful remained out of several hundred before the onset of the disease – died out completely. The list below of those I named includes them, but it is very doubtful if stocks exist anywhere from those that were sold before the trouble began – over 20 years ago:

'ARIEL'
Semi-double 'anemone-centred', light salmon-pink, erect growing at 60 cm.

'BELLARION'
Much the same colour as 'Evenglow', single bright salmon-pink, but larger flowered and more upstanding (all died).

'INFERNO'
A single with some magenta in with the salmon, to give such intensity of colour as to choose such a name (none survived).

'PROSPERO'
A deeper salmon-pink than 'Ariel', this too is anemone-centred and a few survived.

'TAURUS'
Although I had grown several single red varieties, this was the richest blood red and the largest flowered I had ever seen; a few survived but it still lacks vigour.

'VANESSA'
This is fully double, a carmine rose which has a golden flush at the centre; like some other doubles the stem, though 60–75 cm, is rather weak, but more of it survived than any other.

'VENUS'
Also fully double, but with somewhat quilled petals of a delicate, clear pink. It was my favourite but only one plant showed signs of life when I took back the remnants from the nursery and it continued to languish and soon died.

'BRESSINGHAM RED'
This is added by way of explaining that I did not raise it. It was offered as an unamed stock by Mr R.O. Walker of Leeming Bar, Yorks. He was about to retire and wished to dispose of it. As a very good single he himself suggested the name.

A sorry tail piece must be added. Having found pyrethrums responded to extra care I continued to grow them and fuss them somewhat on the five-acre nursery field near my home. By 1987 the 18 varieties I was growing were in some cases in sufficient quantity to accept orders. The stock, by the way, included several old favourites such as the fine double red 'J.N. Twerdy' and some newly imported dwarfs barely 30 cm tall from Germany. In August 1987 heavy rains came and caused severe flooding on our valley bottom fields, on one of which the largest quantities of the strongest growing were planted – some 2,000 plants. All perished because the flood stayed for several days. Those on higher ground made extra lush growth but this appeared to be at first some slight compensation. The following winter was excessively wet and my concern was aroused when spring came because many were failing to make new growth. More than half never did, and the sad conclusion was that the previous late summer surge of late growth weakened them to the extent of being unable to survive the renewed wetness when in winter dormancy.

## SALVIA

One of the most rewarding perennials is *Salvia* × *superba*, with its long succession of violet-blue flowers. It is believed by some to be itself a hybrid, and equally useful variations have come from it, all much the same colour, but less tall from the 50 cm 'May Night' to the 75 cm 'Lubeca'. Another salvia species, but lighter in colour and a more open branching habit is *S. haematodes*, but in my garden it proved less reliably perennial though reproducing freely from seed. In an effort to induce a paler blue on the *superba* type, a plant of this and *haematodes* were placed side by side. From the resultant seedlings a part-way cross appeared, but instead of its being a lighter blue *superba*, it was more like a deeper blue *haematodes*. It was more robust as a perennial, however, than either, with spikes of about 1.2 m, flowering from June onwards into September if faded stems were removed. As *S.* 'Indigo' it has continued to flourish for many years.

## SAPONARIA

It will be noticed that the alpines I have raised and introduced are not only far fewer than border perennials, but are not in any way to be considered choice. *Saponaria* 'Bressingham' is the one exception to this and it remains something of a mystery how it came about. I remember suggesting to Percy

Piper that a cross between the bright but rather common *S. ocymoides* with *S.* × *olivana* might yield another hybrid. They too were very different in habit; the former being almost too vigorous in spread and *olivana* – itself a hybrid – too compact, with no spread at all, but a tuft on which its stemless pale-pink flowers continued for several weeks. Very few seedlings germinated and all but one were either *S. ocymoides* or *olivana*.

That singleton was totally different from either. It took a year to decide on how to classify its habit and behaviour, for it was very slow growing. From a small central rootstock, short prostrate branches with leaves dark green barely 1 cm long, it formed a mat no larger than 4 cm in diameter. In May and June this was almost covered in small but intense pink flowers. It appeared to offer no scope for propagation for it set no seed and scarcely any shoots capable of taking as cuttings. Much as it appealed to me, I doubted if it had a future and feared that it might be short-lived – with no possibility of division, but after flowering two or three minute shoots emerged and as cuttings they rooted under mist. I named it simply 'Bressingham Hybrid', but the latter word soon struck me as superfluous. The mystery is that of being so unlike either parent – if indeed Percy used both for the cross. At the time there were no others, species or hybrids, he could have used, nor should I doubt his assertion that they alone produced the hybrid. It is less easy to grow than either, but in a humus-rich but gritty soil its deep-green mat expands eventually to no more than 15–20 cm across and is winter hardy – though it makes a good subject for a pan in an alpine house.

## SAXIFRAGA

When rebuilding stocks of both alpines and perennials after the war, it was noticeable that my range of mossy saxifrages was rather limited. As easy to grow, showy little plants, they sold freely in bud and flower each spring, but as some trade customers hinted, the buying public liked to have plenty of choice. It was an easy matter to save seed I had already, and within two years I was able to pick out six, all different from the existing 'standard cultivars. They ranged in height from

8 cm to 25 cm and before long a total of 20 were on offer, to include those below which I named. As a section of this wide-ranging alpine subject they are so bright, with little sprays of up-facing flowers on evergreen rosetted mats, and for the producer are so easy that they can be still profitable at low prices:

'CARNIVAL'
Glowing carmine pink, 15 cm.

'DUBARRY'
The tallest at 25 cm, large flowered crimson.

'ELF'
Later than most, deep pink, 10 cm.

'FAIRY'
Similar, but white flowered.

'GAIETY'
Clear pink, 15 cm.

'PEARLY KING'
A dense and rapid carpeter, pearl-white flowers, 10 cm.

'SPRITE'
Also later flowering, compact habit, rosy crimson, 10 cm.

The only other saxifraga I raised and named comes under *kabschia* section. These flower earlier than the *mossy*, some having tight silvery rosettes hard to the touch, and mat or hummock formation. A seedling proved to be freer to send up its 8 cm little sprays of yellow than any other. They covered the green hummock and 'Gold Dust' appealed as a good choice of name.

## SCABIOSA

The mainly blue *Scabiosa caucasica* varieties were top favourite cut flowers which market growers chose to follow pyrethrums. There was quite a spate of new varieties from 1930 to the 1950s but very few stood the test of time for one reason or another. Some were very much alike in any case, and now very few other than the old 'Clive Greaves' are to be seen. Virtually the only white for years was the even older cultivar 'Miss Willmott'. This appeared to be losing vigour in the 1950s and from a batch of seedlings – many of which came blue – I picked out what I saw as an improved white. This judgement appeared to be confirmed after trying it out as stocks were increased by spring division, until I decided to offer it as 'Bressingham White'. It is still in production but so is 'Miss Willmott', and to myself I have to admit that there is very little to choose between the two.

*Scabiosa graminifolia* is a very different subject from the above. Its charms and virtues are still not fully appreciated for it is adaptable as a frontal border plant or for the rock garden. It is long-lived and easy to grow in any well-drained soil, preferring sun, and is also drought resistant. A long succession of light-blue pincushion flowers nestle above a mound of silvery leaves, about 15–20 cm above ground, giving a total height of 25–30 cm. My garden group has been thereabouts undisturbed for 25 years, and though it will divide, seed has been relied upon for nursery produce. To my great surprise a few years ago, one lone seedling appeared which was of a soft pink shade. The plant was carefully nursed, partly because of its novelty value, and because it was less vigorous than the blue. It took several years to have sufficient to offer, since its scanty seed produces only blue, but as 'Pinkushion' its future seems now to be assured.

## Schizostylis

These autumn-flowering plants, something like miniature gladioli, are not 100 per cent hardy and enjoy some shade and a moist rich soil. For many years I grew such named varieties as 'Mrs Heggarty' and 'Viscountess Byng', light and deep pink, 50 cm tall. Then amongst them about 1960 there appeared a single plant that was not only taller, but had larger flowers as near to red as could be. I imagined it must be a sport, for it could scarcely be a species or natural hybrid, and therefore I labelled it *S. coccinea* 'Major', under which it was given an RHS Award of Merit. Since then it has produced another variation without any prompting from me. It was of similar height, but pink, and taller and finer than the old cultivars; it was named 'November Cheer'.

# THYMUS

This genus comes also in the category of being common, whether as alpine carpeters or the more upright growers. One post-war introduction in the carpeting range was *T. doefleri*, a close-growing and somewhat silvery woolly species. I can claim no credit whatever in producing a clearer pink, freer flowering hybrid of it, for it appeared on the nursery plunge beds and Dick Self, the alpine foreman, brought it to me as a chance seedling. This too was given the name 'Bressingham'.

# TRADESCANTIA

Although I have tried out two or three species other than the well-known *T. virginica*, none offered scope for improvement or variation on the latter. It is by no means choice and yet it is distinctive for all its being somewhat common. Those in circulation are probably all named cultivars – from white to blue shades and purple magenta. I grew several but at one time a good deep blue seemed to be lacking. Being variable from seed, one such appeared in a batch which I named 'Isis'. It has since become quite widely grown and still is in modest demand, but one that has since appeared from the Continent, 'Zwannenberg Blue', has proved to be identical.

# TROLLIUS

Much as I love these glorified buttercups (which some folk call them), I have been hesitant to attempt crossing any and have only once or twice raised seedlings from the best cultivars in hopes of finding any improved variations. One such attempt was made in the late 1960s. At the time we had a dozen or so cultivars of the best-known species *europaeus* from the very pale-yellow 'Alabaster' to the rich orange 'Commander-in-Chief'. I also grew the distinctive *T. ledebouri* 'Golden Queen', which flowers a little later in June and July, but stocks of this were dwindling for it did not lend itself so well as others to division, nor did it come fully true from seed. I asked Percy to cross it with a good deep-orange *europaeus* type. This he did, but there was a poor germination and two years elapsed before an assessment could be made. Again, only one was outstanding and in my estimation the finest trollius I had ever seen. The distinctive upstanding stamens characteristic of *T. ledebouri* were shorter, but the flowers were larger with good straight stems of a rich deep orange.

When taken away from the other seedlings, I planted it near my house where the visiting public on open days would not see it, but there it stood for three years because it failed to bulk up sufficiently to increase by division. It then made three, but three more years passed before there were nine. Such slow growth was baffling and very disappointing, the more so because they seemed resentful at being moved at all and for some inexplicable reason made no growth at all where they then were, and in fact four of them died. It had to be a case of kill or cure, so well into the 1980s I prepared a fresh place, adding lime, sharp sand, peat and old manure. They responded to this until at last, in 1989, there are a dozen plants about to be lifted as I write, with hopes that this lovely plant will be my pleasure to name and distribute.

Seed from the above has been saved and sown along with 'Alabaster' and one or two others, including the best medium-yellow 'Goldquelle', which appeared to be losing some vitality. One seedling selected had all the qualities of 'Goldquelle' but was so vigorous that I considered it worthy of naming. As 'Bressingham Sunshine' it has eclipsed all others for vigour and two others are being tested from evidence that they are stronger growing than the rather weakly, small-flowered 'Alabaster'. One is an equally pale yellow and the other a light but glistening canary yellow – an improvement I believe on the old cultivar 'Canary Bird'. I am also hoping to find variations on that charming species *T. yunnanense* which has flattish flowers of pure yellow, dwarfer and later than the boss of the parentage described above. *Yunnanense* is only 45 cm compared with the 75 cm of others.

# VERONICA

This very diverse genus appeared to offer some scope for hybridising many years ago. Blue was the predominant colour, whether in the taller herbaceous species or the low-trailing or carpeting kinds. Pink and white were to be seen only in a very few of the species which varied in colour, as different forms. These were *V. spicata* in the 25–50 cm range of height, and the low-spreading *prostrata*. At the time I grew only one pink *V. spicata* named 'Erica', but it was not a good doer. A sub-species *incana* had only blue-flowered spikes, and seed was collected by including this in hopes of its silver-grey foliage being passed on to a hybrid with 'Erica'.

As was to be expected, when the seedlings flowered blue was dominant, mostly violet or lavender shades, but one of the pinks had grey leaves and this was quite exciting for it also had the somewhat pad formation as a base to the 38 cm tapering spikes of clear pink. In giving it the name 'Minuet' I had in mind once again that it might have a link with the other two. 'Barcarolle' was green leaved but flowers were a deeper pink than 'Erica', on which it was a decided improvement, 30 cm tall and very free. The third, named 'Pavane', was also green leaved, though I did not rate it so highly as the others. I thought there was room for it, being unlike any other. It was a little taller at 45 cm and all three flowered from June onwards for many weeks.

A few years later I decided to fill another lack – of a free-flowering silver-leaved *V. spicata incana* type by crossing it, with help from bees, with *V.* 'Wendy', which that fine plantsman Tom Carlisle named after his daughter. The result was a fourth musical name 'Saraband'. This makes a slowly expanding mat and gives an abundance of violet-blue spikes 50 cm high above grey summer foliage. All but 'Pavane' have proved to be reasonably good survivors, but I have had losses with both 'Minuet' and 'Barcarolle' due to excessive winter wet. They are shallow rooting and indeed do not make large plants in soil that tends to congeal.

There are several variations in height though less in colour, of *V. teucrium* – from under 15 cm up to 60 cm. All die back to clumpy growth in winter but make a bright show of short spikes in June-July. 'Shirley Blue' is probably the best known, but this is only 15–20 cm tall. From the tallest I grew, 'Royal Blue' at 45 cm, came a seedling which finally settled down at 60 cm and possessed a more vigorous spread than any. I named it 'Blue Fountain' because in having my first group on a slope, the intense blue spikes tended to arch over.

One other veronica was obtained as unnamed from a botanic garden, and in this context perhaps ought not to be included, but I was advised to give it a cultivar name and as 'Blue Eyes' it has given that impression as well as pleasure ever since. It has the same habit as a *teucrium*, but with lighter blue than any, as well as being earlier. Only 23 cm high, its flowers closely resemble the wild species known as 'Blue Eyes', but keeps to a compact clumpy growth like the *teucriums*.

Finally the record has to end with another foundling – probably a self-sown seedling of the mat-forming *V. prostrata* species. 'Blue Sheen' could well have come as a seedling from 'Spode Blue'. It is a little paler than this and another difference lies not only in the sheen effect, but its vigour. The little 8 cm spikes cover the mat completely, but though spreaders, these types are shallow rooting and easy to control, making a brave show in May and June.

All the cultivars which have so far been mentioned have been named and introduced by me. All but a very few have been selectd as seedlings raised under my direction, and it has been my pleasure to give them names. Many, as I have admitted, came about as a result of natural agency – such as bees, but if my experience was of value in knowing the possibilities inherent in the various subjects chosen, it was Percy Piper who mostly saved and raised the seed, and in cases where flowers had to be manipulated in order to encourage cross-pollination, it was Percy who provided the means. He worked somewhat furtively and preferred to memorise rather than keep written records. Nor could I blame him, for much of what he called his 'fiddling' was done in his own time after a day's work. Percy retired at 70. He was gardener-cum-handyman to the previous owners of Bressingham Hall, who took no interest whatever in what little garden there was before I bought the property in 1946.

Percy's love of plants and flowers was so deep that he confessed to buying seeds out of his own slender earnings, because the then owners were not interested. Flowers meant nothing to them, but they meant a great deal to Percy. His response to me as his new employer as a professional plant producer was quite whole-hearted, and for nearly 40 years he was tireless in his output and enthusiasm, yet was never pushing or demanding in his attitude and had an open, enquiring mind. He still visits us one or twice a week and we make him welcome, as indeed we should. Incidentally, his father also worked for me in various capacities for nearly 30 years. Such men are sadly becoming thin on the ground.

Naturally Percy enjoyed those times when we examined the seedlings he had raised as they came into flower, and I took account of his opinions as to their merits or whatever. The final selections to be segregated, tested further and propagated were of course my prerogative, but there were never disagreements between us on such occasions. He preferred me to choose names, but the one chosen for the kniphofia he liked so much was at the suggestion of Peter Sare, who took over from him when he retired. A major annual task was seed collecting and raising to fill the requirements of the nursery, from the garden collection of plants growing in its 47 island beds. Peter, who has been with me for over 20 years since he left school, also works unobtrusively and is deeply interested.

The reason I left so much to Percy in raising new cultivars was largely because until 1970 I was also in charge of the nursery. Then when my two sons, Robert and Adrian took over, I was involved in what had begun as a hobby – old-time steam traction-engines – and which was then becoming a live steam museum. It was a rather absorbing diversion for a few years until it became a Charitable Trust with its own staff to restore and display over 50 steam-engines of many types and to lay down five miles of railway track on which visitors can ride round the nursery and woodlands on the 500-acre holding as it is now.

Now the museum with its permanent staff of 15 allows me to spend 90 per cent of my time with my plants. It has always been a pleasure for me to add to my collection of plants, with an extra incentive of having a nurseryman's eye for what might be worthy of growing in quantity for sale. At times I have had to resist any urge to collect for the sake of possessing, regardless of sale potential. Indeed my garden contains a few hundred subjects which I know are not fully garden worthy, but whilst I have room for them, I will let them be.

Many additional species were collected during the period 1957–63 coinciding with converting a five-acre meadow into a garden whenever I could spare the time from running the farm and nursery. The latter was at that time devoted entirely to perennials and alpines, with about 2,000 species and cultivars grown for sale, wholesale only. The developing garden was almost entirely of island beds because there was a vital need to break away from the conventional one-sided herbaceous border and the traditional rock garden. Both these forms were labour-intensive and people were going in so much for shrubs and ground cover that sales of perennials were difficult to maintain. Rather cussedly I stuck to my own preferred speciality, and realising that specialists in hardy plants were dwindling, it was up to me not only to display them to advantage, but to write about them and do whatever I could to restore them to favour. Out of this determination came the formation of the Hardy Plant Society in 1957 and I was elected as its first chairman.

Many of the new cultivars raised at Bressingham emerged during the same period during which I collected a large number of species. The incentive was not only a love of plants, but with an ever-present eye for subjects that would enhance the range of garden-worthy kinds. Some, which after trial proved their worth, were propagated and offered via my trade catalogue – with mostly disappointing rewards. It simply did not pay to grow a few hundred of a subject because I rated it highly, if only a dozen or two were purchased, but this did not put a damper on my enthusiasm for collecting. This, more often than not, involved garden visiting and making swops, not only in Britain and Ireland but to most western Europe countries as well. Botanic gardens were especially rewarding and many a species came from their family Order Beds whilst the several specialist German nurseries were a source of new cultivars.

It struck me as rather strange that during a period from 1950 when interest in perennials in Britain was at a low ebb, there was so much evidence that in Germany it was the other way round. There were more specialist nurserymen setting up and expanding to meet the demand, and they were as keen to augment their range from me as I was from them. The Dutch and Danes on the other hand were busy producing shrubs, a large proportion of which were for export to Britain.

The tide began slowly to turn about the mid-1960s so far as interest in Britain towards perennials was concerned. The reason I decided to open the door to direct sale to the gardening public in 1965 was mainly from the demand by the increasing number of visitors on open days at Bressingham, coupled with the reluctance of trade customers to purchase new or unusual kinds. The vast majority of them, it seemed, perused the wholesale catalogue with its 2,000 or so items, only to pick out and order what they would sell freely to their customers. At the first exhibit at the Chelsea Show for 30 years in 1965, there was no lack of interest from the gardening public and orders booked were such that the way ahead was clearly indicated.

Another pointer at that time and in the following years was that of a slow but steady increase in the number of people setting up in business as specialists in hardy plants. Most of them appeared to have a background as amateur enthusiasts with gardens or space large enough on which to grow plants for sale, learning as they progressed. One of the pioneers in this respect was the late Margery Fish, and another who has come a long way was Beth Chatto, who often visited and made purchases at Bressingham. Some offered small plants or pieces at low prices, as did Margery Fish, but not so many went in for quality. It was variety which came first for them, catering more and more for the resurgent interest in hardy plants away from the common range. Now there are many who are following the lead given by such as Beth Chatto, and most of them are also members of the flourishing Hardy Plant Society which gave me the honour of becoming President.

The National Council for the Conservation of Plants and Gardens has also emerged to play an active and important part in popularising hardy plants. Some of its members have made their gardens into bases for the species and cultivars of a wide range of genera. Although I have done little to deliberately foster its work and aims, those requesting plants of this or that to add to their section of the national collection are never refused if I have any to spare of what they need. Sometimes it is a reciprocal process, because although my collection is wide-ranging, there is a constant emergence of obscure species and new cultivars coming into circulation which previously sometimes one did not know existed.

# A-Z OF PLANTS DISTRIBUTED
# BY THE AUTHOR

It is with considerable diffidence that I set out to list and describe those subjects that I believe have been distributed as a result of my first collecting and growing them at Bressingham. This would be impossible to prove and only those who grew for sale any of the subjects to be mentioned will know from whom or whence they obtained them in the first place. I have no wish whatever to contend this, much less to pretend, regardless of the probability that some at any rate were obtained through my agency. Nor do I wish to assume credit for those that were, since the greatest likelihood is that the recent interest in less common plants would have led to their introduction by someone, sometime, and in any case many have been introduced for long enough to now be quite widely grown. I have no means of checking whether or not any plant mentioned was obtainable from a nursery. Some might have been, but I believe their number would at least be balanced by others in this context, which I have omitted to mention. A modest number of extra good species and cultivars, which were obtained from abroad on an exchange basis, are included because I am fairly certain that most of them were first distributed in Britain via Bressingham when stocks were built up.

In recent years I have travelled around much less in search of unusual plants. But my son Adrian has ranged more widely than ever I did and even more assiduously. His finds have included hardwood subjects as well as perennials, but none of these are included here even if most of the latter are under my care to assess and increase for ultimate distribution. A few, however, are still in the offing, yet to be distributed. Of these some are only included as a matter of possible interest, but which lack in my opinion full garden worthiness for one reason or another.

Garden worthiness is a matter on which opinions might well differ. In an earlier book of mine, *Hardy Plants of Distinction*, I used merit marks for each subject, with ten as maximum. Not many were given full marks for what I see as the criteria. These are: (1) overall elegance including foliage, (2) long flowering, (3) long-living without becoming invasive, (4) ability to stand unsupported, (5) adaptability to most types of soil, (6) hardiness in most temperate climates. Although I am tempted to employ this method again, on balance I think it would serve no useful purpose in this context, but will merely state merits and debits on the score of habit and adaptability. No unworthy plants are included. My regret is that no record was kept until fairly recent years of where accessions were obtained. I can remember the origin of most, but only those and later acquisitions are given.

## ACHILLEA

On a visit to Beth Chatto's garden in Essex I noticed a plant labelled *Achillea clypeolata* which was clearly not that plant. On enquiring, I was told that it had been given by Graham Thomas under that name.

I was given stock and having multiplied it up introduced it as 'Moonbeam' soon after the success of 'Moonshine'. It is taller than 'Moonshine' at about 90 cm with primrose yellow flowers and a running root.

## ACONITUM

*A. vilmorinianum* is of obscure origin although I first obtained it from a botanic garden. It is slender, growing up to 1.5 m, but never needs support, and the somewhat clustered head of 'Monkshood' flowers are a deep violet blue. Jagged leaves of dark green make for some elegance and it is easy enough to grow. *A. japonicum* came to me in 1984, also from a botanic garden. This is shorter at 90 cm, earlier to flower – in June – July – with larger, lighter-green leaves and a rapid increase of its little tubers. Flowers are relatively large of amethyst blue.

## ADENOPHORA

*A. tashiroi*, unlike many of this campanula-related genus, is deep rooting and long-lived. At first glance one would say it was a campanula, for its light-blue bells. They hang on branching stems up to 60 cm for several weeks from June onwards, eventually dying back in winter to somewhat fleshy rootstock having very little spread. Height varies somewhat according to soil and moisture, but it has a preference for some shade if not too dry.

## ADONIS

A very few specialists might have grown some adonis for sale 25 to 30 years ago. At that time I had *Adonis amurensis* from Japan with the cultivar name 'Fukujaika' added, but years later it was proved to be the straight *A. amurensis* which opens its golden cups in January or February. Apart from some helleborus it is the earliest true perennial to flower and is followed by its double form, with a greenish centre. Both are no more than 15 cm tall, with delicate foliage, but become completely dormant by late June. Largely because of being rarely available, I set out to increase the stock and over the years several thousands have been sold. Despite this, stocks have steadily increased until in 'my own' nursery there are about 5,000 plants. The taller, April-flowering *A. vernalis* is very slow to increase and on occasion demand has far exceeded the supply.

Another one I acquired as *A. volgensis* is just a little more responsive to division, but because the only difference I could see between it and *vernalis* was that it flowered a week or two earlier, it brought the conclusion that it is merely a geographical form of *vernalis*.

## AGASTACHE

*A. anisata* species appears to be a better perennial than *A. foeniculum* and *A. mexicana*, which proved to be short-lived.

It grows to about 90 cm with spikes of small purplish flowers June-August, to give a reasonably long display. So far it makes renewed basal growth after flowering which indicates reliability, and is easy to grow in any sunny situation.

## AGROPYRON

*A. magellanica* is a grass with bluer blades even than the well-known *Festica glauca*. It came from Germany some years ago and although it becomes a little untidy by autumn it is a reliable, clump-forming species. The needle-like foliage is about 60 cm long, topped by buff-coloured flowers.

## ANAPHALIS

I came across *A. yedoensis* in Munich Botanic Gardens in 1952 and liked it because it was tall and erect enough to use both as a foil and to dry its papery white flowers on 75 cm stems. Its small leaves are silvery and its roots have a steady but easily controlled spread, July-September.

## ANDROPLEION

*A. scoparius* is a distinctive but rarely seen grass with an upright, very compact habit which seldom flowers. Its shapeliness is enhanced by being evergreen and of a bluish hue and attains 60 cm in height. It is best planted in a warm sunny spot.

## ANEMONE

*A. rivularis* gives a long succession of open, bowl-shaped, white flowers on 60 cm stems. I have grown it in my garden for many years and it always held a quiet charm rather than a bright display. Only recently have I decided it worthy of distribution since it has been rarely seen in gardens and even more rarely listed in catalogues. It makes good growth in sun or light shade and well-drained soil.

## AQUILEGIA

*A. vulgaris* 'Nora Barlow' was sent to me in the early 1980s to grow for distribution, by a friend of the old lady whose name it carries. It has double quilled flowers in which white merges

**16** I named this vigorous *Phlox* after 'Eva Cullum' when she retired from running the retail mail order section

**17** The *Antholyza* parentage of *Crocosmia* 'Lucifer' gives extra hardiness and vigour

**18** *Polygonum affine* 'Dimity' flowers freely and makes good ground cover, with good autumn tints

**19** For good summer brilliance *Kniphofia* 'Bressingham Comet'

**20** The *Perovskia* is one of the few shrubby subjects which fits in with perennials—'Blue Haze' is one of the best

with red and a touch of green. With care it breeds at least 90 per cent true from seed and has been in good demand for several years. Other colours of this type are on trial, all about 75 cm tall. 'Granny's Gold' has similar flowers but pale-yellow leaves mottled in green, while a pure white I received from a Mr Stringer, named 'White Bonnet', should be released in 1991. The problem with aquilegias is keeping the stock true as they hybridise so easily.

## ARUNCUS

A. 'Glasnevin' is so-called because it came from Dublin's 'Glasnevin' Botanic Garden in 1958, where it had no name attached. It appears to be a shorter, more compact, form of *A. dioicus*, growing to about 1.05–1.2 m, with fine creamy-white plumes in June-July. A long-lived deep-rooting and very adaptable plant, as well as being showy.

## CAMPANULA

*C. alaskana*, now thought to be a form of *C. eriocarpa* is one of the showiest taller campanulas with an abundance of light lavender-blue flowers on sturdy 90 cm stems in June-July. It is a leafy plant with strong stems carrying the somewhat bunched head of flowers; rather similar to *C. eriocarpa*. *C. alliarifolia* 'Ivory Bells' came under the name *C. cretica*, but was found to be invalid. It has, however, a more compact habit than *C. alliarifolia* with larger basal leaves, but the bells dangle from arching 60 cm stems as do those of the species. Flowers come for many weeks June-August, and roots are deep and somewhat fleshy, enabling it to flourish in sun or shade and to withstand drought.

The hybrid 'Stella' was sent to me by George Arends as a cross between that pretty but very invasive *C. poscharskyana* and *C. garganica*. It is a splendid plant with long sprays to 38 cm of bright starry flowers above dark-green foliage. Cut back in August after flowering it will mostly give a second crop from a stocky, non-invasive clump. *Campanula trachelium* 'Bernice' is a hybrid of unknown origin that came to me from that very knowledgeable Dutchman, the late Willy van Egmond, in the 1930s. It is neater and more reliable than others of the *C. trachelium* species and probably has other specific blood in its make-up. From a compact chunky rootstock come leafy 20–24 cm stems, carrying large double flowers of powder blue in June-July.

## CAUTLEYA

*C. robusta* is the specific name given as correct by a visiting taxonomist. Tuberous roots which spread in rich soil send up thick stems with large sheathed leaves to 90 cm. In July-August these are tipped with deep-yellow flowers made striking by reddish bracts. A very exotic-looking plant, though I am not entirely convinced of its name being correct.

## CAREX

My original plant of *Carex morrowii* 'Evergold' came from Kew as *C. m. variegata* but was much brighter than the carex species I already had. The blades, about 1 cm wide and 15 cm long, remain colourful year round, but over the years it never flowered – not that it needed to do so. The cultivar name for it was necessary to distinguish it from the similar – though more golden – *Acorus gramineus* 'Ogon'; both are excellent for year-round attraction for either edging or grouping.

## CENTAUREA

*C. hyperleuca* is a name also in doubt because what I have differs greatly from those at Kew under the name. I am in no position to dispute it, but no one has come up with an acceptable name for it. It is a dainty little plant with fine greyish indented foliage, overlapping to form a low mound above which, from May, comes a long succession of pure pink cushion flowers on single stems for many weeks. It is only 30–38 cm tall, whereas at Kew under the name it is a larger and somewhat coarser plant. Mine is in general appearance a larger edition of the mat-forming *C. simplicicaule* which is only 15–20 cm in flower.

## CERASTIUM

As 'Snow in Summer', with its silvery leaves and white flowers, this has ruined many a rockery. It is just as invasive as couch grass and equally difficult to eradicate, especially amongst rocks. I came across another species in Switzerland named *columnae* which was obviously a more compact grower and was assured that its slow spread put it in a different class from *C. tomentosum*. It does not flower quite so freely but its hummocky foliage is dense and even more silvery, as well as being more evergreen. The white flowers come on 8 cm sprays in June. I can, however, make no claims that I was the first to introduce it to Britain.

## CHELONE

*C. obliqua alba.* The deep-pink 'Turtle Head' was for long one of my favourites before I saw its albino form which makes such a display in late summer, with its densely leaved 75 cm stems and short spikes of plump, tight-lipped flowers. The white has lighter green privet-shaped foliage, growing just as erectly as a dense little bush at 60 cm, but its expanding roots spread more slowly. Both are fully hardy and easy to grow.

## CHRYSANTHEMUM

*C. corymbosum* is still sometimes referred to as *Pyrethrum*, which its delicate lacy leaves do resemble, as does its root system and time of flowering. However, we are now told we must call it *Tanacetum*. As a tall white daisy-flowered subject for early summer, it stands out with considerable distinction, and if cut back in July as with pyrethrums, it will mostly flower again in September. The foliage is slightly grey and I have never known its 1.2 m stems to need supporting.

*C. parthenium plenum.* There are at least three variations of the double-flowered 'Feverfew'. One had the name 'White Bonnet' but it is short-lived and even though it seeds freely it is not a pure white. Another, which hailed from Rowallane, is taller at 90 cm and the button-type flowers are a clearer white, but it has a weak constitution and makes bottom growth too scantily to survive wet winters.

The third is one which my father grew in quantity as a cut flower for market in June-July, with a steady demand by florists for wreath making. It had no cultivar name and was only referred to as 'Stinker' because of the astringent odour of its leaves, which are in fact like those of an ordinary chrysanthemum, even if then under pyrethrum or sometimes

Matricaria. As I went out of market growing in the 1930s, I did not keep up a supply of plants for sale, and by 1940 had lost it with few regrets. Twenty years later I sought it again, but by sheer coincidence Mr Richard Wainwright of Adel near Leeds, let it be known that he grew and liked it as a border perennial. This stirred a memory, for after exhibiting at Leeds Roundhay Show in 1928, the then Show President bought a variety of plants after the event from me and I recalled his name as Mr H.S. Wainwright who, Richard told me, was his father. Now that 'Stinker' is back and valued as a garden-worthy plant, it needs to have the more attractive cultivar name of 'White Bobbles'. The odour is only noticeable if leaves are pressed and do not fit the term 'Stink'. It is an odour said to alleviate migraine headaches.

## CICHORIUM

The blue-flowered chicory is a pretty plant which one is likely to see growing only in the wild. Because its pink form *C. intybus roseus* is rare, it has an appeal as a garden plant. I first saw it in the RHS Wisley Gardens and the then Director, Frank Knight, suggested I should have it and work up a stock for distribution. Its fleshy roots were used for propagation and over the past 30 years the bright-pink tufty-petalled flowers have not lost their appeal. Stiffly branching stems up to 75 cm with jagged leaves bear a display for several weeks of high summer. Sun and good drainage are its only requirements.

## DEINANTHE

*D. bifida* is still rare and quite distinct from the dwarf *D. coerulea*. The erect stems run to 60 cm or more in the moistish rich soil it prefers, with some shade, to carry terminal clusters of small waxy cup-shaped ivory flowers in June-July. It is a leafy plant, largely hiding the stems, and dies down in autumn to a slowly expanding clump. Whilst it makes no brilliant display, it lacks nothing in elegance.

## DIASCEA

*D. rigescens* came to me from Logan as a new South African species collected by Dr Burtt. In hopes of its proving hardy, I propagated it intensively from tip cuttings whilst enjoying the fine show in my garden. Others were similarly attracted, and I did much the same for the dwarfer pink *D. elegans* a year later. But although neither lack vigour, they have proved to lack reliability on the score of hardiness. Because they grow with a mat-like base, winter covering with litter outdoors appears not to be the answer, so much as to take summer cuttings to plant out the following spring. They are far more likely to survive as perennials in light soil in our warmer counties.

## DISPORUM

*D. flavum*, although quite unrelated, is not unlike the deinanthe above in habit and likes the same conditions. It spreads a little faster and the erect 90 cm stems carry light-yellow bell-shaped flowers in early summer. I find it does quite well in sun, given good soil.

## DORONICUM

I first saw *D. caucasicum* 'Spring Beauty' in Denmark in 1953 under the name 'Frulingspracht'. This indicates a German origin, but at the time no one in Germany appeared to list it. As a double doronicum of the dwarf *caucasicum* species it appealed to my commercial instincts sufficiently to invest in a quantity. The flowers in April and May are fully double, of a pure yellow over 5 cm across. In recent years, however, it has been less thrifty in growth and in the floods of 1987 our entire nursery stock was killed.

## ECHINACEA

*E. purpurea* 'White Lustre' is a cultivar from America and is probably the best of the rarely seen whites, but even so my strong preference is for the rosy-purple cornflower. The rayed petals droop a little, making the yellow-tinged black cone more prominent on the 90 cm upward-branching stems in late summer. My son Adrian found the variety 'Magnus' on the Continent and I am now working up a stock. The flowers are twice the size of other varieties with the petals held horizontally.

## EPIMEDIUM

*E. sagittifolium*, as the name denotes, has arrow-shaped foliage unlike others. It forms a low mound of fresh greenery all year round with a modest spread. As with most epimediums the foliage is of more value than the flowers. In this case they are pink, coming in spring on 15 cm stems. Being a recent acquisition, distribution has scarcely begun.

## CHEIRANTHUS

The original plant of *C. (Erysimum)* 'Constant Cheer' was sent as a gift by F.J. Lamb many years ago, and I gave it the name because it was seldom out of flower. These come on small terminal heads of a light-lavender shade. The habit is that of a fairly erect little bush of dark-green narrow leaves, but as with nearly all these 'perennial' wallflowers it is rather short-lived, though renewable from autumn cuttings. They are best in poor stony soil and need full sun.

## EUPHORBIA

*E. longifolia* was at first believed to be *E. wallichii*, but now we know that the two are quite distinct. Of the two, *longifolia* is to be preferred, although quite tall at about 1.2 m it stands unaided to produce, in June-July, wide heads of sulphur yellow, which retain their unfading attraction for many weeks. The stems carry long narrow leaves coming from a long-lived rootstock, which in time becomes quite large but has no invasive tendency. Two other euphorbias are on the way which we have been asked to distribute under contract with the ladies who raised them. Both are of the evergreen *wulfeni* species – of bush-forming habit. One is to be named 'Burrow Silver' for its brightly variegated leaves. It occurred as a chance seedling in the garden of Judy Benger of Burrow Farm near Axminster and has typical grey-green leaves with silver margins. The young shoots are lime green with gold edges and the mature stems dark pink. It was originally called 'Benger's Silver'. Since we have had this plant on trial it has produced self-sown seedlings of its own but all have normal leaves. Propagation from cuttings is slow. The other has reddish buds as the large flower heads develop in early spring and this flushes the texture of the sulphur yellow when open in March and April. A dwarf form of *E. wulfeni* under 90 cm, received from Ms Pat Perry, is also on the way.

## FILIPENDULA

*F. ulmaria* 'Aurea' is a golden-leaved 'Meadow Sweet', but is much dwarfer than the wild species. Its rather dull buff-white flowers are, however, unattractive and the value lies entirely with the deep-golden foliage which stands out all the more if flower stems are detached from the low pad made by the leaves. Another prettily variegated form (*F. u.* 'Variegata') is a new acquisition, which deserves its own cultivar name. The leaves are streaked with yellow on the bright-green lobed base, and the flowers on 60 cm stems have enough merit to leave on until they begin to fade. After being cut off the leaves take over. This form does not object to some sun but *aurea* is best in a shady situation and both are partial to moist soil.

## FUCHSIA

*F.* 'Oetnang' is named after a place in Austria where it was raised long ago, but was sent to me as a cultivar worth introducing. It has large somewhat globular flowers of shell pink and red, but has never exceeded more than 30 cm in my garden, though it has survived without protection for 25 years.

## GENTIANA

I am a little dubious about including *G. doeringiana* even though it appeared to be virtually unknown when I first offered it in the early 1950s. It is closely related to *G. septemfida*, but for me is an improvement not only in the size and blueness of the trumpet flowers, but also in its dwarfer neater habit. All these summer-flowering gentianas are excellent alpines, reliable to flower and adaptable in any sunny situation.

In 1986 one of my long-standing trade customers, now retired, Mr F.C. Lambe, sent me seed of a new gentian he had raised by crossing *G. septemfida* with I believe, the later-flowering *G. sino-ornata*. He named it 'Blackboys' and it should have a future for being a long-flowering dwarf, royal blue in colour on its semi-prostrate stems.

## GERANIUM

I owe G. 'Ann Folkard' to the raiser, the Revd Folkard, then living near Wisbech. He had set out to collect and hybridise geraniums that appealed to him, but I have to confess that for two or three years 'Ann Folkard' did not appeal greatly to me. This was because it made such a wide carpet of lush summer growth and because the colour, an intense magenta purple, was somewhat violent. But visitors saw it and liked it and yet for all its vigorous summer spread, the root did not divide at all well, so that increase fell far short of the demand. I believe I have now found a more rapid means of propagation even if I have to deplete the somewhat golden-hued vernal growth for cuttings. A single plant is capable of covering almost a square metre in a season before dying back to its compact rootstock, and neither foliage nor its nestling flowers exceed 50 cm. A second hybrid from Mr Folkard, 'Kate Folkard', is named after his other daughter, and is not a spreader. It offers scarcely any material for propagation of its 10 cm mound of bronzy green, studded with lilac-pink flowers, and after seven years I still have only a score of plants. G. wvlossovianum is a species I have valued for many years, having first listed it in 1957 after obtaining stock from Munich Botanic Garden. It has strong clumpy growth with masses of rounded leaves and a long season of soft-lavender-blue cups only about 38 cm high, June-September.

## HELIANTHEMUM

H. 'Annabel' also first came to me as a gift, from a Devonshire lady who had raised it from seed. When the cuttings she sent rooted and flowered, I was very taken with its pure-pink fully double flowers, the like of which I doubted had been seen before. I was on the point of writing to ask her if she would like to choose a name for it when there came an appealing letter from a Surrey customer. A close relation had just lost a baby girl through the mysterious cot-death syndrome and would I consider naming a plant in her memory? Such a coincidence was an opportunity too good to miss. Permission from the raiser was sought and readily given, and as a result of our giving 10 per cent of receipts from sales of 'Annabel', several hundred pounds have been donated to research into cot-death syndrome.

## HEUCHERA

Hybrids from *H. cylindrica* have already been described, but as a species it is worthy of mention. The light-green marbled leaves give good ground cover because the plant's habit gives more spread than any other in sun or part shade. The 60–75 cm stems carry clustered spike-ends of flowers in which both green and white are seen. *H. villosa* is a late-flowering species of vigorous growth. Although the 60 cm open sprays carry tiny white flowers, they come in great profusion from July to September, much later than other heucheras, to give a charming airy effect. I can imagine it as a boon to flower arrangers.

## HOSTA

In my opinion *H. rectifolia* is the finest and most imposing of all hostas for its flowering qualities. The deep-green shining leaves form not only a shapely base – not over-large but overlapping – but decorate the 1.2 m flowering stems as well. The flowers, somewhat trumpet shaped, are lavender blue and make a show for several weeks from late June onwards. My stock came from Edinburgh Royal Botanic Gardens over 30 years ago at which time it was doubtfully in circulation, but a few years later one appeared in a few catalogues under 'Tallboy', a name given to it by John Bond, unaware that it had a specific name already. Incidentally, it displays itself just as well in sun as in some shade, given good soil in which to penetrate its deep-searching roots.

*H. sieboldiana* 'Bressingham Blue' I first obtained from the late Major Daniels, a landscape architect, who having no name for it agreed to my somewhat diffident choice. It took several years to work up a sufficient stock of what was for me the bluest-leaved hosta. A batch was, however, produced from tissue cuttings, which proved to be more like the ordinary species, and I have to admit that the colour when grown on open ground in the nursery fell short of that of my garden group in fairly deep shade.

*H. ventricosa* 'Variegata' too came to me in an exchange from Edinburgh over 30 yers ago. As a species, *ventricosa* is freer to flower than most, and a sturdy grower. To have a base of rich-green leaves streaked with primrose yellow, to 90 cm stems of mauve-purple flowers, makes for a splendid border plant. Within two years it was on an export order to America where hostas were being exploited, and where hundreds of new cultivars have been introduced. The American Hosta Society award an annual engraved plaque for the best, and in 1987 despite such competition and with no foreknowledge on my part, the award came to me. I do not of course claim the slightest credit as raiser, or for that matter as introducer. This is emphasised by the fact that a few years ago Russell's the well-known Surrey nursery, complained that it was not the true *ventricosa* 'Variegata' and sent me a plant of what they affirmed was the true one, but the only difference lies in the shape and placing of the variegation on the leaves.

# HOUTTUYNIA

My first acquaintance with *H. cordata* 'Chameleon' was being handed a plant after giving a talk at Longwood Gardens in America. I had grown the green-leaved species (the smell of which remind one of ripe Seville oranges) in both its single- and double-flowered forms. It was invasive in damp soil and one had to be careful. The heart-shaped leaves with pointed tips become the summer base for small white flowers only a few centimetres high. This new one had coloured leaves – several colours in fact, reddish, yellow and shades in between on the leaves. I found it variable, however, some leaves being plain, but gradually worked up a stock from cuttings only of the most colourful. Meantime Hopley's nursery had also been at work in the same way and came out with their 'Harlequin' before our 'Chameleon' by a matter of months. I would prefer not to judge between the two, but can say that in 1988 more 'Chameleon' were sold than any other plant we grew. Its fault is not only its invasiveness in damp soil, but in making new leaves rather belatedly in spring after losing them over winter.

# HYDRANGEA

I could not resist Herr Arends's request to distribute his splendid *H.* 'Preziosa' hybrid in Britain. Most of his stock had been destroyed by Allied bombing, but were on the way to being restored when I visited his Ronsdorf nursery in 1952. It is not tall at 1.05 m nor does it expand widely. The stems terminate above a compact bush in heads of almost sparkling deep pink, a mere 10–13 cm across, and with lasting brilliance. My original planting remains a joy after over 35 years in one place. I give an occasional light mulch but very little pruning. The leaves have a purplish hue.

# HYSSOPUS

*H. aristatus* is recorded largely because it came from a monastery garden in South Wales, when a little exchange was arranged with a gardening 'Brother'. It has Biblical connections but may not be the 'hyssop that springeth out of the wall' referred to in I Kings. As a semi-shrubby plant with tiny, near-evergreen foliage, it is as undemanding as it is unspectacular, barely 30 cm tall with tiny deep-blue flowers along its short spikes in summer. It prefers a dryish sunny place but is quite hardy.

# INULA

The easy-to-grow yellow daisy-flowered *I. barbata* did not meet with brisk enough demand to keep it listed after working up a stock, but were it to be re-introduced with a colour picture in the catalogue it might do so now after a lapse of several years. It spreads fairly quickly, has small hairy leaves and an abundance of 5 cm-diameter rayed flowers of butter yellow, June-August. A taller species with the interesting name of *I. oculis christii* has not yet been offered for lack of outstanding qualities.

# KIRENGESHOMA

Until fairly recent years it was believed that this Japanese-based genus was confined to one species, *K. palmata*. It came as a surprise to discover another, *K. koreana*, in a botanic garden, and it was several years before the piece I was given was in good enough supply to distribute. It differs from *K. palmata* in having more erect and less leafy growth, the leaves being somewhat fingered and in verticillate formation along the 90 cm stems. The flowers are light yellow, bell shaped, but not open mouthed, which fault is more pronounced in *K. palmata*. Both prefer good soil, not dry, and in such conditions shade is unnecessary.

## LIRIOPE

The species *L. muscari* was for long recommended as useful for a dry, shady place. I soon found, however, that it flowers much better in sun and was so impressed by its display of thin pokery spikes carrying bead-like purple-lilac flowers from August to November along evergreen bladed clumps, that I felt sure a demand for it would eventually come. It has at last, and several thousands now leave the nursery every year. A surprise gift of a large-flowered cultivar arrived from a Texas nursery some years ago labelled 'Majestic', said to be an improvement. Perhaps it is, but not in our climate, for over the years it has scarcely ever flowered. In America variegated forms flourish, as no doubt does 'Majestic', but none I have tried do more than survive at best, as if to indicate that hotter summers than ours are the secret of growth, winter survival and reliable flowering. However, I still have a collection on trial.

## LYCHNIS

I am recording *L. chalcedonica* 'Plena' with a certain feeling of sadness because just now I have but a handful of plants. I first had a few under this name over 40 years ago as the double form of the well-known scarlet-headed plant. It was, however, a weakling and defied all efforts to entice good growth. It was in fact so lacking in garden worthiness that I gave up. A few years later I was offered a single plant which the donor assured me was a good grower, and he was right. Over a period of ten years or so, by careful annual division, there were sufficient to offer and too many for me to hold on my little 'inner' nursery where hand work is practised. I was somewhat out of touch for the next three to four years except for the group in my garden. There it made a regular display, and though due for replanting in 1988, it was missed and I noticed some deterioration when it flowered that year. It was then that I learned the nursery stock had suffered badly in the floods of August 1987 and with it came the request to have the few remnants back under my care to begin more or less all over again.

## Lychsilene

This cross between *Lychnis viscaria* and a *Silene* species is another subject that I have never felt quite justified in offering. It makes a spread of deep-green narrow leaves, giving ground cover almost evergreen, but its deep-pink flowers on lax stems 38–45 cm are somewhat sparse. It has always struck me as a borderline case, interesting, unusual, undemanding, and yet lacking the kind of display most lychnis and silenes give so unstintingly.

## Macleaya

My original stock of *M. cordata* was also lost. I had first seen it growing in a Cambridge college garden in 1955, looking different from what I and others had been growing under this name. Having acquired a nucleus, a plant was sent for indentification to Cambridge Botanic Garden. There it was proved to be the true *M. cordata* and the species in cultivation already was in fact *M. microcarpa*, the difference being that *cordata* had a 3 cm long tubular white flower, whereas *microcarpa* was minute and brownish. After about ten years, however, stocks at Bressingham died out for some unknown reason, but in 1985 in a Cambridge cottage garden I saw what purported to be a cultivar, by an amateur, under the name 'Flamingo', because of a faint pink flush in the flower. This has now become plentiful, but I have a suspicion that it remains the true *cordata* species. It is only a suspicion because having lost the original stock I have no means of checking.

## Melittis

*M. melissophyllum* is native to Europe, including Britain, and it is difficult to understand why it is so rarely seen or offered. I cannot of course claim to have introduced it, but include it because it is such a good, long-lived subject for cool shade. Deep-rooting, long-living plants emerge with leafy upright stems to about 45 cm in spring, with spikes carrying quite large 'dead nettle' flowers in which white merges into pink. It is at its best in early summer and presents an appealing sight for several weeks.

# MEUM

*M. athamanticum* is also a native, especially in Scotland and is decidedly worthy of garden cultivation. In spring comes a mass of the most delicate lacy foliage of rich deep-green on somewhat lateral sprays to about 60 cm, like a very much refined 'cow parsley'. In June, July and into August wide heads of tiny white flowers add charm to the luxuriant base and fading does not spoil the overall effect. Plants are deep rooting and its slow spread gives no trouble, nor is its 'herby' aroma at all unpleasant.

# MISCANTHUS

Most miscanthus fail to flower except in the warmest parts, but *M. sinensis* 'Silver Feather' never fails to do so. It has 1.8–2.1 m plumes open on strong stems in late summer above a wealth of long bladed foliage. The latter fades in November, but the plumes, which change to a buff shade from near white, often remain a noble sight well into the new year. Although clumps expand to become quite massive, they do not invade.

# NEPETA

In the late 1920s I obtained a *N. grandiflora* from Orleans in France under the name 'Souvenir d'Andre Chaudron'. It had spikes of lavender-blue flowers, 60 cm tall, and apart from a rather rapid spread below ground and a fairly strong catmint odour, it was a showy, easy subject. It was however lost during the war, or in the move afterwards to Bressingham during the grim 1947 winter. When restocking I failed to find it in Britain and decided instead to try out one grown in America named 'Blue Beauty'. It soon proved to be the same plant and the explanation that 'Blue Beauty' was a much better selling name was accepted with no qualms. To keep it in good form, it is advisable to replant every spring due to its wandering habit.

*N. govaniana* was rarely to be seen, but since first offering it in 1975 it has been much in demand. Unique for its pale-yellow flowers, it has a bushy upright habit to a good 90 cm. The flowers are too small to make a splash of colour, but come in modest profusion for several weeks after midsummer above abundant greenery. It has no fads and is not a spreader.

## Oenothera

Two distinct species of perennial 'Evening Primrose' have proved worthy of introducing. Although not spectacular, *O. linearis* has radiating sprays of small yellow flowers close to each stem for many weeks from June onwards. About 38 cm high, its basal growth is neat and clumpy. This came to me from Edinburgh. *O. kunthiana* has fairly recently arrived from America. It has a loosely branching habit and the 50 cm stems carry light yellow flowers for several weeks.

## Ononis

*O. antiquorum* is a rarity I have grown for several years and finally decided that it is worth introducing. The fact that Graham Thomas on a visit in 1988 confessed to never having seen or heard of it, should be sufficient evidence of its rarity. This member of the legume family has a somewhat bushy habit with light-green rounded leaves in which nestle pink pea-shaped flowers for several weeks before dying back to its strong deep roots. In good soil it reaches nearly 60 cm, but given full sun it is quite adaptable and has no vices.

## Ophiopogon

I do not claim more in the case of *O. planiscapus nigrescens* than making it widely distributed before anyone else. At first glance this might appear to be a grass, but is in fact a member of the lily family. The blades 10–13 cm long are as near black as can be, but with a purplish sheen. Once established in sun or shade where not too dry, it has a slow steady spread giving dense year-round ground cover. It has tiny spikes amongst the foliage in late summer of purple bead-like flowers.

## ORIGANUM

*O. vulgare* is the common pot herb 'Marjoram', but two hybrid selections from Germany are well worth a place as decorative plants. Each is named after the garden of origin, 'Nymphenburg' (Munich) and 'Herrenhausen' (Hanover). Both produce masses of narrow-leaved 50 cm stems carrying small violet-purple flowers in later summer. I am building up stocks for distribution, and hope to introduce 'Herrenhausen' in the near future.

## PAEONIA

It is over 20 years ago that someone gave me a cross between *P. tenuifolia* and *P. woodwardiana*. To my regret I now have no record of who the donor was, but it will not be long now before it can be offered. It is May flowering, single flowered, 8 cm across and of a rosy red shade, 45 cm tall. I like it because it has good foliage with flowers just above, and is reliably free to flower although slow to increase, as are most peonies, but it quickly recovers after being divided.

## PENNISETUM

A dwarf grass of considerable charm, *P. orientalis* has erect 25–30 cm bottle-brush pokers for several weeks in summer. It has a tufty habit with bluish-grey blades a few centimetres high and a modest expansion into mounded clumps. Any sunny situation suits.

## PENSTEMON

The species *P. utahensis* is probably not likely to be seen in nurseries or private gardens, but I would like to believe it will be. Having tried many other than alpine species without much success, I had doubts that this one would also fail to adapt to the vagaries of the British climate. Having grown it now for four years I consider it safe to offer as of value. It is not entirely herbaceous of habit but forms a summer dome of shiny deep-green leaves through which come 45 cm spikes carrying rosy-purple flowers for much of the summer. Two other penstemons of the more usual *hartwegii* type are quite well known under the names 'Garnet' and 'Firebird'. I obtained them from a continental source in the 1930s and may or may not have been the first to distribute them in the United Kingdom under their original names. It was not I who changed the plum red 'Andenken en Hahn' to 'Garnet', nor the scarlet red 'Schonholzerii' to 'Firebird'.

## PHLOX

The still popular cultivar with brightly variegated leaves, *P. paniculata* 'Nora Leigh' is named after Mrs Joan Elliott's mother. It was Mrs Leigh who requested me to build up a stock from her garden at Broadwell, Glos., and to submit it to the RHS for an Award. In due course it gained an RHS Award of Merit; however, a few years later when visiting Munich Botanic Gardens there was the same plant under the name *P. paniculata* 'variegated' where it had been for 80 years, and so proved that Mrs Leigh's stock was not so unique as she had believed.

## POLEMONIUM

Somewhat similarly I was told on seeing *P. archibaldae* growing in a Northamptonshire garden that it was a rarity worthy of wider distribution. That the correct name was later stated to be *P. foliosissimum* is not significant in the proof it gave of its virtues. In my garden it began to flower on terminal heads in early June and continued unceasingly until September. The clusters of lavender-blue, yellow-eyed flowers above typical 'Jacob's Ladder' foliage, were very appealing. It does not seed around as do some species but makes respectable clumpy plants. This certainly deserved an RHS award but a plant submitted in June about 1959 was turned down. Another sent four to five weeks later also failed to convince, but when a third was sent in September, still in flower, the accolade was at last given.

## POLYGONUM

Ever since obtaining some choice species well over 30 years ago from Edinburgh, I have felt as impelled to extol their virtues as to ensure having ample supplies. All are choice because they do not lend themselves to rapid increase. It must be said that they need to be grown in good soil which does not become arid.

*P. macrophyllum* has clear-pink poker spikes on 50 cm stems above a wealth of attractive foliage. The latter as a base is somewhat mounded, each leaf loosely overlapping, being up to 25 cm long, wavy and scalloped about 3 cm wide. The plant does not make a massed display at any one time but from June until autumn is seldom out of flower.

*P. milettii* also has a clumpy habit with fairly narrow deep-green leaves, but tends to be more erectly held up to 20–23 cm above ground. By late May or early June stiffly upright 30 cm pokers of almost blood red come to arrest the eye and although this first flush may end after a month or so, given moist rich soil, flowering continues intermittently till October.

*P. regelianum* is my original plant and the only one which came from seed obtained from Leningrad Botanic Gardens about 1957. It grew sturdily but compactly and duly produced short-branching sprays of deep-pink pokers nearly 90 cm tall. On lifting it for division I found that new growth came not from the top of the somewhat rhubarb-like rootstock, but from underneath. This made knifing difficult and as seed is but sparse, increase is unavoidably slow – which matters little in a display garden where it can stay undisturbed to form a large clump. A variation yet to be named and distributed has flowers of a brighter, deeper pink, but it will take many years to build up stock.

*P. amplexicaule* 'Inverleith' also came from Edinburgh Royal Botanic Garden where it occurred as a seedling. Although only 60 cm in height, it makes a wide and leafy summer spread on which a long succession of deep-red pokery spikes continue from July to November.

*P. campanulatum* produces heads rather than spikes of flowers, about 5 cm across. It also makes a wide summer spread as a lax 90 cm bush, but not having deep roots it is easy to curb. The colour is pale pink and the improved stock now grown at Bressingham was first seen making a striking late display in the late Sir David Scott's garden at Boughton House. It is a splendid subject for a dampish place in sun or part shade, lasting in flower from August until cut back by frost.

*P. sphaerostachyum* – whilst retaining the name under which it came to me, I have noticed a different description being used elsewhere. My plant makes an expansive display of small rosy-pink pokers on 60 cm branching stems out of proportion to the size of the plant. It is in fact one of the longest-flowering plants I know. Beginning in May it only needs a trim in July or August to continue until autumn non-stop. Stems are branching from angular knots and though inclined to loll a little, it is not at all straggly. All these species prefer sun but will take part shade.

## POTENTILLA

This large genus has many interesting species not to be seen in gardens. *P. alba* is still relatively rare and although I make no claims, at least I have widened its availability as a very worthwhile subject. It flowers in early summer with quite a show of strawberry-like white flowers above neat tufty growth at less than 30 cm in height. An excellent frontal plant. *P. thurberi* is very different and doubtfully available at present. I first saw it in an American garden centre and it appealed to rather more than my collecting instincts. It grows uprightly to about 50 cm with ample stem and base fingered foliage of soft light green. The 1 cm wide flowers opening on small terminal heads are almost as deep a red as *Cosmos* (Bidens) *atrosanguineus*, appearing from June to August in any sunny position, but it is rather slow to make a clump.

## PRIMULA

The diminutive 'Johanna' was given to me by the raiser – who is in charge of the huge natural rock garden at Gothenburg. Its parents were *P. clarkei* and *P. warshenewskyana*, both of which I had tried and failed to please. 'Johanna' has never failed to please with its small but intense pink flowers in March and April. These are almost stemless, nestling in the somewhat rosetted form of deep-green leaves of virtually no height at all. A choice but rewarding plant for cool, humus soil and some shade.

*P. auricula* 'George Edge' was also a gift. The Dowager Lady Linlithgow sent it with a request to get it going for distribution. The thought behind it was as much, or more, for its being named after her late gardener, as for its clear light-yellow flowers. Although other yellow *auriculas* are not uncommon, this has sufficient attraction to keep the supply unequal to the demand.

A primrose with distinctive attributes is *P. vulgaris sib-thorpii*, from Greece and Turkey. It has reliability and vigour both in growth and flower and often produces a second crop in autumn of a very pleasing lilac-pink shade. It has been growing in the same spot for 20 years, divided every two or three years to keep it vigorous. I have never known it suffer here from attacks of red spider mite which affect so many primrose hybrids.

## Rheum

This hitherto obscure species of rhubarb *R. kailense* came from the Far East and is now on offer for, I believe, the first time. It grows barely 30 cm high with dangling sprays of tiny brownish flowers in early summer. The rounded leaves are plentiful and plants have a steady spread. *R. alexandrae* is included as an example of how certain plants become as it were Cinderellas – and how my one-time policy of 'wholesale only' handicapped efforts to distribute uncommon kinds. Prior to 1965, and for several years, I grew and offered to the trade this rheum with its striking yellow lip-like bracts, but never sold more than about a dozen in any one year. But in showing again at Chelsea after a lapse of 30 years, a group in flower on the exhibit brought orders for over 200 plants, both wholesale and retail. Since then the demand has not slackened but stocks have not been regularly available, though future prospects are now much brighter.

## Roscoea

The species *cautleoides*, *humeana* and *purpurea* were around prior to 1960, but were not at all common. In that year, from Edinburgh, came one named *R. procera* and it has proved a fine plant, much superior to *R. purpurea*. The pointed leaves sheath the erect 50–60 cm stems on which the exotic deep violet-blue flowers appear with lips reminding one of some orchids. They come in July-August, and the foliage remains till frost arrives. The roots are fleshy and brittle with an orange sap, but division of established plants is a case of gently enticing individual crowns apart. *R.* 'Kew Beauty' is something of a mystery. It is a doubtful form of the earlier flowering *P. cautleoides* because its leaves are quite different and the stems much stouter, whilst the flowers are much larger and of a delicate primrose yellow in early summer, about 50 cm. The mystery is that it was sent to me merely as 'Kew Form'. On checking with Kew, they said they knew nothing of it but suggested 'Kew Beauty' for a name in expectation of its being a cultivar – but from whence? Or by whom?

## RUDBECKIA

The German-raised cultivar *R. laciniata* 'Goldquelle' is quite outstanding. Instead of the lanky 1.8 m stems so often a nuisance in most tall rudbeckias, this makes a shapely bush of deep-green divided leaves at about 1.05 m. The flowers, 5–8 cm across, are fully double golden yellow on short stems, adorning the upper parts of the bush during August and September. The plants are clumpy with no invasive spread.

## SALVIA

The only genus, I believe, in which blue, red and yellow are to be found amongst the species. This somewhat curious phenomenon prompted me to try out the yellow, having been familiar with the blues and reds. *S. bulleyana* is distinct, not only for its soft-yellow flowers of good size on 50–60 cm spikes, July-September, but it has abundant basal leaves below, which are freshly green and puckered. Unlike many of the brightest salvias, it has proved to be fully hardy over my 25 years of growing it. That much taller, blue-flowered *S. ambigens* is worth a winter coating of litter in cold districts. Where happy in rich but well-drained soil it makes a stately bush up to 1.2 m. The pure deep-blue flowers do not make a massed display, but continue for many weeks in later summer above the luxuriant greenery. My original stock came from the late Oliver Wyatt in 1957.

## SANGUISORBA

What we knew as *Poterium* are now under this generic name, but I have yet to find any reference to one which came to me as *P. sitchense* many years ago. It is taller and much more graceful than the well-known *S. obtusa* which holds its pink bottle-brush at an angle. *P. sitchense* has thinner pokery spikes on erect 1.2 m branching stems nearer red than pink, in July-September. It has the typical deep, tough roots but keeps to a compact but stout clump.

*P. magnifica* also lacks definition as a specific name, but it lacks nothing in vigour as a plant with masses of fingered leaves to form a dense bush about 90 cm high. Its white bottle-brush spikes are held obliquely, but the whole effect is quite different from the white form of *S. obtusa*. It is not to be recommended where space is precious.

## Scabiosa

The species *S. graminifolia* has been noted earlier along with its pink form as a very good plant still not fully appreciated. Another which is almost pink and not at all well known is *S. lucida* which I first grew from seed. It has a long season of lilac-pink flowers above tufty deep-green clumps, only about 38 cm tall, making a useful frontal subject of easy culture. *S. ochroleuca* is less tidy and a little taller, but its pincushion flowers are of a soft primrose-yellow shade.

For good measure I should include *S. rumelica* for a red. It is also known as *Knautia macedonica*, and although this also grows untidily, its red flowers stand out boldly on thin stalks up to 75 cm for much of the summer.

## Schizostylis

*S. coccinea* 'Snow Maiden' was a gift from Audrey Nash of Littleport, the daughter of the late Fred Barcock, whose knowledge of plants was so vast. It was the first white I had seen, but as a genus liable to throw a sport, as in the case of my 'Major' and 'November Cheer', it was a possibility. All are somewhat tender, having a shallow-root system, and if 'Snow Maiden' is no exception, it is a pleasing sight to see brightening the dreariness of late autumn – sometimes up to Christmas. Although less vigorous than other cultivars, the flowers of 'Snow Maiden' are bigger, 'Maiden's Blush' is a pale pink sport or reversion.

# SEDUM

I have avoided including cultivars that were purchased from nurseries, but I can claim to have introduced to Britain two sedums raised by Georg Arends of Ronsdorf, at his request in 1952. 'Autumn Joy' ranks as one of the top ten cultivars of the past 50 years and now is so widely known and grown as to need no description. In Germany 'Autumn Joy' is known as 'Herbstfeude'. The other Arends's sedum was a cross between the little *S. cauticolum* and a larger *spectabilis* type. He named it *cauticulum robustum* since it was, at 20 cm high, larger in every way, with heads of glistening deep-pink flowers in late summer; but the rules of nomenclature are that cultivars must not bear botanic names and Herr Arends agreed to my suggestion of 'Ruby Glow'.

Another German sedum which I believe I was the first to bring and introduce is 'Weihenstephaner Gold'. This too was a cross, probably between *S. middendorfianum* and *S. kamtschaticum* and it inherits the best of both species. It forms expanding but not invasive pads of leafage and produces a long succession of glistening golden-yellow heads only 8–10 cm high. A larger golden head is seen on the showy *S. aizoon* but in the form *S. a. aurantiacum* the heads, 10 cm wide, are orange. The leaves are tinted bronze as they are in S. 'Weihenstephaner Gold'.

*S. heterodontum* is a rarity for spring flowering, but supposedly now comes under the genus *Rhodiola*, along with what was *Sedum rhodiola* – the rose root sedum. *S. heterodontum* comes up with closely packed light-yellow-tinted heads in spring, followed by fleshy glaucous foliage to about 25 cm. It is an undemanding plant and like all but one sedum is best in sun. The one exception is *S. pulchellum* which I have twice lost and found again after much searching over the years. It is mat forming with light-green needly leaves, and in later summer to autumn produces large cockscomb prostrate heads of shining pink flowers. It likes dampish or even heavy soil but as a very shallow-rooting subject needs to be divided and replanted at least every two years.

## SELINUM

*S. tenuifolium* is included with an admission of failure. The plant itself is a majestic umbellifer with broad white heads on strong 1.2 m stems decked with radiating lacy foliage. It gained an Award of Merit as long ago as 1881 and yet has remained a rarity. My failure lies in not being able to meet the demand because in recent years it has failed to set seed, and no other reliable means of propagation has as yet opened up.

## SENECIO

Although many yellow daisy-flowered subjects exist, *S. dorenicum* 'Sunburst' is one scarcely ever seen. It has deep golden-rayed flowers in early summer on single 45 cm stems, growing from clumpy, compact plants. The cultivar name 'Sunburst' was given to an improved seedling of a deeper yellow than the one I formerly grew. Leaves are tongue-shaped and not at all comparable with ligularias, to which genus so many senecios have been transferred.

## SERRATULA

I grew *S. macrocephala* for many years before deciding to distribute it, because *S. shawii* was already in circulation. The latter is an attractive late-flowering plant with purple thistle-type flowers on 30 cm branching stems above finely cut dark-green foliage. Although *S. macrocephala* is earlier, August-October, it is a little taller at 45 cm and makes a brighter display from sturdy, easy growth. It was partly its appeal to Sir Harold Hillier, who saw it in my garden a few years before he died, which made me re-assess its value.

## SILENE

*S. schafta* 'Robusta' came amongst some rewards for having contributed to the costs of a plant-hunting expedition to eastern Turkey. It was labelled *Saponaria*, but proved to be a strong-growing form of this well-known late-flowering alpine plant. It has been consistently better for freedom and vigour to justify the name I added. Flowering as it does, of a bright deep pink, from August to well into October at about 15 cm, makes it a most deserving rock garden or edging plant, with a slow but steady spread in any reasonable soil.

## SOLIDAGO

This distinctive 'Golden Rod', *S. caesia*, deserves to be more widely grown. It carries no plume to spoil with fading after a week or two, but has a profusion of small deep-yellow flowers along slender spikes giving a much more graceful display than most. At 1.05 m it is not too tall and has no fads or vices. It is at its best in September.

## STACHYS

*S. densiflorum* is another subject that seemed to demand release, as seeing its performance year after year deepened my appreciation of it. It forms a compact clump of somewhat rounded light-green leaves which are puckered. Through the base come stumpy spikes on stiff stems, 45 cm high of clear deep pink for many weeks through June and well into August. It is a very accommodating plant for sun or part shade and is not particular about any type of soil other than very dry.

## STROBILANTHES

At first glance *S. atropurpurea* could be taken for a bushy growing salvia, but it is in no way botanically related. It is a long-lived, fully hardy herbaceous perennial, growing from deep, tough roots to form a quite large clump which will flower without attention for years, in almost any soil. The leaves on its shapely bush, which will become 1.05 m high, are rounded and slightly grey green. For many weeks, July-September, come deep mauve-blue lipped flowers, not large but profuse enough to attract attention as an out of the ordinary plant which harmonises well with the prevailing yellows and reds of the later summer season.

## STYLOPHORUM

The little-known member of the Poppy family *S. diphyllum* is spring flowering. The pure-yellow flowers come above freshly green, deeply cut foliage in April-May, only 23 cm high, to add charm and variety even if it makes no splash of colour.

When, 20 years ago I included it in an article in a gardening weekly, the editor came back questioningly because he could not find a reference book that mentioned it. I find it prefers light soil in sun or part shade and its shallow fleshy roots are best divided and replanted in early autumn.

## SYMPHYTUM

Unlike most comfreys, *S. rubrum* is not a spreader and is slow to make a sizeable clump. Its relatively small leaves have typical comfrey roughness, and it has black fleshy roots, but needs good soil and some shade to encourage its arching sprays of small crimson bell-shaped flowers. It has a longer, but less profuse flowering period than other symphytums. *S. uplandicum* 'Variegatum' is best grown for its foliage and the 90 cm sprays of pale-mauve flowers are best cut away. The leaves are large – up to 30 cm long and 15 cm wide, and are quite spectacular from March to November, in sun or shade. The light yellow takes up more than half the basic green of the leaves. Care must be taken not to damage any of its black fleshy roots as they are likely to sprout to develop all-green leaves.

## THALICTRUM

Along with several other subjects, *T. rochebrunianum* came to me from the Continent before 1939, not having been seen or heard of in Britain. It is an elegant plant with strongly erect stems up to 1.5 m, branching to carry sprays almost horizontally of mauve-blue flowers in which the stamens are as tiny puffs and yellow centred. The separated leaves are rounded, finger-nail size, and both these and the stems have a bluish-glaucous hue. This is not a plant for poor dry soil but very rewarding and long-lived where fertility and moisture are not lacking.

*T. angustifolium* might be a disputed name, but in my opinion it ranks highly amongst the yellow-flowered thalictrums. The deeply cut leaves cling to the slender 1.5 m stems, darkly green, and the heads of fluffy canary-yellow flowers are not so heavy as in *T. glaucum*. For all its height, it needs no support and in June-July makes a pleasing background, which needs neither fussing nor curbing.

# Tiarella

Although *T. collina* is said to be a variant of *T. cordifolia*, I find it difficult to believe because it differs so greatly. It grows quite compactly, unlike *T. cordifolia* which spreads quickly from stolons, and has much larger flowers. They are more prominent from erect 30 cm sprays – rather like a heuchera. The leaves are light green, soft, rounded and overlapping to form a low mound. *T. cordifolia* has but a brief flowering season in May, but *T. collina* is later and flowers for several weeks. *T. trifoliata* is also little known but long-flowering, and of similar habit. Its 23 cm sprays carry tiny white flowers. Another, *T. polyphylla* is taller at 25 cm and carries small pearly white bells above soft mounded foliage in early summer. Both these, incidentally, were offered in our earlier retail catalogues, but lacking illustrations attracted too few orders to justify continued inclusion. All tiarellas prefer light soil and some shade, but I find *T. collina* and *T. polyphylla* doing just as well in full sun, noticeable after the trees shading them blew down in the 1987 October hurricane.

# Tovara

*T. virginiana* 'Painter's Palette' was my choice of a name for what was given to me by a customer for its multicolour foliage. It is a bush-forming herbaceous plant allied to poly-gonums and a reliable, long-lived perennial. The pointed leaves, basically deep green, are striped with subdued yellow, brown, pink and red shades, but are not large enough to be really showy, and if it flowers at all they are mere browny-black mouse-tails. In good soil the bushy habit reaches a shapely 75 cm and can remain undisturbed for years – interesting but not spectacular.

# Trollius Yunnanensis

The species have taken a very secondary place with the cultivars of *T. europaeus* taking almost all the limelight. To an increasing extent in recent years I have been impressed with the beauty of *T. yunnanensis* with its wide open glistening yellow flowers. It comes a little later than the well-known cultivars of *T. europaeus* and is only about 45 cm tall. It lasts in flower over a longer period from June to August, with the terminal flower having others to follow and with dark-green leaves as a background. As with all trollius moist soil is much preferred, but as with almost all moisture-loving plants, humus-rich soil is a safeguard against lack of rainfall.

## VERONICA

The little species *V. filifolia* must not be confused with the pretty weed *V. filicaule*. The former is not at all quick growing but has a clumpy habit of congested roots of no deep penetration. In spring comes a low mound of rich-green dessicated foliage, with a modest seasonal coverage. On this, at only 8 cm, comes an array of light-blue little cup-shaped flowers in June, but the foliage effect lasts until late autumn. *V. virginica* 'Alba' (sometimes classified as *Veronicastrum*) is amongst the best of spike-forming subjects for later summer. In good soil the slender but strong tapering spikes attain 1.2 m in height, tipped, as are the short branches, with white pokery spikes not unlike a cimicifuga. Plants grow into sizeable clumps needing minimum attention for years, in sun or part shade. This is another of those subjects which years ago appealed to me as worthy of wider recognition, but which have since become in short supply due to the demand.

Another veronica recently sent from an American nursery is likely to be soon introduced. It is a cultivar of *V. longifolia* named 'Lilac Beauty' with a succession of 75 cm spikes in later summer. In rich soil these tend to loll somewhat but the background of deep-green leafage is a compensation.

## ZAUSCHNERIA

When visiting Glasnevin Botanic Garden near Dublin in 1958 I was very taken with a zauschneria in a blaze of fiery orange scarlet. It had no label but was obviously an improvement on the well-known *Z. mexicana*. It might in fact have been a different species, for its foliage had no greyness but was pure green, and the stems were close on 60 cm tall. A swop was of course arranged and I could but give it the name 'Glasnevin'. So it has remained ever since and is still unsurpassed in my estimation, especially as it has also proved to be hardier and more vigorous than any others I grow.

## ZIGADENUS

This is a genus that has come to the fore in recent years after long-standing obscurity. The best-known species has been Z. *elegans* with its 50 cm sprays of starry, green-tinged white flowers. The foliage is grassy and not very abundant and this appears to be a feature with others now coming into garden cultivation. There is no striking difference between Z. *elegans* and Z. *nutallii* but the latter is a little more luxuriant. I have also acquired Z. *muscitoxicum* and this holds promise of being stronger growing with purer white flowers. They prefer light, fairly rich soil, and will take to some light shade.

# THE 1939 CATALOGUE

The catalogue I produced in 1939 was the culmination of all
my efforts at building up the nursery. The approach of war
prevented the inclusion of full descriptions and in the event
most of the plants were left unsold and had to be ploughed in.

However, that catalogue is worth reproducing to show the
wide range of varieties I grew at that time. Comparison with
the modern catalogue shows how tastes have changed.

# BLOOMS

## OAKINGTON
### Cambridge

## 1938-1939
## Wholesale Catalogue of
## HARDY PLANTS

# NEW PINK BUDDLEIA
## *"CHARMING"*

This really outstanding novelty was raised in America and introduced in the spring of 1938, and we have received the offer to distribute it in the British Isles during the coming season.

It is far and away the nearest to a pink Buddleia yet raised, and is moreover extremely vigorous and free-flowering, producing a profusion of large lavender-pink trusses continuously throughout the late summer and autumn. It is not only a striking ornament for the garden, but is also extremely valuable as a late summer cut flower. Few other plants have attracted as much attention and favourable comment when shown for the first time.

We have a good stock of strong plants in 3½-inch pots, and these will be available after October.

Price **2/6** each; **27/–** per dozen (for not less than 3 plants); **200/–** per 100 (for not less than 25 plants).

OAKINGTON,

CAMBRIDGE.

September, 1938.

Since last year's Catalogue was issued, a further seven acres of land have been taken into cultivation, and about 250 additional items have been added to stock, many of them being novelties.

We now feel that we have some justification in saying that this Catalogue is the most complete and up-to-date list of Hardy Plants in the Trade.

In common with many other localities, weather conditions have been decidedly trying this year, but our losses have been comparatively light, thanks to an irrigation plant which we installed in the spring.

We are more firmly convinced than ever in our policy of supplying first-class plants at reasonable prices to the TRADE ONLY. This has been borne out by a continued increase in business, and it has been very gratifying to have been able to add a large number of customers to our mailing list during the past year.

BLOOMS

*Alan H. V. Bloom*

Tel: HISTON 44.

---

# TERMS OF BUSINESS

**FOR CASH WITH ORDER (Great Britain and Northern Ireland only)**

Packing and Carriage Paid *plus* 10% if order is under **15/-**.
  ,,      ,,    *plus* 7½% if order is over **15/-** and under **30/-**.
  ,,      ,,    *nett*, if order is between **30/-** and **£4**.
  ,,      ,,    *less* 2½%, if order is between **£4** and **£10**.
  ,,      ,,    *less* 5%, if order is over **£10**.

(These terms do not apply to the Collections on pages 50 and 51 where carriage-paid prices are quoted.)

**FOR MONTHLY SETTLEMENT—**

Carriage costs are added to invoices if sent by **passenger train,** and are charged forward if by **goods train.** The cost price **only** is added for boxes, and **no charge is made for packing.**

5% may be deducted for payment within one month, if invoice amount exceeds **£1** in value. No discount can be allowed on accounts under **£1**.

---

**ALL ACCOUNTS** are due **nett** at three months, and 5% interest will be charged on overdue accounts.

**NEW CUSTOMERS,** when unknown to us, are requested to remit cash with order, or to give trade references.

**DESPATCH** is nearly always effected within 24 hours of receipt of order.

**PACKING.** Every possible care is taken to ensure the safe transit of plants by careful packing, and no charge is made for this, except in cases where special packing is necessary.

**STOCKS.** Having every faith in the quality of our plants, we guarantee to refund cash if dissatisfied, if the complaint is made and goods returned immediately. Every possible care is taken to keep stocks true to name, and although we can give no guarantee on this point, we are always willing to do our best to make restitution should a mistake occur.

All plants are offered subject to being unsold on receipt of order.

**N.B.—CUSTOMERS ARE REQUESTED WHEN ORDERING TO GIVE THE NAME OF THEIR NEAREST RAILWAY STATION.**

---

An increasing number of firms are finding it more profitable to keep only small stocks of Hardy Plants for show purposes, and to obtain their main supplies for sale from us. Many of them issue catalogues based on our stocks, the advantages of which are obvious. For this class of business we are always ready to quote special terms, and are anxious to assist in every way.

2

# General List of Hardy Plants

**N.B.—Not less than 4 plants at dozen rate, nor less than 25 at 100 rate.**

"a" denotes pot-grown Alpines.

| | | doz. | 100 |
|---|---|---|---|
| a | **ACÆNA Buchanani,** forms close mats of grey-green foliage.. | 3/6 | 25/- |
| a | **microphylla,** bronzy crimson leaves, red brachts .. .. | 4/- | 28/- |
| a | **ACANTHOLIMON glumaceum,** short spikes of pink flowers, 4 ins., June .. .. .. .. | 6/- | — |
| | **ACHILLEA argentea,** fine silvery foliage, white flowers, 8 ins., May .. .. .. .. | 4/- | 28/- |
| | **clypeolata,** an attractive new species, silvery foliage, flat heads of light yellow flowers, 1½ ft. .. .. | 10/- | — |
| | **Eupatorium Parker's Variety,** deep yellow, extra fine, 4 ft. .. .. .. .. .. | 3/6 | 25/- |
| | **Spark's Variety,** rich deep yellow, very large heads .. | 3/6 | 25/- |
| | **Wallis' Form,** quite the best in this section, with large heads of bright yellow.. .. .. .. | 3/6 | 25/- |
| | (These three varieties of Eupatorium are all excellent for cutting.) | | |
| a | **Huteri,** tufted growth, white flowers, 3 ins. .. .. | 3/6 | 25/- |
| a | **Jabborneggi,** corymbs of white flowers, grey foliage, 6 ins. | 3/6 | 25/- |
| a | **King Edward,** lemon-yellow, free and very useful, 6 ins. .. | 4/- | 28/- |
| | **millefolia Cerise Queen,** very bright and effective, 2 ft. .. | 4/- | 28/- |
| | **Fire King,** similar to *Cerise Queen* but deeper colour, 2 ft. | 4/- | 28/- |
| | **Perry's White,** double button flowers, 2½ ft. .. ·.. | 3/6 | 25/- |
| a | **Prichardi,** semi-double, white, 6 ins. .. .. .. | 3/6 | 25/- |
| a | **rupestre,** neat silver-grey growth, white flowers, 4 ins. .. | 3/6 | 25/- |
| | **Schwefelblüte,** a new hybrid, similar in growth to *millefolia*, with ferny foliage and stiff stems. The flowers are of a pleasing sulphur-yellow colour, useful for cutting. A valuable border plant, June–August, 2½ ft. .. .. | 8/- | 60/- |
| | **taygetea,** very free-flowering over a long period, with flat heads of lemon-yellow flowers, resembling an enlarged *King Edward*, 1–1½ ft. .. .. | 6/- | 42/- |
| a | **tomentosa,** bright yellow heads, very free, 8 ins. .. .. | 3/6 | 25/- |
| | **W. B. Childs** (syn, *alpina*), single white, June–July, 2 ft. .. | 4/- | 28/- |
| | **ACONITUM bicolor,** soft blue and white, June–July, 3 ft. | 4/6 | 30/- |
| | **Fischeri,** spikes of pale blue flowers, August–October, 2½ ft. | 4/6 | 30/- |
| | **lycoctonum,** pale yellow, 3½ ft. .. .. .. | 4/- | 28/- |
| | **Spark's Variety,** deep violet blue, very showy, 4 ft. | 4/6 | 30/- |
| | **Wilsoni,** porcelain-blue flowers, fine spikes.. .. .. | 5/- | 35/- |
| | **Barker's Variety,** bold branching spikes of deep blue flowers, September–October, 5 ft. .. .. | 9/- | 70/- |

3

| BLOOMS' HARDY PLANTS | doz. | 100 |
|---|---|---|
| a **ÆTHIONEMA jucundum,** bright pink, very free-flowering, 6 ins. | 6/– | 42/– |
| a **Warley Rose,** smothers itself in deep pink flowers over a long period, dwarf bushy habit, May–June, a really good selling plant | 4/– | 28/– |
| a **Warley ruber,** similar to the above, but with flowers of a deeper shade | 6/– | 42/– |
| a **AJUGA Rainbow,** forms mats of coloured foliage, very effective in autumn and winter | 3/6 | 25/– |
| a **ALYSSUM saxatile compactum,** deep yellow, 6 ins. | 3/6 | 25/– |
| a **saxatile flore pleno,** double deep golden yellow | 4/6 | 30/– |
| a **Silver Queen,** beautiful lemon form, almost identical with *citrinum* | 4/– | 28/– |
| a **spinosum,** shrubby growth, white, 9 ins. | 6/– | — |
| a **ANAGALLIS collina,** close trailing habit, intense orange flowers | 6/– | — |
| a **vilmoriniana,** similar to above but bright blue | 6/– | — |
| (The above *Anagallis* need protection in winter.) | | |
| **ANAPHALIS triplinervis,** silvery foliage, white, ever-lasting-like flowers, August–September, 1 ft. | 4/6 | 30/– |
| **ANCHUSA Dropmore,** blue, 4 ft. | 3/6 | 25/– |
| **Morning Glory,** the finest deep blue variety | 3/6 | 25/– |
| **Opal,** beautiful light blue, 4 ft. | 3/6 | 25/– |
| **Pride of Dover,** soft sky blue | 4/6 | 30/– |
| **myosotidiflora,** sprays of light blue, quite distinct from the the foregoing, April–June, 2 ft. | 4/6 | 30/– |
| a **ANDROSACE Chumbyi,** greyish rosettes, pink flowers, 4 ins. | 4/6 | 30/– |
| a **lanuginosa,** trailing habit, bright pink | 6/– | — |
| a **primuloides,** rosy-pink flowers on neat rosettes | 4/6 | 30/– |
| a **sarmentosa,** rose with white eye, 4 ins. | 4/6 | 30/– |
| a **sempervivioides,** bright pink | 5/– | — |
| a **villosa,** flowers snow-white, very close-growing, 2 ins. | 5/– | — |
| a **Watkinsii,** a good form of *sarmentosa*, bright and free | 4/6 | — |
| **ANEMONE JAPONICA**—Strong open-ground stock, 2–3 ft. September–October. | | |
| **Charmeuse,** large flowers, deep lilac-rose | 4/6 | 30/– |
| **Coupe d'Argent,** semi-double, white | 4/6 | 30/– |
| **Couronnement,** light rose-pink | 5/– | 35/– |
| **Frau Mary Manhardt,** fine new white | 4/6 | 30/– |
| **hupehensis,** rosy-red, early, dwarf, 1½ ft. | 4/– | 28/– |
| **splendens,** a very bright form of the above | 4/6 | 30/– |
| **Kriemhilde,** bright pink, semi-double | 4/6 | 30/– |
| **Louise Uhink,** the finest semi-double white variety | 5/– | 35/– |
| **Max Vogel,** large semi-double flowers, rich rose pink | 5/– | 35/– |
| **Mont Rose,** semi-double, pink, extra good, | 4/6 | 30/– |
| **Prince Henry,** a really fine variety, flowers rich deep red | 4/6 | 30/– |
| **Profusion,** semi-double red, quite dwarf | 4/6 | 30/– |
| **Queen Charlotte,** bright rose, semi-double, free | 4/6 | 30/– |
| **rubra,** deep red, compact habit | 4/6 | 30/– |
| **Whirlwind,** semi-double, pure white.. | 4/6 | 30/– |

*"a" denotes pot-grown Alpines*

4

| | doz. | 100 |
|---|---|---|
| BLOOMS' HARDY PLANTS | | |
| **ANEMONE pulsatilla,** the purple *Pasque* flower, 6 ins., April–May .. .. .. .. | 5/- | 35/- |
| a **ANTENNARIA dioica,** grey carpenter, bearing white flowers | 3/6 | 25/- |
| **ANTHEMIS nobilis alba plena,** a form of the true *Camomile*, bearing a profusion of pure white double button-like flowers, which should be useful for cutting, 18 ins. .. .. .. .. | 7/- | 50/- |
| **Sancta Johannis,** true, rich orange-yellow, a really good border plant .. .. .. .. .. | 4/6 | 30/- |
| **tinctoria,** a profusion of bright yellow flowers, 2½ ft. .. | 3/6 | 25/- |
| **Mrs. E. C. Buxton,** lemon-yellow, fine for cutting, 2½ ft. June–August .. .. .. .. .. | 4/- | 28/- |
| **Perry's Variety,** deep golden-yellow, a fine plant .. | 4/6 | 30/- |
| **Roger Perry,** green ferny foliage, brightest orange-yellow flowers all summer, 2½ ft., new .. | 14/- | — |
| **Thora Perry,** greyish foliage, large yellow flowers freely produced, June–September, 2½ ft. .. | 14/- | — |
| a **ANTHYLLIS montana rubra,** silvery foliage, heads of deep pink flowers, 4 ins. .. .. .. | 5/- | 35/- |
| a **AQUILEGIA alpina,** beautiful hanging dark blue flowers, 9 ins. .. .. .. .. .. .. | 6/- | — |
| a **Crimson Star,** an outstanding variety, 1½ ft. .. .. | 4/- | 28/- |
| a **discolor,** blue and white, a rare and pretty dwarf species, 4 ins. .. .. .. .. .. .. | 5/- | 35/- |
| **glandulosa major,** blue and cream, extra good, 1½ ft. ... | 5/- | 35/- |
| **Copenhagen Variety,** rich purple, new, 1½ ft. .. .. | 4/6 | 30/- |
| a **Vera,** large blue flowers, 1 ft. .. .. .. .. | 6/- | 42/- |
| a **Hensoll Harebell,** an improved form of *alpina* .. | 4/6 | 30/- |
| a **longissima,** a rare and beautiful yellow species .. | 6/- | 42/- |
| a **Mrs. Nicholls,** a large blue variety .. .. .. | 5/- | — |
| **Mrs. Scott Elliott's Hybrids,** a fine long-spurred strain.. | 3/- | 22/- |
| a **ARABIS alpinus coccineus,** a novelty of merit, bright crimson-rose flowers .. .. .. .. | 12/- | — |
| a **aubrietioides,** pretty pink flowers in early spring .. .. | 4/- | 28/- |
| a **Sturri,** masses of white flowers on neat cushions .. .. | 3/6 | 25/- |
| a **ARENARIA balearica,** forms close green mats with white flowers .. .. .. .. .. .. | 3/6 | 25/- |
| a **cæspitosa aurea,** golden moss-like foliage, always effective | 3/6 | 25/- |
| a **montana grandiflora,** beautiful white flowers, trailing habit .. .. .. .. .. .. | 4/6 | 30/- |
| a **purpurascens,** close-growing, flowers rosy-lilac .. .. | 3/6 | 25/- |
| **ARMERIA Bees' Ruby,** true stock, large glistening pink flower heads, 1½ ft. .. .. .. .. | 5/- | 35/- |
| a **corsica,** deep reddish-orange, on grassy tufts, 6 ins. .. | 3/6 | 25/- |
| a **Laucheana,** rich rosy-red, fine for edging, etc. .. | 3/6 | 25/- |
| a **Merlin,** grassy hummocks, heads of deep pink .. .. | 3/6 | 25/- |
| a **Vindictive,** beautiful crimson-red, 6 ins. .. .. | 5/- | 35/- |
| **ARTEMESIA lactiflora,** attractive plumes of creamy-white, a most useful border plant, 4 ft. .. .. | 3/6 | 25/- |

5

BLOOMS' HARDY PLANTS — doz. 100

**ASCLEPIAS tuberosa,** heads of brightest orange flowers, 18 ins., July–August .. .. .. .. 5/– 35/–

a **ASPERULA nitida** (syn. *Gussoni*), bright pink flowers on green tufts .. .. .. .. 4/6 30/–

a **suberosa,** masses of clear pink flowers, a really choice Alpine .. .. .. .. .. .. 8/– —

**ASPHODELUS luteus,** spikes of golden-yellow flowers, June–July, 3 ft. .. .. .. .. 4/6 30/–

# ASTERS
## Aster Amellus

All the varieties in this section grow from 2 to 3 ft., with large flowers; invaluable for late-flowering. Strong open-ground plants.

| | doz. | 100 |
|---|---|---|
| **Advance,** might be described as an improved *King George*, but flowers later, 2 ft. | 6/– | 42/– |
| **Beauté Parfaite,** violet-blue, 2 ft. | 5/– | 35/– |
| **Beauty of Ronsdorf,** very large rosy-lilac flowers | 6/– | 42/– |
| **Bessarabicus,** violet-blue | 5/– | 35/– |
| **Bessie Chapman,** intense violet-blue, 2 ft., September-October | 6/– | 42/– |
| **Frikarti,** distinct branching habit, deep blue flowers in great profusion over a long period, 2½ ft. | 6/– | 42/– |
| **Wonder of Stäfa,** brilliant blue with orange centre | 7/– | 50/– |
| **Gen. Pershing,** beautiful large pink, one of the best | 5/– | 35/– |
| **Herman Lons,** fine mauve-blue | 5/– | 35/– |
| **King George,** the best-known of this class, violet-blue | 4/6 | 30/– |
| **lilacina,** pleasing shade of lilac-mauve | 5/– | 35/– |
| **Mme. Besnard,** large-flowered, pink, compact habit | 8/– | — |
| **Mrs. Elliott,** soft lilac-rose, large flowers | 7/– | — |
| **Pink Pearl,** light clear pink, neat bushy habit | 5/– | 35/– |
| **Rose of Ronsdorf,** fine clear pink | 6/– | 42/– |
| **Rotfeuer,** deep rosy-red | 7/– | 50/– |
| **Rudolf Goethe,** lavender-blue | 6/– | 42/– |
| **Sonia,** beautiful rose-pink, a popular variety | 6/– | 42/– |
| **The Shirley,** sky-blue, extra large flowers | 4/6 | 30/– |
| **Ultramarine,** deep violet-blue, distinct habit | 5/– | 35/– |
| **Wells' Favourite,** a good deep rose variety | 5/– | 35/– |
| **Wienholtzii,** light rose-pink | 5/– | 35/– |
| **Wm. Robinson,** rich deep pink, 2½ ft. | 6/– | 42/– |

**COLLECTIONS, our selection: 50 in up to 8 sorts for 18/6 ; 100 for 36/–.**

## Aster Novæ Belgii (Michaelmas Daisies)

| | doz. | 100 |
|---|---|---|
| **Acme,** pale lavender, very large flowers, 3 ft., October | 3/6 | 25/– |
| **Alderman Vokes,** bright pink, 3 ft., early | 3/6 | 25/– |
| **A. M. Carr,** intense violet flowers, very neat habit, September–October, 3 ft., new | 5/– | 35/– |
| **Anita Ballard,** double powder blue, 4 ft. | 3/6 | 25/– |

6

BLOOMS' HARDY PLANTS          doz.   100
**Aster Novæ Belgii—continued.**

| | doz. | 100 |
|---|---|---|
| **Autumn Glow,** deep rosy-red, very late | 3/6 | 25/- |
| **Autumn Queen,** deep blue, also late | 3/6 | 25/- |
| **Barr's Pink** (*Novæ Angliæ*), the best deep pink variety | 3/6 | 25/- |
| **Beechwood Beacon,** bushy growth, smothered in large deep crimson-rose flowers, 2½ ft. | 20/- | 150/- |
| **Beechwood Belle,** flowers bright pink with yellow eye, distinct bushy habit, 3 ft. | 6/- | 42/- |
| **Beechwood Challenger,** A.M.R.H.S., glowing crimson-magenta flowers; forms a strong bush; a really outstanding novelty; 3½ ft. | 6/- | 42/- |
| **Beechwood Ray,** bright pink, a really fine variety | 3/6 | 25/- |
| **Blue Eyes,** the nearest approach to a real blue, good habit | 4/- | 28/- |
| **Blue Gem,** very bright, semi-double, and a good habit, late | 4/- | 28/- |
| **Blue Gown,** very large flowers, an improvement on *Climax*, September–October, 4–5 ft. | 4/6 | 30/- |
| **Blue Plume,** flowers almost double, deep purple-blue, produced in tall sprays, 4 ft., late | 12/- | 90/- |
| **Brighteyes,** a novelty of great merit | 15/- | — |
| **Brimstone** (*ericoides variety*), bushes of starry yellow flowers, 2½ ft. | 3/6 | 25/- |
| **Charles Wilson,** a deep pink, good in every way, mid-season | 3/6 | 25/- |
| **Col. F. R. Durham,** flowers rich clear mauve, double, neat habit, 3½ ft., September | 5/- | 35/- |
| **Countess,** fine rose-pink, semi-double, extra good | 4/- | 28/- |
| **Delight** (*ericoides variety*), starry white flowers, 3 ft. | 3/6 | 25/- |
| **Dick Ballard,** double lilac-blue, neat dwarf habit, October, 2½ ft. | 3/6 | 25/- |
| **Dr. Eckener** (*Novæ Angliæ*), a bright salmon-carmine; a welcome addition to this section | 10/- | 72/- |
| **Duchess,** light rose-pink, 3 ft., October | 3/6 | 25/- |
| **Elizabeth Bright,** attractive pink flowers tinged yellow, semi-double, excellent for the border, 3 ft., early-flowering | 4/6 | 30/- |
| **Elta,** double lavender-mauve | 3/6 | 25/- |
| **Empress of Colwall,** fine double heliotrope-blue, September–October | 3/6 | 25/- |
| **Esther,** showy small pink flowers, useful for cutting, 2½ ft. | 5/- | 35/- |
| **Ethel Ballard,** soft shade of pink, 4 ft. | 4/- | 28/- |
| **Gayborder Blue,** an outstanding variety, intense blue | 6/- | 42/- |
| **Gayborder Pride,** semi-double, attractive violet shade, branching habit, 4 ft., September | 4/6 | 30/- |
| **Gayborder Supreme,** large semi-double flowers, a fine shade of violet-rose, useful for cutting, 3½ ft., September | 12/- | — |
| **Golden Spray** (*ericoides*), small white flowers with golden centre, 3 ft., October | 4/- | 28/- |
| **Grey Lady,** distinct blue-grey flowers, 3½ ft., late | 3/6 | 25/- |
| **Heather Glow,** warm deep rose, a first-rate variety, October | 3/6 | 25/- |
| **Hilda Ballard,** a very large-flowered novelty, lavender-blue | 20/- | 150/- |

7

| BLOOMS' HARDY PLANTS | doz. | 100 |
|---|---|---|
| **Aster Novæ Belgii—continued.** | | |
| **King of the Belgians,** lavender-blue, 4 ft. .. .. .. | 3/6 | 25/– |
| **Lil Fardell** (*Novæ Angliæ*), very deep pink .. .. .. | 3/6 | 25/– |
| **Little Boy Blue,** neat bushes of rich blue, very popular .. | 4/6 | 30/– |
| **Little Pink Lady,** the pink counterpart of the above, September–October, 2½ ft. .. .. .. | 4/6 | 30/– |
| **Maggie Perry,** soft mauve, semi-double, 3 ft. .. .. | 3/6 | 25/– |
| **Maid of Athens,** beautiful clear pink, 5 ft. .. .. .. | 3/6 | 25/– |
| **Mammoth,** large semi-double light lavender flowers, new, 5–6 ft., September–October .. .. | 20/– | 150/– |
| **Margaret Ballard,** rich rosy-mauve, semi-double, extra fine, September–October .. .. .. | 4/– | 28/– |
| **Mars,** an early-flowering variety, large pale pink flowers, neat habit, 3 ft., early .. .. .. | 4/6 | 30/– |
| **Melbourne Lad,** branching habit, purple-violet flowers, 4½ ft., September-October .. .. | 6/– | 42/– |
| **Mother of Pearl,** silvery-lilac, late, 4 ft. .. .. .. | 3/6 | 25/– |
| **Mount Everest,** a really fine white variety, 4 ft., September .. .. .. .. .. | 3/6 | 25/– |
| **Mrs. Geo. Monro,** one of the best whites, 4 ft. .. .. | 3/6 | 25/– |
| **Mrs. Lewis Evans,** large deep rosy-red, pyramidal habit, 3½ ft. .. .. .. .. .. | 4/6 | 30/– |
| **Mulberry,** deep red, compact habit, extra good, October .. | 4/– | 28/– |
| **October Dawn,** beautiful lilac-blue, large flowers, September-October .. .. .. .. | 3/6 | 25/– |
| **Owen Wells,** very large clear lavender flowers .. .. | 3/6 | 25/– |
| **Perry's White,** a really good variety, 3 ft. .. .. | 3/6 | 25/– |
| **Pink Nymph,** large rose-pink flowers, tall, September–October, F.C.C. 1936 .. .. .. | 6/– | 42/– |
| **Pink Pearl,** 3½ ft., mid-season .. .. .. | 3/6 | 25/– |
| **Pink Perfection,** very free-flowering, 3½ ft. .. .. | 3/6 | 25/– |
| **Pink Profusion,** flowers of medium growth on long hanging sprays, mid-season, popular .. .. | 3/6 | 25/– |
| **Queen Mary,** rich blue, after the style of *Climax* but deeper colour, October, 4–5 ft. .. .. .. | 3/6 | 25/– |
| **Radiant,** bright rosy-red, semi-double, October, 4 ft. .. | 6/– | 42/– |
| **Red Rover,** one of the finest red varieties, strongly recommended, mid-season .. .. .. | 4/6 | 30/– |
| **Red Star,** small deep rosy-red flowers, late .. .. | 4/– | 28/– |
| **Rev. C. Lunn,** a good deep blue, 3 ft. .. .. .. | 3/6 | 25/– |
| **Ringdove** (*ericoides variety*), light blue, useful for cutting, 3 ft. .. .. .. .. .. | 4/6 | 30/– |
| **Robinson V.C.,** deep mauve blue .. .. .. | 3/6 | 25/– |
| **Rosette,** an attractive semi-double, deep pink, late .. | 3/6 | 25/– |
| **Royal Blue,** bright blue, very early, 3 ft. .. .. | 3/6 | 25/– |
| **Ruby Tips,** deep rose merging into ruby-red, 3½ ft. .. | 3/6 | 25/– |
| **Ruth Bide,** an outstanding novelty, deep rosy-mauve with amber eye .. .. .. .. .. | 6/– | 42/– |
| **St. Egwin,** branching habit, pink flowers .. .. | 3/6 | 25/– |
| **Silver Spray** (*cordifolius*), pale lavender flowers, very distinct .. .. .. .. .. | 4/6 | 30/– |

8

BLOOMS' HARDY PLANTS                                                    doz.    100

**Aster Novæ Belgii—continued.**

| | doz. | 100 |
|---|---|---|
| **Snowdrift,** pure double white  .. .. .. .. | 3/6 | 25/– |
| **Strawberries and Cream,** clear pink, recommended  .. | 4/– | 28/– |
| **Sunset Glow,** rich deep pink, good habit  .. .. .. | 5/– | 35/– |
| **Taplow Spire,** new deep rose-pink flowers on tall pyramidal spikes  .. .. .. .. .. | 4/6 | 30/– |
| **Walkden's Pink,** very fine early variety  .. .. | 3/6 | 25/– |
| **Wonder of Colwall,** a pretty pale blue, 3½ ft.  .. .. | 3/6 | 25/– |

COLLECTIONS, our selection: 50 in up to 10 sorts for
13/6; 100 for 25/–.

## Aster, Dwarf Hybrids

A race of miniature Michaelmas Daisies, which can be strongly recommended. Growing from 6–12 ins. Equally useful for the rock garden or front of the border.

| | doz. | 100 |
|---|---|---|
| **Blue Bird,** clear deep lavender-blue, 10 ins., October  .. | 5/– | 35/– |
| **Constance**  .. .. .. .. .. .. .. | 5/– | 35/– |
| **Countess of Dudley,** clear pink, yellow eye  .. .. | 3/6 | 25/– |
| **Diana,** soft pink semi-double flowers, 9 ins., September  .. | 5/– | 35/– |
| **Hebe,** a good blue variety  .. .. .. .. | 4/6 | 30/– |
| **Lady Henry Maddocks,** pale pink, very free, early  .. | 3/6 | 25/– |
| **Lavenda,** lavender-blue  .. .. .. .. | 4/6 | 30/– |
| **Lilac Time,** pretty shade of lilac  .. .. .. | 3/6 | 25/– |
| **Little Blue Baby,** like a miniature *Little Boy Blue*, a really good thing  .. .. .. .. .. | 5/– | 35/– |
| **Marjorie,** very compact, bright rose  .. .. .. | 4/– | 28/– |
| **Nancy,** flesh-pink, very free  .. .. .. .. | 3/6 | 25/– |
| **Niobe,** pure white, compact habit  .. .. .. | 5/– | 35/– |
| **Peter Pan,** very dwarf and compact; clear soft pink flowers, 6 ins., September  .. .. .. | 5/– | 35/– |
| **Ronald,** rosy-lilac, recommended  .. .. .. | 3/6 | 25/– |
| **Snowsprite,** pure white flowers in rich profusion, 1 ft.  .. | 3/6 | 25/– |
| **Victor,** clear lavender-blue, extra dwarf  .. .. .. | 3/6 | 25/– |

COLLECTIONS, our selection: 25 in up to 5 sorts
for 8/-; 50 for 15/-; 100 for 28/-.

## Aster, Species, etc.

| | | doz. | 100 |
|---|---|---|---|
| | **acris,** very attractive bushes of light blue flowers, 2½ ft.  .. | 3/6 | 25/– |
| | **nanus** (*ramosus*), dwarf form, 9 ins., compact, recommended.. .. .. .. .. | 4/– | 28/– |
| | **roseus,** lilac-rose, dwarf  .. .. .. .. | 4/6 | 30/– |
| a | **alpinus albus,** white, 9 ins., May  .. .. .. | 3/6 | 25/– |
| a | **Nancy Perry,** beautiful light blue variety  .. .. | 4/6 | 30/– |
| a | **Rose King,** large lilac-pink flowers, 9 ins.  .. .. | 4/6 | 30/– |
| | **Farreri,** violet-blue, rayed petals, orange centre, 1 ft.  .. | 5/– | 35/– |
| | **hybridus luteus,** masses of small yellow flowers, 2½ ft.  .. | 4/– | 28/– |
| | **linosyris** (*Goldilocks*), heads of bright yellow, 2 ft. .. .. | 4/6 | 30/– |
| | **oreophilus,** various shades of blue, 1 ft.  .. .. | 4/– | 28/– |
| | **subcœruleus Star of Wartburg,** deep lilac-blue with conspicuous orange centre, 1 ft., May–June | 4/– | 28/– |

*"a" denotes pot-grown Alpines*

9

BLOOMS' HARDY PLANTS        doz.   100

**ASTILBE HYBRIDS** (*Spiræa*)—We offer strong planting size, not forcing clumps.

| | doz. | 100 |
|---|---|---|
| **Betsy Cuperus,** long sprays of white flowers | 4/6 | 30/– |
| **Ceres,** pale pink | 4/6 | 30/– |
| **Etna,** new deep red | 10/– | 72/– |
| **Fanal,** glowing red, the deepest of all | 10/– | 72/– |
| **Granat,** rich crimson, fine spikes | 5/– | 35/– |
| **Jo Ophorst,** dark purple-red | 6/– | 42/– |
| **Kriemhilde,** bright rose | 4/6 | 30/– |
| **Moerheimi,** creamy white | 4/6 | 30/– |
| **Pink Pearl,** fine pink variety | 4/6 | 30/– |
| **Professor van der Wielen,** pure white | 4/6 | 30/– |
| **Silver Sheaf,** tall spikes of silvery-white | 4/6 | 30/– |
| **Wm. Reeves,** bright crimson-red, a fine variety | 12/– | 90/– |

**ASTILBE crispa Perkeo** (syn. *Peter Pan*), deep pink spikes, very dwarf   ..   12/–   —

**sinensis pumila,** dwarf-growing, rosy-lilac flowers, 9 ins.   5/–   35/–

**simplicifolia rosea,** a beautiful little plant, pale pink, 6 ins.   6/–   42/–

# AUBRIETIAS

### All extra strong pot-grown plants

| | | doz. | 100 |
|---|---|---|---|
| a | **Aubrey Prichard,** fine large mauve-blue | 4/– | 28/– |
| a | **Barker's Double,** a new break, fine crimson-purple | 7/– | 50/– |
| a | **Belisha Beacon,** fine bright red | 4/6 | 30/– |
| a | **Bridesmaid,** pale rose, compact habit | 3/6 | 25/– |
| a | **Brighteyes,** light blue with white eye | 3/6 | 25/– |
| a | **Cambria,** a really good large-flowered red variety, early | 3/6 | 25/– |
| a | **Carnival,** quite the best violet-purple | 3/6 | 25/– |
| a | **Clio,** fine deep lilac | 3/6 | 25/– |
| a | **Crimson Queen,** deep red, large flowers and good habit | 4/6 | 30/– |
| a | **Dr. Mules,** popular violet-blue | 3/6 | 25/– |
| a | **Excelsa,** crimson-purple, compact growth | 4/– | 28/– |
| a | **Fire King,** bright red | 4/– | 28/– |
| a | **Fire King Improved,** red, larger flowers than above | 4/– | 28/– |
| a | **Gloriosa,** the best pink of all | 5/– | 35/– |
| a | **Godstone,** deep violet-purple, one of the best | 4/– | 28/– |
| a | **Gurgedyke,** intense crimson-purple, new | 7/– | 50/– |
| a | **H. S. Baker,** rich purple-blue, self colour | 3/6 | 25/– |
| a | **Lilac Time,** a fine shade of clear lilac, extra large flowers, early, strongly recommended | 3/6 | 25/– |
| a | **Magician,** deep reddish-purple, a fine variety | 6/– | 42/– |
| a | **Magnificent,** rich deep red with brown eye, large flowers | 6/– | 42/– |
| a | **Maurice Prichard,** light rosy-mauve | 6/– | 42/– |
| a | **Mrs. Lloyd Edwards,** a good violet-blue, early | 3/6 | 25/– |
| a | **Mrs. Rodewald,** large crimson flowers, very brilliant and showy, new | 8/– | 60/– |
| a | **Oakington Lavender,** a strong grower with large light lavender flowers | 3/6 | 25/– |

*" a " denotes pot-grown Alpines*

10

BLOOMS' HARDY PLANTS        doz.   100

**Aubrietias—continued.**

| | | doz. | 100 |
|---|---|---|---|
| a | **Peter Barr,** deep crimson-purple | 3/6 | 25/- |
| a | **Prichard's A.1,** deep violet-blue | 4/- | 28/- |
| a | **Red Carnival,** very bright red | 4/6 | 30/- |
| a | **Riverslea Pink,** clear pink, strong habit | 4/- | 28/- |
| a | **Rose Queen,** light pink with white eye | 3/6 | 25/- |
| a | **rosea splendens,** fine soft pink flowers, compact habit | 3/6 | 25/- |
| a | **Ruddigore,** deep red flowers, compact growth | 4/6 | 30/- |
| a | **Russell's Crimson,** deep red | 4/- | 28/- |
| a | **Russell Vincent,** the deepest red of all | 6/- | 42/- |
| a | **Studland,** pretty shade of light blue | 3/6 | 25/- |
| a | **Triumphant,** the nearest approach to true blue, extra fine | 5/- | 35/- |
| a | **variegata splendens,** blue flowers, pretty variegated foliage | 4/6 | 30/- |
| a | **Vindictive,** deep rosy-red | 4/- | 28/- |
| a | **Violet Queen,** deep violet, strong grower | 4/- | 28/- |
| a | **Wallacei,** light mauve | 3/6 | 25/- |
| a | **Warbarrow,** deep pink | 4/- | 28/- |

> **COLLECTIONS OF AUBRIETIA, our selection:**
> 24 in up to 8 sorts for 8/-; 50 in up to 10 sorts for
> 14/6; 100 for 27/-; 100 in up to 20 sorts for 30/-.

| | | doz. | 100 |
|---|---|---|---|
| a | **AURICULA alpina,** mixed varieties, pot-grown plants | 3/6 | 25/- |
| a | **BELLIS Dresden China,** double clear pink, 4 ins. | 3/- | 20/- |
| a | **Eliza,** flowers larger than above | 3/6 | 25/- |
| a | **Rob Roy,** double red, 4 ins. | 3/- | 20/- |
| a | **White Dresden China** | 4/- | 28/- |
| | **BETONICA grandiflora robusta,** a little larger than *superba* | 3/6 | 25/- |
| | **grandiflora superba,** short spikes of pink flowers, 1½ ft. | 3/6 | 25/- |
| | **BOCCONIA cordata,** effective sprays of brownish-cream, 6 ft. | 4/6 | 30/- |
| a | **CALAMINTHA alpina,** produces mauve flowers, very free, 6 ins. | 3/6 | 25/- |
| a | **CALCEOLARIA Hall's Variety,** large deep yellow flowers, red markings, an improvement on *John Innes*; hardy in most localities | 6/- | 42/- |
| | **CALTHA palustris monstrosa plena,** a fine form of double Kingcup | 6/- | 42/- |

> *For COLLECTIONS of ALPINES and HERBACEOUS*
> *PLANTS see pages 50 and 51.*

11

# CAMPANULAS

| | | | doz. | 100 |
|---|---|---|---|---|
| a | **abietina,** deep violet flowers on green tufts, May–June, 6 ins. .. .. .. .. .. .. | | 4/– | 28/– |
| a | **Abundance,** lavender-blue, upright habit, 6 ins, June–July | | 5/– | 35/– |
| a | **Allioni,** light blue cup flowers, 3 ins, May–June .. .. | | 6/– | 42/– |
| a | **grandiflora,** flowers much larger and better than the type | | 8/– | 60/– |
| a | **Blue Tit,** a new hybrid, crossed between *Hallii* and *Profusion,* having large open blue flowers of the *Hallii* type; freer flowering than either ; June–August .. .. .. .. .. | | 5/– | 35/– |
| a | **carpatica,** the blue Carpathian Harebell, 9 ins, July–August | | 3/6 | 25/– |
| a | **alba,** white form of the above, .. .. .. .. | | 4/– | 28/– |
| a | **pelviformis,** rich blue saucer-shaped flowers, very attractive .. .. .. .. .. | | 4/– | 28/– |
| a | **Riverslea,** a large-flowered form .. .. .. .. | | 5/– | 35/– |
| | **celtidifolia atro-cœrulea Prichard's Variety,** new dark blue variety, 2½ ft., July–August .. .. | | 8/– | — |
| a | **cochlearifolia,** dainty blue bells, 4 ins. .. .. | | 4/– | 28/– |
| a | **collina,** deep purple, erect stems, 1 ft., May–June .. .. | | 4/– | 28/– |
| a | **garganica,** trailing sprays of starry-blue flowers .. .. | | 4/6 | 30/– |
| a | **W. H. Paine,** violet-blue, with white eye .. .. | | 6/– | 42/– |
| a | **G. F. Wilson,** large violet bells, very free, 4 ins. .. .. | | 4/– | 28/– |
| | **glomerata superba,** larger than the above, very showy, 2 ft. .. .. .. .. .. .. | | 3/6 | 25/– |
| | **grandis Highcliffe Variety,** a new variety with intense deep blue flowers, 2½ ft., June–July .. | | 5/– | 35/– |
| a | **Hallii,** erect habit, pure white flowers, 6 ins. .. .. | | 4/– | 28/– |
| a | **hypopolea,** a choice plant with greyish foliage and light blue bells, 4 ins. .. .. .. .. | | 5/– | 35/– |
| a | **Incurva** (syn. *Leutweinii*), large silvery-lavender bells, 9 ins., July-August .. .. .. | | 4/6 | 30/– |
| | **lactiflora,** pale blue flowers, bushy growth, 3 ft. .. .. | | 4/6 | 30/– |
| | **latifolia macrantha,** spikes of deep blue, 3 ft., June–July | | 4/– | 28/– |
| | **macrantha alba,** a pretty white form .. .. .. | | 4/– | 28/– |
| | **Brantwood,** deep blue trumpets .. .. .. | | 5/– | 35/– |
| a | **Molly Pinsent,** dwarf branching habit, medium blue flowers in profusion, 6 ins. .. .. .. | | 4/6 | 30/– |
| a | **muralis** (*Portenschlagiana*), blue, 4 ins, really good .. | | 4/– | 28/– |
| a | **nitida alba,** stumpy spikes of large white flowers, 6 ins. .. | | 4/6 | 30/– |
| a | **plena,** double blue flowers, 6 ins. .. .. .. | | 5/– | 35/– |
| a | **Norman Grove,** fine free-flowering hybrid, light blue, 4 ins., July–August .. .. .. | | 4/– | 28/– |
| | **persicifolia,** blue, 2–2½ ft. .. .. .. .. .. | | 4/– | 28/– |
| | **Fleur de Neige,** the finest double white variety .. | | 5/– | 35/– |
| | **Pride of Exmouth,** rich double blue .. .. .. | | 5/– | 35/– |
| | **Queen of June,** large pale blue flowers, freely produced, 2 ft. .. .. .. .. | | 4/6 | 30/– |

*" a "  denotes  pot-grown  Alpines*

12

BLOOMS' HARDY PLANTS           doz.    100

**Campanulas—continued.**

| | | doz. | 100 |
|---|---|---|---|
| | **Telham Beauty,** large deep blue, single, always in demand, 3 ft. .. .. .. .. .. | 6/- | 42/- |
| | **The King,** large deep blue cup-and-saucer flowers on strong stems .. .. .. .. .. | 7/- | 50/- |
| a | **Poscharskyana,** lavender-blue flowers, a useful species .. | 3/6 | 25/- |
| a | **Profusion,** blue, erect habit, very free, 6 ins. .. .. | 3/6 | 25/- |
| a | **pseudo-Raineri,** deep blue cup-like flowers, 4 ins. .. | 4/6 | 30/- |
| a | **pulla,** dainty purple bells, 4 ins., June–July .. .. | 4/- | 28/- |
| a | **pulla x Waldsteiniana,** deep mauve, 2 ins., uncommon | 4/- | 28/- |
| a | **pulloides,** larger and taller than *pulla* .. .. | 3/6 | 25/- |
| a | **pusilla** (*Bellardii*), pretty blue hanging bells, 4 ins. .. | 3/6 | 25/- |
| a |    **alba,** very useful white form, June–August .. .. | 4/- | 28/- |
| a | **Cambridge Blue,** describes the colour, a really lovely thing and worth having, 3 ins. .. .. | 5/- | 35/- |
| a | **Cloudy Blue,** colour between *Cambridge Blue* and *Miss Willmott*, 3 ins., very free .. .. .. | 3/6 | 25/- |
| a | **Fosteri,** pretty white form with branching sprays of large white flowers .. .. .. .. | 4/- | 28/- |
| a | **Miranda,** broad, silvery-blue bells, 3 ins. .. .. | 3/6 | 25/- |
| a | **Miss Willmott,** deep blue, attractive and popular | 4/- | 28/- |
| a | **Oakington Blue,** the same shaped flowers as *Miranda,* but a much deeper and richer colour; it is very free-flowering with a good constitution, and can be strongly recommended, 4 ins. .. | 4/- | 28/- |
| a | **Raddeana,** violet-purple, 8 ins., May–June .. .. | 3/6 | 25/- |
| a | **Raineri hirsuta,** deep blue cups, choice, 4 ins. .. | 4/6 | 30/- |
| a | **Rhomboidalis,** pale blue, 1 ft., late .. .. | 4/- | 28/- |
| a | **R. B. Loder,** a choice and attractive hybrid, double blue, 6 ins. .. .. .. .. .. | 6/- | 42/- |
| a | **Robsoni,** giant form of Wild Harebell .. .. .. | 4/6 | 30/- |
| a | **rotarvatica,** starry lavender flowers, very profuse, one of the best hybrids yet raised, 3 ins. .. .. | 6/- | — |
| a | **rotundifolia Olympica,** large bright blue hanging bells, 9 ins. .. .. .. .. .. | 4/6 | 30/- |
| a |    **Spetchley White,** a very fine variety, 9 ins. .. .. | 4/6 | 30/- |
| a | **Stansfieldii,** violet-purple, very free, 6 ins. .. .. | 5/- | 35/- |
| a | **Steveni nana,** mat-like foliage, short stems of blue bells, May–June, 3 ins. .. .. .. .. | 5/- | 35/- |
| a | **turbinata** (true), deep blue, cup-shaped flowers .. .. | 4/6 | 30/- |
| a |    **albescens** (*pallida*), large pale blue flowers, 3 ins. .. | 4/- | 28/- |
| a | **valdensis,** deep blue flowers on slender stems, 1 ft. .. | 4/- | 28/- |
| a | **van Houttei,** large blue trumpets, 2 ft. .. .. | 4/- | 28/- |
| a | **Warleyensis,** large double pale blue, a first-rate late-flowering variety, 6 ins., July–August .. | 4/6 | 30/- |
| a | **Warley White,** double flowers, even larger than *Warleyensis,* pure white, a rare and beautiful form | 8/- | 60/- |
| a | **Wockii,** a rare and pretty species, deep mauve, 3 ins. .. | 5/- | 35/- |

**COLLECTIONS of ALPINE CAMPANULA, our selection: 24 in up to 8 sorts for 8/-; 50 in up to 10 sorts for 15/-; 100 for 28/-.**

13

BLOOMS' HARDY PLANTS                                              doz.    100

a **CARDAMINE pratensis lilacina flore plena,** double
      *Cuckoo flower* .. .. .. .. ..                            4/6     30/-

  **CATANANCHE cœrulea major,** deep lavender-blue double
      flowers, very free, 2 ft.     .. .. ..                    5/-     35/-

  **CENTAUREA dealbata,** rosy-pink flowers, fine foliage
      effect  .. .. .. .. ..                                    4/6     30/-

    **macrocephala,** large yellow flowers on tall stems ..  ..  4/6    30/-

    **montana rosea,** pink perennial cornflower  .. ..         4/-     28/-

    **pulchra major** (syn. *Rhaponticum*), handsome pink
        border plant .. .. .. .. ..                            5/-     35/-

    **Ruthenica,** lemon-yellow, branching habit, 3 ft. ..  ..  4/6    30/-

  **CENTRANTHUS** (see *Valeriana*).

a **CHEIRANTHUS Harpur Crewe,** old-fashioned double
      yellow Wallflower  .. .. .. ..                            4/-     28/-

a   **Moonlight,** bright clear yellow  .. .. .. ..             4/6     30/-

a   **Rufus,** deep orange, almost perpetual, 9 ins.  .. ..     5/-     35/-

  **CHELONE** (*Pentstemon*) **barbata,** spikes of orange-scarlet
      tubular flowers, 2½ ft.  .. .. ..                         3/6     25/-

a **CHRYSANTHEMUM arcticum,** pretty pink daisy
      flowers, 9 ins. .. .. .. .. ..                            3/6     25/-

a   **Mawii,** rose-pink flowers on wiry stems, very free and
        pretty, 9 ins. .. .. .. .. ..                           5/-     35/-

  **CHRYSANTHEMUM azaleanum** (*Pink Cushion*), a dwarf
          bushy plant not exceeding 18 ins. in height,
          spreading outwards in perfect shape and
          covered with a mound of deep pink flowers
          from July onwards. The colour pales
          somewhat with age, but this enhances rather
          than detracts from its beauty. Invaluable
          for the front of the border, for massing effect
          and as a pot plant .. .. .. ..

    **Bronze Cushion,** a fine bronze, similar to the above

    **Deep Pink Cushion,** a deep FADELESS pink variety ..

    **Red Cushion,** a bright red form  .. .. .. ..

    **White Cushion,** pure white .. .. .. ..

    **Yellow Cushion,** a fine new yellow variety  .. ..

        **The varieties of Azaleanum mentioned above will be
        available in rooted cuttings in the spring. Watch for
        further announcements.**

  **CHRYSANTHEMUM ERUBESCENS**, strong bushy
          growth, bearing a profusion of rose-pink
          flowers, 3 ft., open-ground plants .. ..             5/-     35/-

  **Clara Curtis,** a really fine form of the above, the colour
          being much brighter. Rooted cuttings in
          Spring .. .. .. .. .. ..                             12/-    90/-

  **CHRYSANTHEMUM KOREANUM, etc.**
      Korean Chrysanthemums are proving to be a very useful addition to
  the border. Flowering late, they provide a wide range of colour at a time
  when there is very little else to be seen, added to which, they are perfectly
  hardy.

      **Apollo,** bronze-red with gold and salmon shades giving a
          glowing effect, flowering mid-September
          onwards, 2½ ft.  .. .. ..

                                14

BLOOMS' HARDY PLANTS

## Chrysanthemum Koreanum, etc.—continued.

**Arcadia,** double white pompon, large flowers, vigorous growth, 3½ ft., mid-October. An excellent novelty. .. .. .. ..

**Astrid,** a distinct variety with soft pink flowers, shaded apricot, with yellow centres, produced on long stems. The dark green foliage is firm and glossy. Proved to be one of the most outstanding plants introduced into the U.S.A. in 1938 .. .. .. ..

**Athalie,** an early-flowering novelty. Single flowers of deep bronzy-yellow with 2 or 3 rows of petals ..

**Carmen,** gleaming reddish-bronze flowers; a great improvement on Mercury .. .. ..

**Daphne,** a beautiful golden-rose shade, with centre of pure gold; very hardy, 2½ ft. .. ..

**El Dorado,** a novelty of merit, fine bronzy-yellow flowers

**Ember,** a new double variety, deep bronze flowers of 2½ inches diameter .. .. ..

**Fireflame,** a good single variety, deep blood red, suffused carmine .. .. .. ..

**Hestia** semi-double rose-pink flowers, having a white halo around the small yellow centre. Bushy plants of medium height, compact habit. Very free-flowering, and early .. ..

**Indian Summer,** very bright coppery-orange flowers deepening towards the centre. Fully double, 3 ins. in diameter, with attractive slightly shaggy petals. Somewhat late in flowering, it provides colour when most other flowers are dead. The growth is stiff, and no supports are needed for the plants .. ..

**Juno,** single coppery-red flowers in profusion, paling with age to a light salmon-pink; very dwarf and compact, early flowering .. .. ..

**Louise Schling,** a beautiful beep warm red variety, with a double row of petals .. .. ..

**Mars,** wine red, but with the lustre peculiar to Koreans. Large single, well-shaped flowers, with bright yellow centres which add to the brilliant effect of the petals. Very free, of good bushy habit and excellent for cutting. Thoroughly recommended ..

**Mercury,** bright salmon-red, deepening to a tawny effect with age. Large flowers with 3 or 4 rows of petals, free-flowering, height 2½ ft. ..

**Nysa,** single flowers of clear rosy-lilac in profusion, 3 ins. in diameter. Upright plants, 2½–3 ft. high

**Orion,** the long flowering period of bright canary-yellow gives brilliance at a time when other yellow flowers are becoming dull. Single flowers, 3 ins. in diameter, with distinct rayed petals

**Psyche,** dainty single flowers of a warm shell-pink colour, 4 to 5 ins., on wiry stems. The plants are strong and of medium height .. ..

**Romany,** rich bronzy-red flowers, lightened and brightened by an orange tint in the reverse of the petals. Larger than *Indian Summer*, double and of perfect shape. It is very free, of good habit, about 2½ feet high with strong wiry stems. Excellent for cutting as the flowers last for 2 or 3 weeks in water ..

15

BLOOMS' HARDY PLANTS                                           doz.   100

**Chrysanthemum Koreanum—continued.**

**Sappho,** pure yellow single flowers, dwarf, compact plants ;
    a welcome new variety in this colour  ..

**Saturn,** a very bright orange-bronze, the golden yellow
    centre surrounded with a golden-orange
    halo, giving the effect of true autumn
    colours. This is an outstanding variety,
    the flowers being of excellent texture,
    fragrant, in large graceful sprays, height
    2½ ft. ..    ..

**Sultan,** a fine rosy-salmon, single, dwarf and very free
    flowering  ..    ..

**The Moor,** an excellent late-flowering variety of a brilliant
    port-wine-red colour, fully double, flowers
    3 ins. across, lasting for a long time when
    cut. Strongly recommended as a very
    hardy grower, height 2 ft. ..  ..  ..

**Venus,** the perfect Korean and the best pink. The beau-
    tiful deep rose-pink flowers with a silvery
    lustre, have 3 or 4 rows of petals and a small
    bright yellow centre. The bright effect
    continues throughout the long-flowering
    period from about the third week of August
    until November. It is unspoilt by weather
    or unsightly dead flowers. The plants are in
    perfect bushy form, 2½ ft. high, and the wiry
    stems with a profusion of flowers make it
    invaluable as a market variety ..  ..

**Vulcan,** ray-like petals in a double row form an attractive
    flower of crimson-red changing to crimson-
    bronze on opening, with a golden centre.
    In growth and habit, very much like *Venus*,
    but later-flowering. Strongly recommended
    for cutting ..  ..  ..  ..

**Wildfire,** a handsome rust-orange pompon, fully double,
    on strong shapely sprays. An outstanding
    sturdy grower ..  ..  ..  ..

> **Offers of the above will be made at very reasonable
> prices early in the New Year. Of some varieties we
> can supply open-ground stools in limited quantities.
> Prices on application.**

**CHRYSANTHEMUM MAXIMUM** (*Marguerite* or *Shasta Daisy*)

| | | | |
|---|---|---|---|
| **Beauté Nivelloise,** very large shaggy flowers  ..  .. | 4/6 | 30/- |
| **Crusader,** a giant white variety  ..  ..  .. | 4/6 | 30/- |
| **Esther Read,** double white, a fine florists' flower .. | 4/6 | 30/- |
| **Mayfield Giant,** large pure white, July  ..  .. | 3/6 | 25/- |
| **Phyllis Smith,** a very fine white variety with attractive finely-cut petals  ..  ..  .. | 4/6 | 30/- |
| **Rentpayer,** early white *Marguerite*, best for cutting  .. | 3/6 | 25/- |
| **V. L. Harkness,** a new variety of great merit  ..  .. | 8/- | 60/- |
| **CHRYSOBOLTONIA pulcherrima,** starry pink flowers over a long period, useful for cuttings  .. | 5/- | 35/- |
| **CIMICIFUGA japonica,** spikes of white flowers, August-September, 3 ft.  .. | 5/- | 35/- |
| **CLEMATIS recta purpurea,** upright, purple foliage, white flowers ..  ..  ..  .. | 5/- | 35/- |

16

BLOOMS' HARDY PLANTS

|  | doz. | 100 |
|---|---|---|
| **COREOPSIS auriculata superba** (true), masses of golden-yellow flowers, with red blotch in centre, a good plant .. .. .. .. .. | 5/– | 35/– |
| **grandiflora Mayfield Giant,** pure yellow, 2½ ft. .. .. | 3/6 | 25/– |
| **Sunburst,** very bright yellow, semi-double .. .. | 4/– | 28/– |
| **rosea,** finely-cut foliage, pale pink flowers, 1 ft. .. .. | 5/– | 35/– |
| **verticillata,** makes a neat bush of ferny foliage, freely starred with deep yellow flowers, produced for many months during the summer, 18 ins. | 4/6 | 30/– |
| a **COTYLEDON simplicifolia,** short racemes of yellow flowers, very pretty, 6 ins. .. .. | 3/6 | 25/– |
| a **CRASSULA sarcocaulis,** pretty pink heads on stumpy growth, August–September .. .. .. | 5/– | 35/– |
| a **CYANANTHUS integer,** a choice Alpine, soft blue flowers, July–October, 4 ins. .. .. | 10/– | — |
| **CYNOGLOSSUM nervosum** (Benth), rich gentian-blue, July–August, 2 ft. .. .. .. .. | 5/– | 35/– |

# DELPHINIUMS

**We have a particularly fine stock this year, both in quality and quantity**

|  | each | doz. | 100 |
|---|---|---|---|
| **A. J. Moir,** a variety of recent introduction with large semi-double cornflower-blue flowers with white eye .. .. | 3/6 | 40/– | — |
| **Baldershage,** light blue, semi-double falls, long spikes .. .. .. .. .. | 1/– | 11/– | 84/– |
| **Blue Beauty,** bright deep blue with a black eye .. | 4/6 | 52/– | — |
| **Blue Bird,** full deep blue, semi-double .. .. | 1/– | 11/– | 84/– |
| **Blue Boy,** splendid deep blue, single .. .. | 10d | 9/– | 70/– |
| **Blue Gown,** a really fine variety, ultramarine-blue, semi-double, strong grower .. .. | 1/6 | 16/– | 120/– |
| **Blue Princess,** branching habit, light blue, single .. | 9d | 8/– | 60/– |
| **Cambria,** semi-double mauve-blue, vary large flowers and spike, still one of the best varieties .. .. .. .. | 10d | 9/– | 70/– |
| **Constance,** very bright gentian-blue with white eye, single, a good spike, early-flowering .. | 10d | 9/– | 70/– |
| **Coquette,** a deep violet-blue, vigorous growth .. | 10d | 9/– | 70/– |
| **Dawn,** sky-blue, overlaid mauve, semi-double, long spike .. .. .. .. | 2/– | 22/– | 180/– |
| **D. B. Crane,** deep lavender, shaded blue, semi-double large spikes .. .. .. .. | 1/6 | 16/– | 120/– |
| **Duchess of Portland,** ultramarine-blue, semi-double with small white eye, a variety of great merit .. .. .. | 3/6 | 40/– | 300/– |
| **Duchess of Westminster,** large pale blue flowers with black centre, tall spike.. | 1/6 | 16/– | 120/– |
| **Dusky Monarch,** purple, deeper centre, semi-double, good spike .. .. .. | 11d | 10/– | 80/– |
| **Edward Bromet,** rich violet-blue with white eye, an improved *Rev. Lascelles* .. | 1/10 | 20/– | 156/– |
| **F. W. Smith,** pure gentian blue, white eye, outstanding .. .. .. .. | 10d | 9/– | 70/– |

17

# ALAN BLOOM'S HARDY PERENNIALS

BLOOMS' HARDY PLANTS

each  doz.  100

**Delphiniums—continued.**

| | each | doz. | 100 |
|---|---|---|---|
| **Harry Smetham,** rich porcelain-blue, semi-double | 11d. | 10/- | — |
| **Hunsdon Dell,** bright gentian-blue, semi-double | 1/8 | 18/- | 136/- |
| **Ida R. Elliott,** semi-double, amethyst-blue | 9d | 8/- | 60/- |
| **Ivorine,** creamy-white, semi-double | 10d | 9/- | 70/- |
| **Jenny Jones,** purple and violet-blue, semi-double, a better grower than *Sir Douglas Haig* | 2/- | 22/- | 180/- |
| **King of Delphiniums,** rich blue, plum centre, semi-double | 9d | 8/- | 60/- |
| **Lady Edith,** semi-double, lavender with dark eye | 4/6 | 48/- | — |
| **Lady Eleanor,** double light blue, a good selling variety | 1/4 | 14/- | 100/- |
| **Lady Elizabeth,** lavender, overlaid bright blue, semi-double, recommended | 1/6 | 16/- | 120/- |
| **Lady Grace,** semi-double, cornflower-blue with black eye | 1/6 | 16/- | 120/- |
| **Lady Holt,** deep sky-blue, semi-double, small white eye | 2/6 | 28/- | 210/- |
| **Lady May,** large pale mauve-blue flowers | 1/8 | 18/- | 136/- |
| **Lilian Bishop,** beautiful cornflower-blue self, semi-double, strong spike, mildew proof | 5/- | 54/- | — |
| **Lize van Veen,** light azure blue, single | 9d | 8/- | 60/- |
| **Lord Derby,** lilac-mauve, semi-double, fine spike | 10d | 9/- | 70/- |
| **Lord Lansdowne,** single deep blue with white eye | 1/2 | 12/- | 90/- |
| **Lorenzo de Medici,** large flowers of soft lilac-blue shade | 1/2 | 12/- | 90/- |
| **Millicent Blackmore,** blue and mauve with large black eye | 3/3 | 36/- | — |
| **Monarch of Wales,** violet-mauve and bright blue, tall spike | 1/6 | 16/- | 120/- |
| **Mrs. Foster Cunliffe,** light mauve, shaded sky-blue, fully double | 3/6 | 40/- | — |
| **Mrs. H. Kaye,** rich indigo-blue flushed with purple | 1/6 | 16/- | 120/- |
| **Mrs. Newton Lees,** a fine shade of mauve and light blue, very large flower and spike | 1/4 | 14/- | 100/- |
| **Mrs. Paul Nelke,** brightest cornflower blue | 2/3 | 24/- | 180/- |
| **Mrs. Townley Parker,** beautiful sky blue, white eye | 9d | 8/- | 60/- |
| **Nell Gwyn,** semi-double, rosy-mauve | 3/6 | 40/- | — |
| **Nora Ferguson,** light blue, shaded rose, really good | 9d | 8/- | 60/- |
| **Pompadour,** clear brilliant blue, semi-double, sepia eye, fine spikes | 2/9 | 30/- | 220/- |
| **Queen Mary,** soft pale blue with showy centre | 1/- | 11/- | 80/- |
| **Rev. Chas. Storr,** rich bright blue, shaded rosy-mauve | 2/3 | 24/- | — |
| **Rev. E. Lascelles,** deep blue with white eye, striking | 41d | 10/- | 80/- |
| **Rijnstroon,** semi-double, lilac-mauve with white eye | 1/- | 11/- | — |
| **RUYSII PINK SENSATION.** *See page 19* | | | |
| **Sir Douglas Haig,** deep purple and blue, immense spike | 2/6 | 27/- | 200/- |

18

| BLOOMS' HARDY PLANTS | each | doz. | 100 |
|---|---|---|---|
| **Delphiniums—continued.** | | | |
| **Smoke of War,** reddish-purple, very effective   .. | 9d | 8/– | 60/– |
| **The Alake,** deep violet-purple, shaded blue     .. | 1/2 | 12/– | 90/– |
| **The Shah,** rosy-lavender, semi-double, very fine .. | 2/– | 22/– | 170/– |
| **Turquoise,** pure light blue, long spikes   ..     .. | 1/2 | 12/– | 90/– |
| **Van Veen's Triumph,** soft blue  ..    ..    .. | 9d | 8/– | 60/– |
| **Violet Robinson,** rich violet-blue with white eye, semi-double, flowers often 3 ins. across  ..    ..    ..    ..    .. | 3/9 | 42/– | 320/– |
| **Welsh Boy,** semi-double, gentian-blue  ..    .. | 3/6 | 40/– | — |
| **Hybrid Delphiniums Mixed,** seedlings from best-named varieties  ..    ..    .. | — | 3/– | 20/– |

## Belladonna Varieties

| | each | doz. | 100 |
|---|---|---|---|
| **Blue Bees,** beautiful light blue, one of the best for cutting, 3 ft...   ..    ..    ....    .. | | 4/6 | 30/– |
| **Cliveden Beauty,** Cambridge-blue, 3 ft., double.. | | 6/– | 42/– |
| **Elstead Blue,** rich bright blue, 3 ft...   ..    .. | | 12/– | 90/– |
| **Isis,** rich deep violet-blue, strongly recommended.. | | 9/– | 70/– |
| **Lamartine,** rich deep blue, one of the best, 3 ft. .. | | 5/– | 35/– |
| **Orion,** clear cornflower-blue, large flower ..    .. | | 5/– | 35/– |
| **Naples,** A.M. 1935, rich deep blue, a novelty worth having | | 9/– | 70/– |
| **semi plena,** light blue, semi-double    ..    ..    .. | | 4/6 | 30/– |
| **Theodora,** very bright gentian-blue    ..    ..    .. | | 6/– | 42/– |
| **Wendy,** deep cobalt-blue, flecked purple  ..    ..    .. | | 12/– | 90/– |

| | each | doz. | 100 |
|---|---|---|---|
| **RUYSII PINK SENSATION** a real break in Delphiniums, growing after the style of Belladonnas, but very erect. The colour is really pink, and it flowers almost continuously from June onwards. Vigorous growth. Height 3–4 ft. It is a plant which can be strongly recommended for the border or for cutting..    ..    ..    .. | 2/6 | 27/– | 200/– |

## Dwarf Alpine Species

| | | each | doz. |
|---|---|---|---|
| a | **Cashmirianum,** silvery-blue flowers, dwarf and distinct | 4/6 | 30/– |
| a | **Chinense Blue Butterfly,** a really showy plant, perennial | 3/6 | 25/– |
| a | **Tom Thumb,** Cambridge-blue, white centre  ..    .. | 4/– | 28/– |
| | **formosum,** deep blue, useful for cutting, 3 ft. ..    .. | 4/– | 28/– |
| a | **nudicaule,** flowers orange-scarlet, 1½ ft. ..    ..    .. | 5/– | 35/– |
| a | **Lemon Gem,** a lemon-yellow form    ..    ..    .. | 5/– | 35/– |

*" a " denotes pot-grown Alpines.*

---

*See terms for SPECIAL DISCOUNTS on Cash Orders—page 2.*

# DIANTHUS

| | | | |
|---|---|---|---|
| a | **Albatross,** a *cæsius* hybrid of real merit. The flowers are large, fully double and pure white, height 6 ins. .. .. .. .. .. | 4/6 | 30/- |
| a | **arvernensis,** pink flowers on close grey-green mats .. | 4/6 | 30/- |
| a | **cæsius Baker's Impr.,** deep pink with red zone, 6 ins. .. | 4/6 | 30/- |
| a | **fl. pl.,** neat double pink with trace of red zone .. | 4/6 | 30/- |
| a | **Mrs. Holt,** neat growing, single clear pink, 6 ins. .. | 4/6 | 30/- |
| a | **caucasicus,** brilliant single carmine flowers, 10 ins. .. | 6/- | — |
| a | **Crossways,** forms neat tufts of dark green foliage with bright cerise flowers, fragrant and continuous ; a *neglectus* hybrid of great merit, 4 ins. | 9/- | 70/- |
| a | **deltoides Brilliant,** deep rose, trailing habit .. .. | 3/6 | 25/- |
| a | **erectus,** a new break in this section .. .. | 4/- | 28/- |
| a | **Major Stern,** deeper coloured flowers and foliage .. | 3/6 | 25/- |
| a | **Dew,** neat grassy growth, pale pink, fringed fragrant flowers.. .. .. .. .. .. | 5/- | 35/- |
| a | **Diana,** a beautiful hybrid raised here, deep rose-pink with crimson zone, flowers over a long period, 6 in. | 5/- | 35/- |
| a | **Donizetti,** bright crimson, with deeper zone .. .. | 7/- | 50/- |
| a | **Duchess of Fife,** masses of fragrant pink flowers, 6 ins. .. | 3/6 | 25/- |
| a | **Forbes' Variety,** a plant of obscure parentage, but of real merit ; 4 in. stems rising from dark green foliage, bearing large flowers of a rich deep pink ; a variety which is sure to meet with a good demand .. .. | 6/- | 42/- |
| a | **Highland Queen,** rich red with crimson centre, 1 ft. .. | 5/- | 35/- |
| a | **Integer,** sweet-scented white flowers, fringed petals, 6 ins. | 3/6 | 25/- |
| a | **Lemsii,** single rose-pink, very free, 8 ins. .. .. .. | 4/6 | 30/- |
| a | **Little Jock,** large single pink flowers, compact habit, recommended .. .. .. .. .. | 3/6 | 25/- |
| a | **Mars,** a wonderful variety, with fine double crimson clove-scented flowers, 6 ins., May–October .. | 12/- | 90/- |
| a | **musalæ (microlepis),** tiniest cushion growth, deep rosy-red flowers, 1 in. .. .. .. .. | 8/- | 60/- |
| a | **neglectus,** petals pink with reverse buff, a good dwarf variety .. .. .. .. .. .. | 6/- | 42/- |
| a | **Oakington Hybrid,** fragrant double flowers of a lovely deep salmon-rose colour, 6 ins., a plant of real merit and strongly recommended .. | 4/- | 28/- |
| a | **Prichardi fl. pl.** (sometimes sold as *Aubrey Prichard*), a pleasing shade of rose-pink, quite double, 6 ins. .. .. .. .. .. .. | 4/- | 28/- |
| a | **Spark,** fiery crimson, always sells well, tender .. .. | 7/- | 50/- |
| a | **Spencer Bickham,** neat tufts with pretty pink flowers, 4 ins. .. .. .. .. .. | 4/- | 28/- |
| a | **superbus nanus,** white, very fragrant, 9 ins. .. .. | 4/- | 28/- |

*" a " denotes pot-grown Alpines*

20

BLOOMS' HARDY PLANTS        doz.   100

**Dianthus—continued.**

a   **The Dubarry,** a charming *cæsius* hybrid, producing large double flowers on 6-in. stems ; rich rosy-lilac deepening to crimson ..   ..   4/-   28/-

a   **Winnie Lambert,** bright cerise, semi-double, 9 ins.   ..   6/-   42/-

> **COLLECTIONS of DIANTHUS, our selection:**
> 24 in up to 6 good showy sorts for 8/6; 50 in up to
> 10 for 15/6; 100 for 29/-.

**DICTAMNUS fraxinella,** spikes of deep rose, 2 ft., young plants ..   ..   ..   ..   ..   4/6   30/-

**DIELYTRA** (*Dicentra*) **formosa,** short sprays of rosy-red flowers, 1 ft. ..   ..   ..   ..   5/-   35/-

    **spectabilis,** deep rose, the well-known *Bleeding Heart*, medium-sized plants..   ..   ..   6/-   42/-

**DIGITALIS The Shirley,** the best strain of Foxglove   ..   3/6   25/-

a   **DODECATHEON meadia,** purple hanging flowers, 8 ins...   4/6   30/-

**DORONICUM austriacum,** bright yellow flowers, March–May, 2 ft.   ..   ..   ..   ..   4/-   28/-

    **Harpur Crewe,** large yellow daisy flowers in spring, 2½–3 ft.   ..   ..   ..   ..   3/6   25/-

a   **DRABA bruinæfolia,** neat cushions, yellow flowers, early spring ..   ..   ..   ..   ..   3/6   25/-

**DRACOCEPHALUM virginianum** (see *Physostegia*)

**ECHINACEA** (syn. *Rudbeckia*) **purpurea,** rosy-red-rayed flowers, 2½ ft., July–September, a good plant for the border ..   ..   ..   4/6   30/-

    **purpurea Abendsonne,** deep rose ..   ..   ..   10/-   75/-

      **Earliest of All,** bright deep rose, 2½ ft., July–September   8/-   60/-

    **The King,** deep crimson-red, very large flowers, 3½ ft., the finest of all   ..   ..   10/-   75/-

**ECHINOPS humilis Taplow Blue,** glistening blue heads, 4 ft.   ..   ..   ..   ..   ..   6/-   42/-

    **ritro,** blue thistle heads, fine for cutting, 3 ft.   ..   4/-   28/-

**EREMURUS Bungei,** spikes of bright yellow flowers   ..   8/-   60/-

    **Himalaicus,** snowy-white flowers on 6 ft. spikes, young plants ..   ..   ..   ..   ..   10/-   75/-

**ERIGERON**

    **Antwerpia,** mauve-blue, 2 ft.   ..   ..   ..   4/-   28/-

    **Asa Gray,** orange-buff, 1 ft. ..   ..   ..   ..   6/-   42/-

    **aurantiacus,** shades of orange and deep yellow, May–June, 9 ins.   ..   ..   ..   ..   4/6   30/-

    **Azure Beauty,** large flowers, almost double, mauve shades   4/-   28/-

    **Beauty of Hale,** rich mauve, bright golden centre, 1½ ft.   5/-   35/-

    **B. Ladhams,** pink with orange buds, a really good seller ..   5/-   35/-

a   **caucasicus,** light blue, dwarf and very free, 6 ins ..   ..   4/-   28/-

    **Fontainebleau,** lavender-blue, 2 ft. ..   ..   ..   3/6   25/-

a   **leiormerus,** very dwarf species, light mauve, 3 ins.   ..   3/6   25/-

    **Merstham Glory,** good habit, deep violet flowers, 2 ft. ..   4/-   28/-

    **mesa-grande,** large deep blue flowers, erect habit, good for cutting, 2 ft.   ..   ..   ..   3/6   25/-

21

BLOOMS' HARDY PLANTS       doz.   100
**Erigeron—continued.**

**Moonlight,** quite dwarf, large light-blue flowers ..    4/–   28/–
**Mrs. F. H. Beale,** dwarf and free, deep mauve, 1 ft. ..   4/–   28/–
**Pink Pearl,** an attractive shade of rosy-pink, June–August, 2 ft. ..     5/–   35/–
**Quakeress,** large lavender-rose flowers, 2 ft. .. ..   3/6   25/–
**Sommerneuschnee,** appears to be identical with *White Quakeress* .. .. .. ..   4/–   28/–
a **ERINUS alpinus Dr. Hanæle,** brilliant crimson-red form   4/6   30/–
a **ERODIUM chamædrioides roseum** (syn. *Reichardii*), bright pink flowers on green tufts, all summer .. .. .. .. ..   4/–   28/–
**ERYNGIUM planum,** steely-blue thistle-like flowers and stems, excellent for cutting .. .. ..   4/–   28/–
**tripartitium,** deep blue, fine branching habit ..   4/6   30/–
**Violetta,** dark lilac-blue, large flower .. ..   6/–   42/–
**EUPATORIUM purpureum,** stiff stems, heads of deep purple flowers, August–September, 4 ft. ..   4/6   30/–
a **FRANKENIA lævis** (*Sea Heath*), mats of dark green foliage, pink flowers .. .. .. ..   3/6   25/–
a **FUCHSIA pumila,** attractive Alpine form, purple and red, 8 ins. .. .. .. .. ..   4/6   30/–
a **Tom Thumb,** large rose and light purple flowers, neat bushy habit .. .. .. ..   6/–   42/–
(The above Fuchsias are all quite hardy in most localities.)
**FUNKIA japonica lutea variegata,** attractive variegated foliage, 1½ ft. .. .. .. ..   5/–   35/–
**japonica undulata, variegata** .. .. ..   5/–   35/–
**Sieboldii,** large ornamental leaves and lilac flowers, 1½ ft.   5/–   35/–
**GAILLARDIA grandiflora,** best hybrids mixed ..   3/–   20/–
**Ipswich Beauty,** fine crimson and yellow flowers ..   4/6   30/–
**Mrs. H. Longster,** in our opinion the best yet raised. Flowers large and of great substance, deep yellow with small red zone on strong long stems .. .. .. .. ..   4/–   28/–
**Mrs. Lascelles,** mahogany-crimson petals, tipped orange   4/–   28/–
**Robin Hood,** golden-yellow, early and very free ..   3/6   25/–
**Tangerine,** bright flame colour, true stock ..   5/–   35/–
**GALEGA, Her Majesty,** bushy growth, short spikes of lavender blue flowers, 3 ft. .. ..   4/–   28/–
**GAURA Lindheimeri,** graceful spikes of white and rose flowers, July–August, 3 ft. .. ..   4/–   28/–

**GENTIANA**

a **acaulis,** blue trumpets, flowers in spring .. ..   4/6   30/–
a **Farreri,** beautiful sky-blue flowers, late .. ..   10/–   72/–
a **Lagodechiana,** rich blue trumpets, late summer ..   5/–   35/–
a **Macaulayi Wells' Variety,** bright turquoise-blue, of easy growth .. .. .. ..   10/–   72/–
a **prolata,** resembles a small *Lagodechiana* .. ..   6/–   42/–

" a " *denotes pot-grown Alpines*

22

| BLOOMS' HARDY PLANTS | doz. | 100 |
|---|---|---|

**Gentiana—continued.**

| | | doz. | 100 |
|---|---|---|---|
| a | **septemfida,** bright blue trumpets, August-September .. | 5/– | 35/– |
| a | **hascombensis,** a very vigorous attractive form .. | 5/– | 35/– |
| a | **sino ornata,** rich blue, late-flowering .. .. .. | 4/– | 28/– |
| a | **verna,** the blue spring gentian, always in demand .. | 7/– | 50/– |
| | **GERANIUM grandiflorum,** violet-blue, useful dwarf border plant, 1 ft. .. .. .. .. | 3/6 | 25/– |
| | **Russell Prichard,** deep rose flowers, freely produced all summer, 9 ins. .. .. .. .. | 6/– | 42/– |
| | **GEUM** | | |
| | **Borisii,** very deep orange, 1 ft. .. .. .. .: | 4/6 | 30/– |
| | **Dolly North,** rich orange, 1 ft. .. .. .. | 4/6 | 30/– |
| | **Fire Opal,** dazzling bronzy-scarlet, first-rate plant .. | 4/6 | 30/– |
| a | **Gladys Perry,** A.M., semi-double orange-yellow flowers in profusion, very dwarf, 4 ins. .. .. | 20/– | 150/– |
| | **Heldreichii superbum,** deep orange, single .. .. | 4/6 | 30/– |
| a | **Jenny Ross,** deep yellow, dwarf and very useful .. .. | 5/– | 35/– |
| | **Lady Stratheden,** double golden-yellow .. .. .. | 3/– | 20/– |
| | **Mrs. Bradshaw,** double red .. .. .. | 3/– | 20/– |
| | **Princess Juliana,** fine large orange, 2 ft. .. .. | 4/6 | 30/– |
| | **Red Wings,** similar to *Fire Opal* but bright scarlet .. | 8/– | 60/– |
| | **rivale Leonard's Variety,** pendant salmon-rose flowers, 18 ins. .. .. .. .. .. | 4/6 | 30/– |
| a | **sibiricum,** pretty orange-scarlet flowers, 9 ins, May .. | 3/6 | 25/– |
| a | **GLOBULARIA cordifolia,** deep green leaves, blue heads, 4 ins. .. .. .. .. .. | 4/6 | 30/– |
| a | **incanescens,** a real gem, close green tufts covered in May–June with pale blue "powder-puff" flowers, 2 ins. .. .. .. .. | 5/– | 35/– |
| a | **nana,** tiny green mats, blue flowers, 1 in. .. .. | 4/6 | 30/– |
| a | **nudicaule,** a little larger growth than above .. .. | 4/6 | 30/– |
| a | **GYSOPHILA cerastioides Cooper's Variety,** larger and freer than the type, white .. .. .. | 3/6 | 25/– |
| a | **fratensis,** very bright pink flowers, trailing habit .. | 4/6 | 30/– |
| | **pacifica,** light rose, 3 ft. .. .. .. .. .. | 4/– | .28/– |
| | **paniculata,** single white .. .. .. .. .. | 3/6 | 25/– |
| | **Bristol Fairy,** large pure double white, stock is grown from cuttings .. .. .. .. .. | 7/– | 50/– |
| a | **repens rosea,** pretty pink creeping species .. .. | 3/6 | 25/– |
| | **Rosy Veil** (*Rosenschleier*), a valuable variety smothered in summer with double pink flowers, 18 ins. .. | 5/– | 35/– |
| a | **HEDERA conglomerata,** miniature ivy of very slow growth | 5/– | 35/– |
| | **HELENIUM.** | | |
| | **autumnale rubrum,** coppery-red, 4 ft. late .. .. | 3/6 | 25/– |
| | **Baronin Linden,** a lovely variety, the colour being rich orange-flame, flowers very large with small centre .. .. .. .. .. .. | 5/– | 35/– |
| | **Braungold,** rich bronze with golden-yellow edge, new .. | 12/– | — |
| | **Chipperfield Orange,** recommended, 4 ft., August–September.. .. .. .. .. .. | 3/6 | 25/– |

23

| BLOOMS' HARDY PLANTS | doz. | 100 |
|---|---|---|
| **Helenium—continued.** | | |

| | | doz. | 100 |
|---|---|---|---|
| **Crimson Beauty,** a very useful dwarf variety, 1½ ft. .. | .. | 4/– | 28/– |
| **Dorothy Perfield,** orange-red, good habit, 3 ft. .. | .. | 3/6 | 25/– |
| **Gartensonne,** bright yellow, 4 ft. .. .. | .. | 3/6 | 25/– |
| **Goldene Jugend** (*Golden Youth*), rich golden-yellow flowers | | 4/6 | 30/– |
| **grandicephalum striatum,** brown and orange striped flowers | | 4/– | 28/– |
| **Hoopesii,** bright orange flowers in May, quite distinct, 18 ins. .. .. .. .. | .. | 3/6 | 25/– |
| **July Sun,** orange and brown streaked, 3 ft... .. | .. | 3/6 | 25/– |
| **Mme. Canivet,** flowers yellow with deep red centre, recommended .. .. .. .. | .. | 4/6 | 30/– |
| **Moerheim Beauty,** rich wallflower-red, outstanding | .. | 4/– | 28/– |
| **pumilum magnificum,** deep yellow self, good habit, 2 ft. | | 3/6 | 25/– |
| **Riverton Gem,** bronzy-orange, late, 4 ft. .. .. | .. | 3/6 | 25/– |
| **The Bishop,** deep yellow with a dark centre .. | .. | 7/– | 50/– |
| **Wesergold,** bright orange-yellow, fine upright habit, 2½ ft., July–August .. .. .. .. | .. | 3/6 | 25/– |
| **Wyndley,** yellow and bronze large flowers, fairly dwarf, 2½ ft. .. .. .. .. | .. | 4/– | 28/– |

**COLLECTIONS of HELENIUM, our selection:
24 in up to 6 sorts for 7/6; 50 in up to 10 sorts for
14/-; 100 for 26/-.**

### HELIANTHEMUM (Rock Rose).

| | | | doz. | 100 |
|---|---|---|---|---|
| a | **Ben Alder,** flowers terra-corra, single | .. .. .. | 3/6 | 25/– |
| a | **Ben Heckla,** orange-brick shade with red centre.. | .. | 3/6 | 25/– |
| a | **Ben Lawers,** light orange with deeper centre | .. | 3/6 | 25/– |
| a | **Ben Mare,** deep flame, shaded cerise | .. .. | 4/– | 28/– |
| a | **Ben Nevis,** golden-yellow, maroon centre.. | .. | 3/6 | 25/– |
| a | **carneum,** single pink, fairly upright growth | .. | 3/6 | 25/– |
| a | **chamæcistus,** distinct habit, large flowers of port wine colour .. .. .. .. | .. | 3/6 | 25/– |
| a | **Brilliant,** lighter but brighter in colour than the foregoing, strongly recommended .. | .. | 4/– | 28/– |
| a | **croceum,** rich orange-yellow | .. .. | 3/6 | 25/– |
| a | **Double Chocolate,** coppery-brown.. | .. .. | 3/6 | 25/– |
| a | **Double Salmon** .. .. .. | .. .. | 3/6 | 25/– |
| a | **Fireball,** double scarlet | .. .. | 3/6 | 25/– |
| a | **Firebrand,** single red .. | .. .. | 3/6 | 25/– |
| a | **Huntsman's Pink,** a pretty shade .. | .. .. | 3/6 | 25/– |
| a | **Jubilee,** double yellow | .. .. | 3/6 | 25/– |
| a | **lunulatum,** tiny upright bushes covered with yellow flowers. This is quite a distinct species.. | | 4/– | 28/– |
| a | **luteum,** large golden single flowers .. | .. .. | 3/6 | 25/– |
| a | **Mrs. Clay,** coppery-orange, single .. | .. .. | 3/6 | 25/– |
| a | **Mrs. Earle,** fine double scarlet, very free.. | .. | 3/6 | 25/– |
| a | **Old Gold,** semi-double | .. .. | 3/6 | 25/– |
| a | **Peach,** fine large flowers | .. .. | 3/6 | 25/– |
| a | **præcox,** bright yellow, grey foliage.. | .. .. | 3/6 | 25/– |

*"a" denotes pot-grown Alpines*

24

BLOOMS' HARDY PLANTS                                                    doz.    100

**Helianthemum—continued.**

a   **Rose Queen,** clear pink      ..     ..     ..     ..     ..   3/6   25/-
a   **Salmon Queen,** salmon-pink   ..     ..     ..     ..       3/6   25/-
a   **Sudbury Gem,** deep terra-cotta   ..     ..     ..     ..   3/6   25/-

COLLECTIONS of HELIANTHEMUM, our selection:
24 in up to 8 sorts for 7/6; 50 for 13/6; 100 for 25/-.

HELIANTHUS multiflorus Bouquet d'Or, large deep yellow
    flowers with close double centre, produced
    from August to October   ..     ..     ..   4/-   28/-

**multiflorus Loddon Gold,** rich yellow, perfectly double,
    5 ft. ..     ..     ..     ..     ..     ..   4/-   28/-

    **Soleil d'Or,** bushes of double yellow flowers, 5 ft.   ..   4/-   28/-

    **rigidus Miss Mellish,** large deep single yellow flowers ..   3/6   25/-

    **sparsifolius,** huge golden flowers, 6 ft.   ..     ..     ..   3/6   25/-

    **Monarch,** flowers even larger than the above ..     ..   6/-   42/-

a **HELICHRYSUM bellidioides,** little white everlasting
    flowers ..     ..     ..     ..     ..     ..   4/-   28/-

HELIOPSIS scabra Incomparabilis, A.M.R.H.S. Intro-
             duced by us. Admitted to be one of the
             finest border perennials of recent years. The
             flowers are a wonderful rich golden-yellow,
             nearly double and over 3 ins. in diameter.
             It is of easy growth, attaining a height of
             2½–3 ft., and is in flower continuously from
             July to autumn   ..     ..     ..     ..   6/-   42/-

    **scabra Golden Sun,** has more, though smaller, petals than
        *Incomparabilis,* new ..     ..     ..     ..   8/-   60/-

    **vitellina,** deep yellow imbricated petals, 2½ ft.   ..     ..   6/-   42/-

HEMEROCALLIS (*Day Lily*), **Apricot,** flowers apricot-
    yellow, 2½ ft. ..     ..     ..     ..     ..   4/6   30/-

    **Dr. Regel,** rich orange flowers, graceful foliage ..     ..   4/6   30/-

    **Gold Dust,** deep orange-yellow, 1½ ft., July   ..     ..   4/-   28/-

    **Margaret Perry,** brilliant orange-scarlet, 3 ft., July–
      September   ..     ..     ..     ..     ..   7/-   50/-

    **Orangeman,** deep orange trumpet flowers, 1½ ft. ..     ..   4/-   28/-

    **Queen of May,** large apricot-yellow flowers, 2½ ft., June ..   4/6   30/-

    **Sovereign,** rich yellow, 1½ ft., June–July ..     ..     ..   4/-   28/-

    **Viscountess Byng,** grassy foliage, rosy-silver flowers with
      orange-yellow base   ..     ..     ..     ..   18/-   —

*"a" denotes pot-grown Alpines*

# HEUCHERAS

As a result of the new varieties we have introduced in recent years, Heucheras have now regained the popularity which they lost owing to the shyness with which the older varieties flower. For border decoration, all are invaluable, whilst many are particularly suitable for cut-flower purposes. Further recommendation has been given by the Royal Horticultural Society this year to four of our varieties. *Freedom* and *Oakington Jewel* received Awards of Merit, and *Corallion* and *Gaiety* Highly Commended certificates after trial at Wisley.

## BRIZOIDES SECTION

Best for cutting and market work, although equally effective for the border.

**Blooms' Variety,** A.M.R.H.S., Produces long sprays, each carrying dozens of dainty coral-red flowers, and, whether used as a cut flower for decoration or as a border plant, the effect is really wonderful. The advantage of its free-flowering habit, coupled with its unique charm and usefulness for decoration, go to make an ideal plant for cutting. For the border or for cutting, this is a plant worth having. June–July .. .. .. ..   6/–   42/–

**Coral Cloud,** somewhat brighter than *Blooms' variety*, with larger flowers .. .. .. .. ..   15/–   100/–

**Crimson Cascade,** bright crimson-scarlet, new, very free   12/–   90/–

**erubescens,** produces long sprays of creamy-white flowers   3/6   25/–

**gracillima,** masses of deep rosy-red sprays, 2½ ft. .. ..   3/6   25/–

**Mary Rose,** bears a profusion of clear pink flowers, very neat habit and most effective, June–August   7/–   50/–

**Pink Spray,** lighter colour than *Blooms' variety*, but not quite so free .. .. .. .. ..   4/6   30/–

## SANGUINEA SECTION

**Apple Blossom,** describes the colour, a very strong grower and free-flowering, 2½ ft. .. .. ..   6/–   42/–

**Corallion,** highly commended R.H.S. Wisley Trials, 1938. Old rose and coral, large flowers freely produced and a first-rate variety, 2 ft., July–August .. .. .. .. .. ..   8/–   60/–

**Dainty,** pale pink, almost continuous flowering, 2½ ft. ..   5/–   35/–

**Edge Hall Hybrid,** rather dull pink flowers on short spikes   4/6   30/–

**Freedom,** A.M.R.H.S. Wisley Trials, 1938. Large bright rose-pink flowers, comparatively dwarf growth, but amazingly profuse, 1½ ft., June–September   10/–   75/–

**Gaiety,** highly commended R.H.S. Wisley Trails, 1938. Extra large, rich coral-scarlet flowers. This is a first-rate variety in every way, and is strongly recommended .. .. ..   9/–   70/–

26

**Heucheras (Sanguinea Section) continued.**

| | doz. | 100 |
|---|---|---|
| **Honeybell.** This variety is identical with *Pink Delight*, which was raised at Wisbech several years ago at the same time as *Honeybell* was raised here. For description see under *Pink Delight* ..   ..   ..   ..   .. | | |
| **Isobell,** flowers bright carmine-rose, dwarf habit ..   .. | 6/- | — |
| **Jubilee,** a great improvement on *Edge Hall*, the flowers being half as large again and the colour a glistening rose-pink, more freely produced, 1½ ft., June–July   ..   ..   ..   .. | 7/- | 50/- |
| **Oakington Jewel,** A.M.R.H.S. Wisley Trials, 1938, deep coral-red, tinged copper, on strong stems, extremely free-flowering with robust growth and distinct bronzed foliage ..   ..   .. | 7/- | 50/- |
| **Pink Delight,** A.M.R.H.S. Wisley Trials, 1938. Large flowers of a deep old rose shade. Sturdy growth and free flowering ..   ..   .. | 6/- | 42/- |
| **Pluie de Feu,** bright scarlet, 2 ft.   ..   ..   .. | 5/- | 35/- |
| **Red Pimpernel,** flowers of bright crimson-red   ..   .. | 6/- | 42/- |
| **sanguinea grandiflora,** large crimson-red flowers borne on long spikes ; this is a really outstanding variety which is seldom offered   ..   .. | 6/- | 42/- |
| **Scarlet Beauty,** a real scarlet, 2 ft. ..   ..   .. | 10/- | — |
| **Shere Variety,** very attractive and free-flowering, producing short spikes of bright scarlet flowers during most of the summer ..   ..   .. | 7/- | 50/- |
| **Snowflakes,** quite the best white variety yet seen, large flowers freely produced, 2½ ft.   ..   .. | 6/- | 42/- |
| **tiarelloides,** distinct early-flowering variety, rose-pink, 1 ft. | 4/- | 28/- |
| **White Giant,** often produces sprays, 3 ft. long   ..   .. | 7/- | — |
| a **HIERACEUM villosum,** bright yellow flowers, grey foliage, very showy, 8 ins. ..   ..   ..   .. | 4/6 | 30/- |
| **HOLLYHOCKS,** all doubles—appleblossom, bright rose, crimson, golden yellow, scarlet, sulphur yellow and mixed   ..   ..   ..   .. | 2/6 | 18/- |
| a **HUTCHINSIA alpina,** forms deep green cushions covered with white flowers in spring ..   ..   .. | 3/6 | 25/- |
| a **HYPERICUM Coris,** deep golden flowers in profusion from June onwards ; an attractive and useful plant, 6 ins. ..   ..   ..   ..   .. | 4/6 | 30/- |
| a   **grandiflorum,** prostrate habit with huge yellow flowers, new, an extra good plant, June–July   .. | 5/- | 35/- |
| a   **polyphyllum,** yellow, very showy, 6 ins. ..   ..   .. | 3/6 | 25/- |
| a **HYPSELLA longiflora,** close dark green foliage, pink and white flowers, 1 in., June–August ..   .. | 4/6 | 30/- |
| a **IBERIS corræfolia Snowflake,** head of pure white flowers, 9 ins. ..   ..   ..   ..   .. | 4/- | 28/- |
| a   **jucundum** (see *Aethionema*). | | |
| a   **Little Gem,** dwarf, bushy growth, smothered in white flowers, a most useful plant ..   ..   .. | 3/6 | 25/- |
| **INCARVILLEA grandiflora,** deep pink trumpets, 1 ft. .. | 4/6 | 30/- |

| BLOOMS' HARDY PLANTS | doz. | 100 |
|---|---|---|
| **INULA glandulosa,** fine yellow rayed flowers, 2 ft. .. | 4/6 | 30/– |
| **Golden Beauty,** bushes of yellow flowers, 2 ft., June–September .. .. .. .. | 4/– | 28/– |
| **Royleana,** large orange-yellow flowers, 2 ft. .. .. | 5/– | 35/– |

### IRIS GERMANICA

| | | |
|---|---|---|
| **Afterglow,** lilac-bronze suffused amber-yellow .. .. | 4/– | 28/– |
| **Alcapal,** a cross between *Alcazar* and *pallida,* very large flowers, mixed violet, purple and blue ; the flowers are of great substance and will last well when cut .. .. .. .. .. | 6/– | 42/– |
| **Alcazar,** lavender and violet .. .. .. | 3/6 | 25/– |
| **Ambassadeur,** fine violet-red with ruby falls, tall .. | 4/6 | 30/– |
| **Ann Page,** lavender-blue self .. .. .. .. | 5/– | 35/– |
| **Archeveque,** rich violet, light blue standards .. .. | 3/6 | 25/– |
| **Ballerine,** silvery-lavender-blue, large flowers .. .. | 4/6 | 30/– |
| **Bruno,** bronze and deep purple-maroon .. .. | 12/– | — |
| **Cambridge Blue,** clear light blue with deeper falls, exceptionally free-flowering, strongly recommended.. .. .. .. .. .. | 6/– | 42/– |
| **Cluny,** lilac-blue with violet falls .. .. .. | 4/– | 28/– |
| **Cresset,** huge reddish-bronze oval flowers, new .. | 24/– | — |
| **Dalila,** white, ruby-red falls .. .. .. .. | 3/6 | 25/– |
| **Dream,** lovely rose-pink .. .. .. .. | 4/6 | 30/– |
| **Eldorado,** bright yellow, tinged violet .. .. | 4/– | 28/– |
| **Empress of India,** lovely soft pale blue self .. .. | 3/6 | 25/– |
| **Flaming Sword,** yellow, crimson falls, a fine variety .. | 5/– | 35/– |
| **Foster's Yellow,** a good yellow variety .. .. | 4/– | 28/– |
| **Fro,** red and yellow suffused brown .. .. .. | 4/– | 28/– |
| **Goldcrest,** deep blue with golden falls .. .. | 4/6 | 30/– |
| **Imperator,** clear violet and purple-red .. .. | 4/6 | 30/– |
| **intermedia Helge,** creamy-yellow, orange falls, early .. | 3/6 | 25/– |
| **Isolene,** silvery-white, shaded violet-rose .. .. | 3/6 | 25/– |
| **Leander,** rich blue .. .. .. .. .. | 3/6 | 25/– |
| **Lent, A. Williamson,** soft violet, velvety-purple falls .. | 3/6 | 25/– |
| **Lord of June,** Cambridge-blue, a good selling variety .. | 4/6 | 30/– |
| **Majestic,** light mauve, velvety-purple falls .. .. | 5/– | 35/– |
| **Mercutio,** light purple self, very free .. .. | 4/6 | 30/– |
| **Mlle. Schwartz,** silvery-mauve self .. .. | 4/– | 28/– |
| **Mrs. Neubronner,** fine golden-yellow .. .. | 4/– | 28/– |
| **pallida macrantha,** large blue flowers .. .. | 4/– | 28/– |
| **Queen of May,** soft rose-pink .. .. .. | 4/– | 28/– |
| **Pioneer,** glowing violet purple .. .. .. | 4/6 | 30/– |
| **Prospero,** bronzy-lavender, falls purple with orange beard | 4/– | 28/– |
| **Quaker Lady,** lavender-blue with bronze and gold .. | 4/– | 28/– |
| **Selma,** ruby-violet .. .. .. .. .. | 3/6 | 25/– |
| **Shelford Chieftain,** light blue and bright violet .. .. | 4/6 | 30/– |
| **Shot Silk,** violet-rose and bronze, new .. .. | 24/– | — |
| **Sir Michael,** lavender-blue with falls of crimson-purple shaded bronze .. .. .. .. | 12/– | 90/– |
| **Souvenir de Mme. Gaudichau,** deep violet-purple .. | 6/– | 42/– |

28

| BLOOMS' HARDY PLANTS | doz. | 100 |
|---|---|---|

**Iris Germanica—continued.**

| | doz. | 100 |
|---|---|---|
| **Standard Bearer,** light reddish-purple .. .. .. | 4/– | 28/– |
| **Susan Bliss,** fine rose-pink .. .. .. .. .. | 4/6 | 30/– |
| **Tom Tit,** deep violet-blue self, dwarf and distinct .. | 4/6 | 30/– |
| **Yellow Hammer,** bright yellow .. .. .. .. | 4/– | 28/– |

**COLLECTIONS of IRIS GERMANICA, our selection:
24 in up to 6 sorts for 8/-; 50 in up to 10 sorts for 14/-;
100 for 26/-.**

**IRIS, VARIOUS**

| | | doz. | 100 |
|---|---|---|---|
| a | **cristata,** rich amethyst-blue, orange markings, 4 ins. .. | 5/– | 35/– |
| | **japonica Ledger's Variety,** beautiful pale blue, orchid-like flowers with gold markings .. .. | 8/– | 60/– |
| | **Kæmpferi Iso-no-Nami,** light blue suffused on white, double .. .. .. .. .. | 6/– | 42/– |
| | **Nishiki Yama,** ruby-rose with lighter centre, double | 6/– | 42/– |
| | **Shippo,** deep violet-blue, feathered white .. .. | 6/– | 42/– |
| | **Tora Odori,** deep purple, flecked white, double .. | 6/– | 42/– |
| | **Zama-no-Mori** (*Morning Mist*), single white, faint blue shading .. .. .. .. .. | 6/– | 42/– |
| | **Mixed**—all colours, single and double .. .. | 5/– | 35/– |
| a | **lacustris,** pale blue, like a miniature flag iris, 3 ins. .. | 5/– | 35/– |
| | **pumila** (*chamæiris*) **atro-cœrulea,** deep blue .. | 3/6 | 25/– |
| | **Campbelli,** a deep violet-blue, 9 ins. .. .. | 6/– | — |
| | **Excelsa** .. .. .. .. .'. .. .. | 4/6 | 30/– |
| | **The Bride,** pure white .. .. .. .. | 3/6 | 25/– |
| | **sibirica Perry's Blue,** tall rush-like growth, small blue flowers .. .. .. .. .. .. | 3/6 | 25/– |
| | **stylosa,** light blue, the first to flower, 1 ft. .. .. | 4/6 | 30/– |
| a | **JASIONE perennis,** pretty blue scabious-like flower, 6 ins. | 4/6 | 30/– |

**KNIPHOFIA (TRITOMA or RED HOT POKER)**

| | doz. | 100 |
|---|---|---|
| **Buttercup,** pure. yellow, early and dwarf, 2½ ft. .. .. | 4/– | 28/– |
| **Galpini,** grass-like foliage, dainty spikes of salmon-yellow, very free, quite hardy but rare .. .. | 20/– | — |
| **Gold Else,** rich deep yellow, very free, 3 ft. .. .. | 4/– | 28/– |
| **June Glory,** bright scarlet heads, freely produced, 3½ ft. | 4/6 | 30/– |
| **Lord Roberts,** brightest orange-scarlet, very free .. | 5/– | 35/– |
| **Royal Standard,** scarlet, changing to rich yellow, 3 ft. .. | 5/– | 35/– |
| **Rufus,** short spikes of yellow, tipped crimson, good dwarf habit, 2 ft. .. .. .. .. .. | 5/– | 35/– |
| **Russell's Gold,** rich yellow, tipped orange-red, 3 ft. July–August .. .. .. .. .. | 6/– | 42/– |
| **Sanderson** ... .. .. .. .. .. | 5/– | 35/– |
| **Sir C. K. Butler,** deep orange and yellow, strong spikes .. | 5/– | 35/– |
| **Star of Baden-Baden,** beautiful orange self .. .. | 8/– | — |
| **The Rocket** (*Mt. Etna*), brilliant orange-scarlet .. .. | 12/– | 90/– |
| **uvaria grandiflora,** fine crimson and gold, 4 ft. .. .. | 5/– | 35/– |
| **LAVATERA olbia rosea,** showy bushes of pink flowers, pot-grown plants .. .. .. .. | 5/– | 35/– |

29

| BLOOMS' HARDY PLANTS | doz. | 100 |
|---|---|---|
| a **LAVENDULA nana alba,** very dwarf white form .. .. | 5/– | 35/– |
| a **nana Backhouse Variety,** fine dwarf deep blue .. .. | 5/– | 35/– |
| a **LEONTOPODIUM alpinum,** an improved strain of *Edelweiss* | 4/– | 28/– |
| **LIATRIS pycnostachia,** tall spikes of bright rosy-purple a striking plant, 4 ft., July–September .. | 5/– | 35/– |
| **spicata,** earlier and more compact than the above .. | 4/6 | 30/– |
| a **LINARIA æquitriloba,** close mats with mauve flowers, all summer .. .. .. .. .. | 4/– | 28/– |
| **dalmatica,** dense spikes of primrose-yellow flowers, 3 ft., June–September .. .. .. .. | 3/6 | 25/– |
| a **globosa,** compact growth, light blue flowers .. .. | 3/6 | 25/– |
| a **rosea,** very pretty pink form .. .. .. .. | 6/– | 42/– |
| a **hepaticæfolia,** pale violet flowers, pretty flat leaves .. | 4/– | 28/– |
| **purpurea Canon Want,** erect spikes of bright rose-pink flowers, very effective, 2½ ft., June–September | 4/– | 28/– |
| a **LINUM arboreum,** dwarf shrubby growth, bright yellow flowers .. .. .. .. .. .. | 4/6 | 30/– |
| a **flavum compactum,** golden-yellow, free and very showy | 4/6 | 30/– |
| **perenne,** the blue perennial Flax, 2 ft. .. .. .. | 3/6 | 25/– |
| a **LIPPIA repens,** creeping habit, pink flower heads .. .. | 3/6 | 25/– |
| a **LITHOSPERMUM graminifolium,** grassy tufts, masses of bright blue flowers .. .. .. .. | 6/– | 42/– |
| a **intermedium,** tufted growth, bright gentian-blue flowers | 6/– | 42/– |
| a **prostratum Grace Ward,** an enlarged form of *Heavenly Blue* .. .. .. .. .. .. | 6/– | 42/– |
| a **Heavenly Blue,** needs no description .. .. .. | 5/– | 35/– |

*"a" denotes pot-grown Alpines*

---

*New PINK BUDDLEIA "CHARMING." See our offer on inside of front cover.*

---

30

# LUPINUS POLYPHYLLUS

| | each | doz. | 100 |
|---|---|---|---|
| **Ada,** yellow, suffused buff | 8d | 7/- | 50/- |
| **Artist,** delicate shade of light blue, recommended | 7d | 6/- | 42/- |
| **Blackpool Tower,** a most striking blue and white variety | 1/2 | 12/- | 90/- |
| **Box Apricot,** deep apricot, tinged bronze.. | 1/6 | 16/- | — |
| **Charming,** an outstanding clear pink | 10d | 9/- | 66/- |
| **Chocolate Soldier,** deep chocolate-purple, yellow standards | 11d | 10/- | 72/- |
| **Cleopatra,** pale coppery-gold and buff | 8d | 7/- | 50/- |
| **C. M. Prichard,** orange, flushed salmon | 10d | 9/- | 66/- |
| **Countess of March,** white, opening to lilac-blue.. | 1/3 | 14/- | 100/- |
| **Elizabeth Arden,** rich orange, first-rate variety | 10d | 9/- | 66/- |
| **Gladys Pearson,** pink with gold standards.. | 1/4 | 15/- | — |
| **Golden Thoughts,** rosy-fawn with yellow wings | | | |
| **Grenadier,** a very fine golden-yellow variety, with orange-red wings changing to deep red | 2/6 | 27/- | — |
| **Hades,** salmon and bronze with golden-bronze standards deepening to red .. | 2/3 | 24/- | 180/- |
| **Happiness,** long spikes of intense indigo-blue | 1/- | 11/- | 80/- |
| **Harry Hartley,** rich rosy-crimson, a very fine spike, strongly recommended | 10d | 9/- | 66/- |
| **Highlander,** a clear light pink | 11d | 10/- | 72/- |
| **Joyce Blackburn,** yellow, shaded bronze .. | 7d | 6/- | 42/- |
| **Lilac Domino,** deep lilac and white.. | 1/- | 11/- | 80/- |
| **Man of War,** deep violet-purple | 9d | 8/- | 60/- |
| **Mrs. Jack Pearson,** wistaria-blue .. | 9d | 8/- | 60/- |
| **Mrs. John Harkness,** quite the best yellow | 1/- | 11/- | 80/- |
| **Mrs. Nicol Walker,** deep orange and rosy-red, shading with yellow, an outstanding variety | 1/6 | 16/- | 120/- |
| **Mrs. Penry Williams,** clear deep rose-red, fine spikes | 1/8 | 18/- | 130/- |
| **Mrs. Siveright,** a lovely cream shade | 7d | 6/- | 42/- |
| **Olympiade,** indigo-blue and yellow .. | 10d | 9/- | 66/- |
| **Orange Glow,** brilliant orange, shading to carmine | 1/6 | 16/- | 120/- |
| **Phyllis Prichard,** distinct shade of claret-rose | 9d | 8/- | 60/- |
| **Powerful,** beautiful salmon-rose, immense spikes.. | 1/9 | 20/- | 150/- |
| **Redgrove,** deep glowing pink, fine spikes .. | 1/- | 11/- | 80/- |
| **Riverslea,** giant crimson, an outstanding variety | 1/6 | 16/- | 120/- |
| **Ruby King,** deep purple-crimson .. | 6d | 5/- | 35/- |
| **Snow Queen (arboreus),** pot-grown plants, pure white | — | 4/6 | 30/- |
| **Sulphur Gem,** light yellow, very free | 6d | 5/- | 35/- |
| **Sunshine,** fine yellow semi-tree lupin | 7d | 6/- | 42/- |
| **21st Lancers,** bluish-yellow .. | 8d | 7/- | 50/- |

31

BLOOMS' HARDY PLANTS       each  doz.  100
**Lupinus Polyphyllus—continued.**

| | each | doz. | 100 |
|---|---|---|---|
| **Zulu,** violet-purple | 7d | 6/- | 42/- |
| **Seedlings from best-named sorts once flowered** | — | 3/6 | 25/- |

**COLLECTIONS OF NAMED LUPINS:** Special prices on application.

RUSSELL LUPINS  We have a fine stock of plants which flowered in July and August. Many inferior types have been rogued out, and we can confidently recommend both the strain and the quality of the plants we are offering .. 6/- 42/-

| | doz. | 100 |
|---|---|---|
| a **LYCHNIS alpina,** deep pink flower heads, tufted growth, 3 ins., May–June | 3/6 | 25/- |
| **chalcedonica,** rich scarlet flower heads, 2 ft. | 3/6 | 25/- |
| **Salmon Queen,** rosy-salmon form | 4/- | 28/- |
| a **viscaria splendens plena,** brightest carmine-red, double, 1 ft. | 4/- | 28/- |
| **LYTHRUM Brightness,** deep rose-pink spikes, 2½ ft. | 4/- | 28/- |
| **Lady Sackville,** fine rosy-red variety | 4/6 | 30/- |
| **Prichard's Variety,** bright rose-pink, 3 ft. | 4/6 | 30/- |
| **Rose Queen,** dwarf habit, bright pink, 2 ft. | 4/- | 28/- |
| **roseum superbum,** tall spikes of pink flowers, 3 ft. | 4/- | 28/- |
| **The Beacon,** A.M.R.H.S., an outstanding variety, producing neat spikes of large deep carmine-red flowers | 7/- | 50/- |
| a **MAZUS reptans** (syn. *rugosus*), close creeping habit, lilac-mauve flowers | 3/6 | 25/- |
| a **MECONOPSIS Baileyi,** bright blue poppy-like flowers | 6/- | 42/- |
| **Dhwojii,** finely cut foliage, lemon-yellow flowers, 2½ ft. | 8/- | 60/- |
| a **Pratti,** clusters of pale blue flowers, 1½ ft. | 5/- | 35/- |
| a **rudis,** clear blue flowers on 18-in. stems | 7/- | — |
| a **MENTHA Requini,** aromatic carpeter, lilac flowers | 4/- | 28/- |
| a **MERTENSIA echioides,** rich blue, flowering in spring, 4 ins. | 4/- | 28/- |
| a **MICROMERIA piperella,** tiny aromatic bush, pink flowers | 5/- | 35/- |
| a **MIMULUS A. T. Johnson,** bright golden flowers, crimson blotches | 3/6 | 25/- |
| a **Chelsea Pensioner,** strong growth, producing large flowers of a crimson-red shade, 8 ins. | 4/6 | 30/- |
| a **Flame of Fire,** dazzling bronzy-scarlet, 6 ins. | 4/- | 28/- |
| a **Hose-in-Hose,** deep yellow flowers, spotted brown | 3/6 | 25/- |
| a **Prince Bismarck,** deep crimson-red | 3/6 | 25/- |
| a **Whitecroft Scarlet,** dwarf compact habit, brilliant orange-scarlet flowers | 4/6 | 30/- |
| **MONARDA Cambridge Scarlet,** well-known *Red Bergamot*, 3 ft. | 3/6 | 25/- |
| **magnifica,** rich salmon-pink, 2 ft. | 6/- | 42/- |
| **Mrs. Perry,** bright rosy-scarlet, an improvement on *Cambridge Scarlet* | 6/- | 42/- |
| **Pink Beauty,** fine clear pink, 3 ft. | 4/- | 28/- |
| **Sunset,** bright crimson-purple, 3 ft., July–September | 5/- | 35/- |

*"a" denotes pot-grown Alpines*

32

BLOOMS' HARDY PLANTS       doz.   100

a **MORISIA hypogea,** deep green rosettes, bright yellow flowers ..    ..    ..    ..    ..    5/–   35/–

a **MUEHLENBECKIA complexa,** masses of green leaves on twining shrubby growth   ..    ..    ..    4/6   30/–

a **MYOSOTIS rupicola,** a real Alpine forget-me-not, rich blue   4/6   30/–

a    **Ruth Fischer,** branching stems of sky-blue, 6 ins., April–June   ..    ..    ..    ..    3/6   25/–

   **NEPETA Mussini** (*Catmint*) ..    ..    ..    ..    3/–   20/–

   **nervosa,** mauve-blue, very pretty compact habit    ..    4/–   28/–

   **Six Hills Giant,** a fine form of *Mussini*, grows 3 ft.    ..    3/6   25/–

   **Souv. d'Andre Chaudron,** large mauve-blue flowers, free   3/6   25/–

a **NIEREMBERGIA rivularis,** close dark green growth, large white flowers   ..    ..    ..    3/6   25/–

a **ODONTOSPERMUM maritimum,** bright yellow flowers all summer, tender ..    ..    ..    ..    6/–   42/–

   **ŒNOTHERA fruticosa,** bright yellow    ..    ..    3/6   25/–

   **fruticosa Yellow River,** the best of the *fruticosa* types. A profusion of yellow flowers, 2 ft., July–October, new   ..    ..    ..    ..    ..    9/–   70/–

   **Youngi,** rich yellow flowers over a long period, 1 ft.    ..    4/–   28/–

a    **glaber Fyrverkerei** new, deep golden-yellow flowers, all summer, 1 ft    ..    ..    ..    ..    8/–   60/–

   **macrocarpa,** (syn. *Missouriensis*), large yellow flowers, dwarf habit, 9 ins. ..    ..    ..    ..    4/6   30/–

a    **pumila,** tiny sprays of deep yellow, 6 ins. ..    ..    ..    5/–   35/–

a    **riparia,** masses of yellow flowers on trailing stems, all summer    ..    ..    ..    ..    4/6   30/–

a **OMPHALODES cappadocica,** sprays of bright blue flowers   5/–   —

a **ONOSMA taurica,** arching sprays of yellow tubular flowers, 9 ins.    ..    ..    ..    ..    6/–   —

a **ORIGANUM dictamnus,** woolly leaves, drooping heads of pink flowers   ..    ..    ..    ..    6/–   42/–

a **hybridum,** flowers like pink hops in late summer, 1 ft.   6/–   42/–

a **OXALIS adenophylla,** compact tufted foliage, masses of lilac-pink flowers, 3 ins., April–June    ..    5/–   35/–

a **florabunda rosea,** bright deep pink, very free, 6 ins.    ..    4/–   28/–

   **PÆONIA,** strong one-year plants, not clumps. Double varieties except where stated.

   **Adolphe Rousseau,** deep purple-red, striking colour    ..    6/–   42/–

   **Albert Crousse,** bright pink, crimson centre    ..    5/–   35/–

   **Avalanche,** extra large white variety    ..    ..    6/–   42/–

   **Bunker Hill,** Tyrian-rose, very free-flowering ..    6/–   42/–

   **Canary,** white, shading to yellow centre    ..    ..    5/–   35/–

   **Duchesse de Nemours,** pure double white..    ..    5/–   35/–

   **Duke of Wellington,** large fully double flowers, pale sulphur-yellow    ..    ..    ..    6/–   42/–

   **edulis superba,** rich silvery-pink    ..    ..    5/–   35/–

   **Felix Crousse,** bright red    ..    ..    ..    6/–   42/–

   **festive maxima,** white with crimson-flecked centre    ..    5/–   35/–

   **Gen. MacMahon,** deep crimson-red, strong grower    ..    6/–   42/–

   **La Tendresse,** creamy-white, centre flecked crimson    ..    6/–   42/–

33

| BLOOMS' HARDY PLANTS | doz. | 100 |
|---|---|---|
| **Pæonia—continued.** | | |
| **Lady Alexandra Duff,** very pale flesh-pink, large double flowers .. .. .. .. .. .. | 6/– | 42/– |
| **L'Indispensable,** lilac-white, shading to pale rosy-mauve at centre .. .. .. .. .. | 5/– | 35/– |
| **Lord Kitchener,** bright cherry-red, very early .. .. | 5/– | 35/– |
| **Mme. Calot,** clear pink, deeper centre, fragrant and early | 6/– | 42/– |
| **M. Charles Leveque** (syn. *Mlle. Leonie Calot*), pale rose-white, deeper centre, lightly tipped carmine | 5/– | 35/– |
| **M. Jules Elie,** silvery-lilac-pink .. .. .. .. | 5/– | 35/– |
| **M. Martin Cahuzac,** the darkest red Paeony .. .. | 6/– | 42/– |
| **officinalis rosea,** double salmon-pink .. .. .. | 7/– | 50/– |
| **rubra plena,** double crimson, early .. .. .. | 6/– | 42/– |
| **President Roosevelt,** bright deep red .. .. .. | 6/– | 42/– |
| **Reine Hortense,** lilac-pink and salmon .. .. .. | 5/– | 35/– |
| **Sarah Bernhardt,** apple-blossom-pink, very early .. | 6/– | 42/– |
| **Solange,** salmon-orange, late .. .. .. .. | 6/– | 42/– |
| **tenuifolia rubra plena,** ferny foliage, double crimson flowers, 1 ft. .. .. .. .. .. | 7/– | 50/– |
| **Victoire de la Marne,** glowing crimson-red .. .. | 6/– | 42/– |
| a **PAPAVER alpinum,** miniature *Iceland Poppy*, various colours, 5 ins. .. .. .. .. .. | 4/– | 28/– |
| **orientale Col. Bowles,** an outstanding variety, brilliant scarlet .. .. .. .. .. .. | 4/– | 28/– |
| **Crimson Brocade,** rich blood-red .. .. .. | 4/– | 28/– |
| **Ethel Swete,** cerise-pink with black blotch .. .. | | |
| **Jenny Mawson,** soft salmon-pink, large open flowers, 2 ft. .. .. .. .. .. .. | 4/– | 28/– |
| **King George,** deeply-fringed scarlet flowers, 2 ft. .. | 4/– | 28/– |
| **Lady Haig,** deep orange-scarlet .. .. .. .. | 4/6 | 30/– |
| **Lady Roscoe,** orange-salmon .. .. .. .. | 4/– | 28/– |
| **Leviathan,** giant mauve, 3 ft. .. .. .. .. | 4/6 | 30/– |
| **Lord Lambourne,** orange-scarlet, black centre, 3 ft. .. | 4/– | 28/– |
| **May Queen,** double salmon-red, dwarf, 15 ins. .. | 4/6 | 30/– |
| **Olive Harkness,** beautiful salmon, blotched crimson .. | 5/– | 35/– |
| **Olympia,** orange-scarlet flowers, quite double .. .. | 4/6 | 30/– |
| **Peter Pan,** very dwarf, bright red .. · .. .. | 4/– | 28/– |
| **Rembrandt,** rich crimson, six-petalled flowers .. .. | 4/6 | 30/– |
| **Stormtorch** (*Sturmfackel*), fiery-red, erect stems .. | 6/– | 42/– |
| **Wunderkind,** cerise-pink, black blotch .. .. | 4/6 | 30/– |
| **nudicaule Sandford's Strain,** one of the best strains of *Iceland Poppies* .. .. .. .. | 3/6 | 25/– |
| **PENTSTEMON Andenken an Hahn,** a new Continental variety, which is absolutely hardy. Forms strong bushes about 2 ft. high, and is extremely free-flowering. The tubular flowers are a brilliant wine-red colour with paler throat. The mere fact that it is hardy makes it a most welcome addition .. .. | 6/– | 42/– |
| **barbatus** (see *CHELONE barbata*). | | |

*"a" denotes pot-grown Alpines*

34

BLOOMS' HARDY PLANTS                doz.   100

**Pentstemon—continued.**

| | | doz. | 100 |
|---|---|---|---|
| a | **heterophyllus,** blue tinged pink | 5/– | 35/– |
| a | **Blue Gem,** shades of blue and rosy-blue | 5/– | 35/– |
| a | **True Blue,** spikes of bright blue, 1 ft. | 7/– | 50/– |
| a | **Scouleri,** bushes of lilac-blue flowers, 9 ins. | 6/– | 42/– |
| a | **Six Hills,** bushy habit, large lilac flowers, 6 ins. | 6/– | 42/– |

**PETROCALLIS** (see *DRABA pyrenaica*).

# PHLOX DECUSSATA

### (Border Varieties)
#### Strong, healthy young plants, free from disease

| | | |
|---|---|---|
| **Admiral,** cerise-red, large truss | 4/– | 28/– |
| **Aida,** compact habit, crimson with purple eye | 5/– | 35/– |
| **Baron van Dedem,** rich salmon-red | 4/– | 28/– |
| **Baron van Heeckeren,** fine clear salmon-pink | 4/– | 28/– |
| **Border Gem,** deep violet-purple, a fine variety | 4/– | 28/– |
| **Camillo Schneider,** a fine crimson-scarlet | 4/6 | 30/– |
| **Caroline van den Berg,** beautiful lavender-blue, huge trusses | 4/6 | 30/– |
| **Commander-in-Chief** (*Hindenburg*), blood-red, very large flowers | 4/– | 28/– |
| **Coquelicot,** bright orange-scarlet | 4/6 | 30/– |
| **Daily Sketch,** fine rose-pink, deeper centre, outstanding | 6/– | 42/– |
| **Dr. Charcot,** the nearest approach to blue | 4/6 | 30/– |
| **Eclaireur,** crimson-purple, very bright | 3/6 | 25/– |
| **Electra,** carmine-red, blotched crimson edge | 4/– | 28/– |
| **Elizabeth Campbell,** beautiful rose-pink with white centre | 4/– | 28/– |
| **Emain Macha,** deep flaming red, dwarf habit, new | 5/– | 35/– |
| **Erntefener,** large heads of bright orange-salmon, late, new | 7/– | 50/– |
| **Europe,** white with conspicuous red eye | 3/6 | 25/– |
| **Eva Foerster,** very large flowers, rich salmon-pink with white eye, new | 7/– | 50/– |
| **Evangeline,** large salmon-pink, improved *Elizabeth Campbell* | 4/– | 28/– |
| **Evelyn,** rich salmon-rose | 4/– | 28/– |
| **Firebrand,** large trusses of bright orange-scarlet | 4/6 | 30/– |
| **Frau A. Buchner,** large pure white | 3/6 | 25/– |
| **Gen. French,** crimson-orange, very fine truss | 4/– | 28/– |
| **Gen. Petain,** very effective, a deep wine colour | 4/6 | 30/– |
| **Gen. van Heutz,** deep salmon with white eye | 4/– | 28/– |
| **Graf Zeppelin,** large white with crimson eye | 4/– | 28/– |
| **Gustav Lind,** early dwarf, red | 4/– | 28/– |
| **H. B. May,** clear pink, very large flower and truss | 3/6 | 25/– |
| **Hauptmann Kohl,** bright crimson-red, very large flowers | 4/– | 28/– |
| **Iris,** purple-mauve with deeper eye | 3/6 | 25/– |
| **Josephine Gerbaux,** white with large red centre | 4/– | 28/– |

35

BLOOMS' HARDY PLANTS                                          doz.    100

**Phlox Decussata—continued.**

| | doz. | 100 |
|---|---|---|
| **Jules Sandeau,** extra large pure pink flowers, dwarf .. | 4/– | 28/– |
| **Karl Foerster,** brilliant deep orange-red, extra fine .. | 4/– | 28/– |
| **Le Mahdi,** very deep violet .. .. .. .. .. | 4/– | 28/– |
| **Leo Schlageter,** bright scarlet-orange, the finest of its colour | 4/6 | 30/– |
| **Lord Lambourne,** quite the best salmon, very free-flowering, new .. .. .. .. | 7/– | 50/– |
| **Louis Ganne,** deep lilac, very large flower and truss .. | 4/– | 28/– |
| **Lucas Schwinghammer,** dwarf habit like *Mia Ruys*, bright deep pink flowers .. .. .. | 4/– | 28/– |
| **Margaret Gavin Jones,** bright red centre, paling to white edge, large flower, strong grower .. | 4/– | 28/– |
| **Marie Jacob,** lilac-mauve, streaked white .. .. .. | 3/6 | 25/– |
| **Mia Ruys,** pure white, large truss and very dwarf .. .. | 3/6 | 25/– |
| **Milly van Hoboken,** rose-pink with deeper centre .. | 3/6 | 25/– |
| **Miss Ellen Willmott,** beautiful lilac-blue .. .. | 4/– | 28/– |
| **Morgenrood,** pure deep rose with red eye .. .. | 4/– | 28/– |
| **Mrs. W. van Beuningen,** salmon-pink self, vigorous growth .. .. .. .. .. | 4/6 | 30/– |
| **Mrs. E. Fitzgerald,** plum-purple .. .. .. .. | 4/– | 28/– |
| **Mrs. Ethel Prichard,** fine lilac self colour, early .. .. | 4/– | 28/– |
| **Mrs. Scholten,** deep salmon-pink .. .. .. .. | 4/– | 28/– |
| **Newbird,** dazzling crimson-red, early, strong grower .. | 4/– | 28/– |
| **Paul Hoffmann,** bright deep carmine-crimson, very large truss and flower .. .. .. | 3/6 | 25/– |
| **P. D. Williams,** soft appleblossom-pink, deeper in the centre, new .. .. .. .. .. | 6/– | 42/– |
| **Professor Went,** deep amaranth-purple .. .. .. | 5/– | 35/– |
| **Rijnstroon,** fine deep pink, self colour .. .. .. | 3/6 | 25/– |
| **Saladin,** dazzling salmon-scarlet, extra good .. | 5/– | 35/– |
| **Salome,** new, deep salmon with crimson centre .. .. | 7/– | 50/– |
| **San Antonio,** deep blood-red, fine truss, new .. | 6/– | 42/– |
| **Selma,** large pink flowers, cherry-red eye .. .. .. | 4/– | 28/– |
| **September Glow,** tall, crimson-red .. .. .. | 4/6 | 30/– |
| **Sir Wm. Lawrence,** clear rosy-red, small white eye .. | 6/– | 42/– |
| **Smiles,** deep rose with deeper eye .. .. .. | 4/– | 28/– |
| **Spätrot,** new, deep vermilion-red, compact habit, late .. | 7/– | 50/– |
| **Sweetheart,** glowing salmon, a very fine variety .. .. | 3/6 | 25/– |
| **The King,** brightest purple-red, an outstanding variety .. | 5/– | 35/– |
| **Thor,** deep salmon-pink, large truss .. .. .. | 3/6 | 25/– |
| **Tigress,** bright orange-scarlet .. .. .. .. | 4/6 | 30/– |
| **Titanic,** deep lilac, purple eye .. .. .. .. | 4/6 | 30/– |
| **Widar,** purple-rose with white eye .. .. .. .. | 4/– | 28/– |
| **Wm. Kesselring,** violet, white centre, very large truss, dwarf .. .. .. .. .. | 3/6 | 25/– |
| **Wm. Ramsay,** rich deep purple, an outstanding variety.. | 3/6 | 26/– |

**COLLECTIONS of PHLOX, our selection: 24 in up to 6 sorts for 7/6; 50 in up to 10 sorts for 13/6; 100 for 25/-.**

36

BLOOMS' HARDY PLANTS doz. 100

# PHLOX (Alpine Species and Varieties, all pot-grown)

| | | doz. | 100 |
|---|---|---|---|
| a | **adsurgens,** heads of large soft pink flowers, distinctive, 4 ins. | 6/- | 42/- |
| a | **amœna rosea,** broad green leaves, pink flowers | 4/6 | 30/- |
| a | **canadensis Laphami,** lovely panicles of lavender-blue, 1 ft. | 5/- | 35/- |
| a | **Perry's Variety,** light blue, free-flowering | 5/- | 35/- |
| a | **Cecil Davies,** creeping habit, heads of rosy-lilac flowers | 3/6 | 25/- |
| a | **subulata (setacea),** very deep rose, trailing habit | 3/6 | 25/- |
| a | **Attraction,** light pink, very dwarf | 4/6 | 30/- |
| a | **Bijou Rose,** bright deep pink | 3/6 | 25/- |
| a | **Brightness,** deep rosy-red, very showy | 3/6 | 25/- |
| a | **Camla,** large deep rosy-red | 6/- | 42/- |
| a | **Cuchlaine,** lilac-blue, quite distinct | 3/6 | 25/- |
| a | **Exquisite,** rose-pink with deeper eye | 3/6 | 25/- |
| a | **Fairy,** lilac-blue, with deeper eye, dwarf | 3/6 | 25/- |
| a | **G. F. Wilson,** well-known lavender-blue | 3/6 | 25/- |
| a | **Lilacina,** bright lilac shade with deeper eye | 3/6 | 25/- |
| a | **Moonlight,** light silvery-blue | 3/6 | 25/- |
| a | **Nelsoni,** pure white, compact grower | 5/- | 35/- |
| a | **Oakington Blue Eyes,** an improved *G. F. Wilson*, very dark foliage and clear lavender flowers, recommended | 4/6 | 30/- |
| a | **Samson,** large deep rose flowers, crimson eye | 5/- | 35/- |
| a | **Sensation,** deep fiery rose-pink, very showy | 4/- | 28/- |
| a | **Sprite,** beautiful salmon-rose | 4/6 | 30/- |
| a | **stellaria,** starry lilac-blue flowers | 3/6 | 25/- |
| a | **Vivid,** brilliant salmon-pink, one of the best | 6/- | 42/- |

**COLLECTIONS of ALPINE PHLOX, our selection:**
24 in up to 6 sorts for 8/-; 50 in up to 10 sorts for 14/-;
100 for 26/-.

| | doz. | 100 |
|---|---|---|
| **PHYGELIUS capensis,** spikes of brick-red flowers | 5/- | 35/- |
| **capensis coccineus** | — | — |
| **PHYSALIS (Cape Gooseberry) Franchetti gigantea,** new, very large flowers, brilliant orange-scarlet, a great improvement on the type | 15/- | — |
| **Franchetti monstrosa,** totally distinct, deep orange-tufted calyces | 15/- | — |
| a **nana,** unique dwarf form of *Franchetti*, 6 ins. | 15/- | — |
| **PHYSOSTEGIA speciosa rosea,** neat spikes of pink flowers, 2 ft. | 3/6 | 25/- |
| **Vivid,** fine deep rosy-red form, 1½ ft. | 5/- | 35/- |
| **PLATYCODON** (syn. *Wahlenbergia*). | | |
| a **POLYGALA calcarea,** bright deep blue, 2 ins, April-June, a first-rate Alpine | 6/- | 42/- |
| a **POLYGONUM polystachyum,** strong bushy growth, spikes of pink flowers | 6/- | 42/- |
| a **vaccinifolium,** shrubby, trailing growth, pink flowers | 4/6 | 30/- |
| a **viviparum,** short spikes of snow-white flowers, 8 ins. | 5/- | 35/- |

*"a" denotes pot-grown Alpines*

37

BLOOMS' HARDY PLANTS                                              doz.    100
### POTENTILLA

|  | | doz. | 100 |
|---|---|---|---|
| | **Gibson's Scarlet,** always in demand, 1 ft. | 5/– | 35/– |
| | **hirsuta,** large clear primrose-yellow flowers, 2 ft. | 5/– | — |
| | **Master Floris,** fine single yellow flowers with dark red centre | 6/– | 42/– |
| | **Miss Willmott,** bright deep pink | 4/– | 28/– |
| a | **nitida, Lissadell Variety,** an improved form of *nitida* | 7/– | — |
| | **Thurberi,** deep red, 1 ft. | 5/– | — |
| a | **Tonguei,** trailing stems, bearing beautiful orange and bronze flowers, a fine late-flowering Alpine | 4/6 | 30/– |
| a | **verna nana,** compact tufts studded with yellow flowers, 1 in. | 4/6 | 30/– |
| | **Warrensii,** bushes of large golden flowers, long-flowering period | 4/6 | 30/– |
| | **POTERIUM obtusum,** feathery spikes of pink flowers | 5/– | 35/– |

# PRIMULA

**Mostly pot-grown.   (m) Denotes moisture-loving.**

|  | | doz. | 100 |
|---|---|---|---|
| | **acaulis croussei plena,** soft double lilac | 5/– | 35/– |
| | **Double Sulphur,** clear sulphur-yellow | 6/– | 42/– |
| | **Double White** | | |
| a | **Asthore Hybrids,** a beautiful strain, embracing some really good colours (m) | 4/– | 28/– |
| a | **auricula (alpina),** mixed shades | 3/6 | 25/– |
| | **Barrowby Gem,** deep yellow polyanthus | 12/– | 90/– |
| a | **Beesiana,** purple with yellow eye, 2 ft. (m) | 4/6 | 30/– |
| a | **Bullesiana Hybrids,** include a wonderful range of colours, 18 ins. (m) | 4/– | 28/– |
| a | **Bulleyana,** beautiful shade of orange, 18 ins., May–June (m) | 4/– | 28/– |
| a | **capitata Mooreana,** heads of Tyrian purple on powdered stems, 9 ins. | 4/– | 28/– |
| a | **Cashmeriana,** large round heads of light blue in early spring | 3/6 | 25/– |
| a | **Chionantha,** fine heads of milk-white flowers | 4/6 | 30/– |
| a | **Cockburniana,** whorls of rich orange, a really beautiful species, 1 ft. (m) | 4/6 | 30/– |
| a | **cortusoides,** bright rose-pink flowers, 9 ins. | 3/6 | 25/– |
| a | **denticulata,** blue and violet heads, early spring-flowering | 3/6 | 25/– |
| a | **Hall's Strain,** extra large heads, good shades of colour, a very fine strain | 4/– | 28/– |
| a | **Florindæ,** like a giant form of *sikkimensis* (m) | 3/6 | 25/– |
| | **Helenæ** (*Primrose Type*), purple flowers in early spring | 4/– | 28/– |
| a | **helodoxa,** whorls of bright yellow flowers on strong stems (m) | 5/– | 35/– |
| a | **japonica Cherry Ripe,** large flowers of deepest cherry-red (m) | 4/6 | 30/– |
| a | **Giant Pink** (m) | 4/– | 28/– |
| a | **Tyrian Red** (m) | 5/– | 35/– |

*"a" denotes pot-grown Alpines*

38

BLOOMS' HARDY PLANTS     doz.   100

**Primula—continued.**

| | | doz. | 100 |
|---|---|---|---|
| a | **Scott Elliott's Strain,** embraces a very wide range of colours | 3/6 | 25/- |
| | **Juliana Gloria** (*Primrose type*), crimson-purple, March–April | 3/6 | 25/- |
| a | **Lichiangensis Highdown Variety,** short heads of bright rosy-red, 9 ins. | 4/- | 28/- |
| a | **microdonta alpicola,** soft primrose-yellow, 1 ft. | 4/- | 28/- |
| a | **violacea,** soft purple, 1 ft., July | 4/6 | 30/- |
| a | **Pam** (*Primrose type*), smaller and brighter than *Wanda* | 4/- | 28/- |
| | **pulverulenta,** crimson-purple, 2 ft. (m) | 4/- | 28/- |
| a | **Bartley Strain,** beautiful soft pink shades, 2 ft. (m) | 4/6 | 30/- |
| a | **Red Hugh,** rich deep red, very popular, 2 ft. (m) | 4/- | 28/- |
| a | **rosea grandiflora,** bright deep pink, early spring, 6 ins. (m) | 5/- | 35 - |
| a | **saxatilis,** sprays of mauve-pink flowers, 9 ins. | 4/6 | 30/- |
| a | **sikkimensis,** pendant heads of scented yellow flowers, 18 ins. (m) | 3/6 | 25/- |
| a | **Veitchii,** heads of bright deep rose, 1 ft. | 3/6 | 25/- |
| | **Wanda** (*Primrose type*), fine for early spring, purple-red | 3/6 | 25/- |
| a | **Wendy** (*Primrose type*), beautiful clear lilac, a fine early variety, very sweetly-scented | 4/6 | 30/- |

COLLECTIONS of PRIMULA, our selection: 24 in
up to 6 sorts for 8/-; 50 in up to 10 sorts for 14/6;
100 for 27/-.

**PULMONARIA**

| | | doz. | 100 |
|---|---|---|---|
| | **saccharata,** marbled leaves, blue flowers in early spring, 8 ins. | 4/6 | 30/- |

**PYRETHRUM** (Double Varieties)

| | doz. | 100 |
|---|---|---|
| **Aphrodite,** one of the best early double whites | 5/- | 35/- |
| **J. N. Twerdy,** fiery crimson, large flower | 6/- | 42/- |
| **La Vestalle,** flesh-pink, good grower | 4/6 | 30/- |
| **Lord Rosebery,** rich velvety-crimson | 6/- | 42/- |
| **Mme. Patti,** soft rose-pink | 4/6 | 30/- |
| **Mont Blanc,** pure double white | 5/- | 35/- |
| **Queen Mary,** rich pink | 3/6 | 25/- |
| **Triomphe de Paris,** glowing carmine-red | 4/6 | 30/- |
| **Victoria,** good strong-growing white | 4/6 | 30/- |
| **Yvonne Cayeaux,** beautiful creamy-yellow shade | 5/- | 35/- |

**PYRETHRUM** (Single Varieties)

| | doz. | 100 |
|---|---|---|
| **Avalanche,** fine large pure white | 3/6 | 25/- |
| **Comet,** bright crimson, early-flowering | 3/6 | 25/- |
| **Countess Poulett,** deep rosy-carmine | 4/- | 28/- |
| **Dr. Bosch,** salmon-pink, a distinct colour | 6/- | — |
| **Eileen May Robinson,** still the finest clear pink | 3/6 | 25/- |
| **Harold Robinson,** large deep crimson | 4/6 | 30/- |
| **James Kelway,** glowing red | 3/6 | 25/- |
| **Kelway's Glorious,** intense glowing crimson, a new market variety | 11/- | 80/- |

39

| BLOOMS' HARDY PLANTS | doz. | 100 |
|---|---|---|
| **Pyrethrum (Single Varieties)—continued.** | | |
| **Margaret Deed,** red with anemone centre, distinct .. | 6/- | 42/- |
| **Marjorie Robinson,** fine large flowers, glowing deep pink.. | 4/- | 28/- |
| **May Queen,** a shade deeper than *Eileen May Robinson* and flowering several days earlier ; an invaluable market variety .. .. .. .. | 5/- | 35/- |
| **Mrs. Bateman Brown,** intense crimson-scarlet .. .. | 3/6 | 25/- |
| **Mrs. James Leake,** fine large deep pink .. .. .. | 4/- | 28/- |
| **Pink Pearl,** pink flowers, dwarf habit .. .. .. | 3/6 | 25/- |
| **Radiant,** glowing crimson, of fine form, early .. .. | 3/6 | 25/- |
| **Scarlet Glow,** rich deep red, immense flower .. .. | 3/6 | 25/- |
| a **RAMONDIA pyrenaica,** pretty mauve flowers, 6 ins., choice | 6/- | 42/- |
| **RANUNCULUS acris plenus,** pretty double yellow butter-cup flowers, 2 ft., May–September .. .. | 3/6 | 25/- |
| a **gramineus,** fine yellow flowers on grassy foliage, 9 ins. .. | 5/- | 35/- |
| a **RAOULIA australis,** tiny silver-grey carpeting plant .. | 4/- | 28/- |

**ROSA (Miniature Alpine Forms)**

These all meet with a continued demand, having an irresistible appeal to the public.

| | doz. | 100 |
|---|---|---|
| a **Oakington Ruby,** A.M.R.H.S., 1934, has proved to be one of the most popular additions to Alpines for some years. It is a real dwarf rose, and in ordinary soils will not attain a height of more than 12 ins. The flowers are fully double, deep crimson in the bud, opening to rich ruby-carmine often 1½ ins. in diameter. It is very free-flowering, commencing in May and continuing until late autumn. It is quite hardy, and will grow in almost any soil, but prefers sun. .. .. .. .. | 8/- | 60/- |
| a **Peon,** a miniature *polyantha* rose, flowers the size of a shilling, bright red with paler centre ; an outstanding novelty .. .. .. .. | 18/- | 136/- |
| a **pumila,** large double rose-pink flowers, a sure seller .. | 8/- | 60/- |
| a **Rouletti,** true stock, much smaller in every way than *pumila,* flowers quite double .. .. | 14/- | 100/- |
| a **Doncaster's Variety,** somewhat larger in growth, and flowers deeper in colour than the above .. | 14/- | 100/- |
| a **ROSMARINUS prostratus,** dwarf creeping form of *Rosemary* .. .. .. .. .. | 4/6 | 30/- |
| **RUDBECKIA Golden Glow,** deep double yellow flowers, a very fine variety, tall.. .. .. .. | 3/6 | 25/- |
| **Herbstsonne** (*Autumn Sunshine*), large deep yellow flowers, 5 ft. .. .. .. .. | 3/6 | 25/- |
| **hirta Herbstwald,** shades of orange and bronze, 2 ft. .. | 4/- | 28/- |
| **My Joy** (*Mon Plaisir*), rich deep yellow, 2 ft., July–October | 4/- | 28/- |
| **Newmanni,** deep golden with black centre, showy, 2 ft. .. | 3/6 | 25/- |
| **purpurea** (see *ECHINACEA purpurea*). | | |
| **SALVIA azurea grandiflora,** slender spikes of pale blue flowers, 3 ft., September–October .. .. | 5/- | 35/- |

*"a" denotes pot-grown Alpines*

40

BLOOMS' HARDY PLANTS          doz.    100

**Salvia—continued.**

| | | doz. | 100 |
|---|---|---|---|
| **patens Cambridge Blue,** pot-grown, very free, intense blue flowers, 2 ft. .. .. .. .. | | 5/– | 35/– |
| **virgata nemorosa,** violet-purple, a fine border plant, 3 ft. | | 5/– | 35— |
| a **SAPONARIA ocymoides,** deep pink, trailing habit .. | | 3/6 | 25/– |
| a **SANTOLINA incana,** yellow flowers on close gray bushes.. | | 4/– | 28/– |
| a    **incana nana,** neat dwarf form of the above, 6 ins... .. | | 4/6 | — |
| a    **viridis,** similar but bright green foliage, 1 ft. .. .. | | 4/6 | — |

# SAXIFRAGA

### All pot-grown

### AIZOON or ENCRUSTED SECTION

| | | doz. | 100 |
|---|---|---|---|
| a | **aizoon Baldensis,** close mats of silver foliage .. .. | 3/6 | 25/– |
| a | **lutea,** lemon-yellow, 4 ins. .. .. .. .. .. | 3/6 | 25/– |
| a | **pectinata,** heavily silvered rosettes, white flowers .. | 3/6 | 25/– |
| a | **Rex,** white, spotted pink, extra fine .. .. .. | 3/6 | 25/– |
| a | **rosea,** light pink .. .. .. .. .. .. | 3/6 | 25/– |
| a | **rosularis,** smaller than *rosea* .. .. .. .. | 3/6 | 25/– |
| a | **Sturmiana,** white, silvery foliage.. .. .. | 3/6 | 25/– |
| a | **Andrewsii,** green rosettes, pink flowers, 9 ins. .. .. | 5/– | 35/– |
| a | **Burnati,** white sprays on silver rosettes, 6 ins., May–June | 4/– | 28/– |
| a | **Caterhamensis,** large sprays of red spotted white flowers, 2 ft. .. .. .. .. .. .. | 5/– | 35/– |
| a | **cochlearis,** true, like sprays of tiny pearls, extra fine .. | 5/– | 35/– |
| a |    **minor,** a very dwarf form of the above .. .. .. | 5/– | 35/– |
| a | **encrustata,** foliage heavily silvered .. .. .. | 3/6 | 25/– |
| a | **Esther,** neat rosettes, large sprays of pale yellow flowers.. | 3/6 | 25/– |
| a | **Icelandica,** very large sprays of white flowers, a fine variety .. .. .. .. .. | 5/– | 35/– |
| a | **Kathleen Pinsent,** graceful sprays of clear rose-pink flowers produced very freely ; a valuable introduction .. .. .. .. .. | 10/– | — |
| a | **lingulata Albertii,** arching sprays of white, 1 ft., May–June .. .. .. .. .. .. | 4/– | 28/– |
| a |    **superba,** flowers spotted crimson .. .. .. | 4/6 | — |
| a | **MacNabiana,** large silver rosettes, flowers white, spotted crimson, 18 ins. .. .. .. .. | 4/– | 28/– |
| a | **paradoxa,** very pretty silvery rosettes .. .. .. | 4/– | 28/– |

### KABSCHIA SECTION

Flowering from February to April.

| | | doz. | 100 |
|---|---|---|---|
| a | **apiculata,** lemon-yellow, 4 ins., March .. .. .. | 3/6 | 25/– |
| a |    **alba,** white form of the above .. .. .. .. | 3/6 | 25/– |
| a | **Aubrey Prichard,** pink, 2 ins. .. .. .. .. | 6/– | — |
| a | **Boston Spa,** yellow, 3 ins., March .. .. .. .. | 4/6 | 30/– |
| a | **Burseriana minor,** tiny white variety, 1 in. .. .. | 6/– | 42/– |
| a |    **sulphurea,** primrose-yellow, very attractive .. .. | 6/– | 42/– |
| a | **Bursiculata,** large white flowers .. .. .. .. | 6/– | 42/– |

41

BLOOMS' HARDY PLANTS       doz.    100
**(Kabschia Section) Saxifraga continued.**

| | | doz. | 100 |
|---|---|---|---|
| a | **Dainty Dame,** full pink, free-flowering .. .. .. | 6/– | 42/– |
| a | **Elizabethæ,** yellow, 3 ins., March .. .. .. .. | 4/– | 28/– |
| a | **Gem,** pearly pink flowers, 2 ins. .. .. .. .. | 7/– | — |
| a | **Jenkinsæ,** larger than above, very free-flowering .. .. | 6/– | 42/– |
| a | **Kestoniensis,** pure white flowers, 1 in. .. .. .. | 6/– | 42/– |
| a | **Kyrilli,** deep yellow, 3 ins., very early .. .. .. | 5/– | 35/– |
| a | **L. G. Godseff,** fine early yellow, 3 ins. .. .. .. | 4/– | 28/– |
| a | **Macedonica,** bright yellow, close green cushions .. .. | 4/6 | 30/– |
| a | **Paulinæ,** yellow flowers, neat hummocks .. .. .. | 5/– | 35/– |
| a | **Salamoni,** neat grey foliage, white flowers .. .. .. | 4/6 | 30/– |
| a | **Sancta,** bright yellow, 2 ins. .. .. .. .. .. | 5/– | — |

### MOSSY SECTION
Flowering in April and May.

| | | | |
|---|---|---|---|
| a | **Clibrani,** deep red, strongly recommended .. .. .. | 3/6 | 25/– |
| a | **CLOTH OF GOLD,** for foliage effect the whole year round, this will prove a valuable introduction. Forms neat golden hummocks with white flowers in April and May, new .. .. | 7/– | 50/– |
| a | **Crimson King,** fine deep colour .. .. .. .. | 3/6 | — |
| a | **decipiens grandiflora,** crimson-red, large flowers | 3/6 | 25/– |
| a | **Diana,** pale pink flowers, very early and free, 4 ins. .. | 3/6 | 25/– |
| a | **Dubarry,** deep crimson variety, producing masses of 6 in. stems, and very large flowers .. .. | 5/– | 35/– |
| a | **Enchantress,** flesh-pink, very free, 4 ins. .. .. .. | 3/6 | 25/– |
| a | **Feltham Queen,** deep rosy-red, 6 ins. .. .. .. | 3/6 | 25/– |
| a | **Fire King,** crimson-scarlet .. .. .. .. .. | 3/6 | 25/– |
| a | **Gen. Joffre,** deep crimson, neat habit, 4 ins. .. .. | 4/– | 28/– |
| a | **Miss Britten,** pure white, neat habit, 4 ins. .. .. | 3/6 | 25/– |
| a | **Mrs. E. Piper,** fine clear pink, 4 ins. .. .. .. | 3/6 | 25/– |
| a | **Pearly King,** neat pure white, strongly recommended .. | 3/6 | 25/– |
| a | **Peter Pan,** bright crimson, very neat and dwarf .. .. | 3/6 | 25/– |
| a | **Pixie,** deep red, dwarf habit .. .. .. .. .. | 3/6 | 25/– |
| a | **Pompadour,** blood red, very large flowers .. .. .. | 3/6 | 25/– |
| a | **Red Admiral,** fine red, better than *Bathoniensis*, 6 ins. .. | 3/6 | 25/– |
| a | **robusta,** strong-growing pink .. .. .. .. .. | 4/6 | 30/– |
| a | **sanguinea superba,** deepest crimson, 4 ins. .. .. | 3/6 | 25/– |
| a | **Sir Douglas Haig,** fine large crimson, 6 ins. .. .. | 4/– | 28/– |
| a | **Stansfieldii rosea,** pale pink flowers on dense cushions, 2 ins. .. .. .. .. .. .. | 3/6 | 25/– |
| a | **Triumph,** quite the best of the red mossy Saxifrages, a rich deep colour, 6 ins. .. .. .. .. | 6/– | 42/– |
| a | **Whitlavii compacta,** forms bright green mats with white flowers .. .. .. .. .. .. | 3/6 | 25/– |

### SAXIFRAGA, VARIOUS

| | | | |
|---|---|---|---|
| a | **aizoides atro-rubens,** browny-red flowers in summer, 2 ins. | 4/– | 28/– |
| a | **oppositifolia splendens,** mats, of purple-rose flowers, March .. .. .. .. .. .. | 5/– | 35/– |
| a | **Wetterhorn,** bright carmine-red, extra good .. .. | 6/– | 42/– |

*"a" denotes pot-grown Alpines*

42

BLOOMS' HARDY PLANTS          doz.    100

**Saxifraga Various—continued.**

| | | | |
|---|---|---|---|
| a | **Primulaize,** short sprays of carmine, June–August  .. | 4/– | 28/– |
| a | **primuloides Elliott's Variety,** like a tiny *London Pride*.. | 4/6 | 30/– |

COLLECTIONS of SAXIFRAGA, our selection:
ENCRUSTED: 24 in up to 6 sorts for 8/-; 50 in up to
     10 sorts for 15/-; 100 for 28/-.
MOSSY: 24 in up to 6 sorts for 7/6; 50 in up to
     10 sorts for 13/6; 100 for 25/-.

| | | | |
|---|---|---|---|
| a | SCABIOSA **alpina,** pretty mauve flowers, all summer, 6 ins. | 4/6 | 30/– |
| a | **Fischeri,** deep mauve pincushion flowers, 18 ins. ..   .. | 4/– | 28/– |
| a | **Parnassi** (*pterocephela*), lilac-pink, grey foliage, 3 ins.  .. | 3/6 | 25/– |

SCABIOSA CAUCASICA—strong one-year plants.

| | | |
|---|---|---|
| **alba magnifica,** pure white ..    ..    ..    ..    .. | 4/– | 28/– |
| **Clive Greaves,** deep blue, flowers of great substance  .. | 5/– | 35/– |
| **Constancy,** rich blue, very free  ..    ..    .. | 5/– | 35/– |
| **Diamond,** very deep violet-blue  ..    ..    .. | 5/– | 35/– |
| **Goldingensis,** fine blue, really good variety for cutting.. | 4/– | 28/– |
| **Ida Stather,** beautiful light blue, large flowers  ..    .. | 4/– | 28/– |
| **Isaac House,** the deepest blue Scabious  ..    .. | 18/– | — |
| **J. Haskins,** a fine novelty ..    ..    ..    ..    .. | 10/– | 72/– |
| **Mildred,** a new variety of lilac shade  ..    ..  ⌐.. | 12/– | 90/– |
| **Miss Willmott,** the finest white of all  ..    ..    .. | 4/– | 28/– |
| **Torwoodlea,** beautiful silvery-blue flowers of great substance | 12/– | 90/– |

| | | | |
|---|---|---|---|
| a | SCHYSOSTILIS **coccinea,** spikes of bright red flowers in autumn, 1 ft. ..    ..    ..    ..    .. | 3/6 | 25/– |
| a | **Mrs. Hegarty,** beautiful satiny rose-pink form of the above | 4/– | 28/– |
| a | SCUTELIARIA **hastata,** neat spikes of violet-purple  .. | 3/6 | 25/– |
| a | **indica japonica,** mauve-blue, a good plant, 4 ins...    .. | 4/6 | 30/– |

**SEDUM**

| | | | |
|---|---|---|---|
| a | **arboreum,** erect shrubby growth, pinkish-white, 6 ins. .. | 3/6 | 25/– |
| a | **Coral carpet,** mats of green foliage, changing to coral-red in winter  ..    ..    ..    .. | 3/6 | 25/– |
| a | **dasyphyllum,** tiny grey cushions, white flowers, 2 ins.  .. | 3/6 | 25/– |
| a | **Ewersii,** pink flower heads, August–September, 8 ins. .. | 3/6 | 25/– |
| a | **Kamtschaticum,** bright yellow, very free, 6 ins...    .. | 3/6 | 25/– |
| a |   **variegatum,** foliage prettily marked  ..    .. | 3/6 | 25/– |
| a | **Lydium,** reddish-bronze cushions, pink flowers  ..    .. | 3/6 | 25/– |
| a | **Maweanum,** yellow, 4 ins. ..    ..    .. | 3/6 | 25/– |
| a | **Middendorffianum,** bronze foliage, golden flowers, 4 ins. | 3/6 | 25/– |
| a | **monstrosum,** curious cockscomb growths..    .. | 3/6 | 25/– |
| a | **murale,** purple foliage, pink flowers, showy, 4 ins...    .. | 3/6 | 25/– |
| a | **obtusatum,** yellow, red-bronze leaves  ..    .. | 3/6 | 25/– |
| a | **pulchellum,** handsome pink trailing heads..    .. | 3/6 | 25/– |
| a | **rupestre,** erect brönzy growth, yellow heads, 6 ins.  .. | 3/6 | 25/– |
| a | **sexangulare,** small yellow species ..    ..    .. | 3/6 | 25/– |
| a | **Sieboldii variegatum,** pretty leaves and pink flowers .. | 4/– | 28/– |
| a | **spathulifolium purpureum,** plum-purple foliage    .. | 4/6 | 30/– |

43

BLOOMS' HARDY PLANTS        doz. 100

**Sedum—continued.**

|  |  | doz. | 100 |
|---|---|---|---|
| | **spectabile Brilliant,** bright deep pink heads in autumn.. | 4/– | 28/– |
| | **roseum,** paler colour than above, showy .. .. | 3/6 | 25/– |
| a | **spurium coccineum,** bright rosy-red trailing heads .. | 3/6 | 25/– |
| a | <u>**Schorbüser Blut,**</u> a novelty which is sure to become popular. The buds and stems are bronzy-red, deep bright carmine-red in flower and dark crimson when finished. Flowers very freely during July, August and September, 3 ins. ..   ..   ..   ..   ..   .. | 7/– | 50/– |

**COLLECTIONS of SEDUM, our selection: 24 in up to 6 sorts for 7/-; 50 in up to 10 sorts for 13/-; 100 for 24/-.**

### SEMPERVIVUM.

|  |  | doz. | 100 |
|---|---|---|---|
| a | **arachnoideum,** the cobweb houseleek .. .. .. | 3/6 | 25/– |
| a | **Laggeri,** a fine form with deep pink flowers, 4 ins. .. | 3/6 | 25/– |
| a | **Brauni,** tiny silvery-grey rosettes .. .. .. .. | 4/– | 28/– |
| a | **cornutum,** rosettes green, tipped bronze .. .. .. | 4/– | 28/– |
| a | **Doellianum,** fine cobweb species, pink flowers .. .. | 4/– | 28/– |
| a | **Hookeri,** pretty little form .. .. .. .. .. | 4/– | 28/– |
| a | **Reufelli,** large green rosettes.. .. .. .. .. | 3/6 | 25/– |
| a | **Ruthenicum,** handsome green rosettes, 4 ins. diameter .. | 3/6 | 25/– |
| a | **triste,** coppery foliage, pale pink flowers, 6 ins. .. .. | 3/6 | 25/– |
| a | **violaceum,** large plum-coloured rosettes .. .. .. | 4/6 | 30/– |

**COLLECTIONS of SEMPERVIVUM, our selection: 24 in up to 6 sorts for 8/-; 50 for 14/-; 100 for 26/-.**

|  |  | doz. | 100 |
|---|---|---|---|
| a | **SENECIO abrotanifolius,** ferny foliage, bright orange flowers, 6 ins., May–June .. .. .. .. | 4/6 | 30/– |
| | **clivorum Orange Queen,** deep orange flowers, large brown leaves, 4 ft. .. .. .. .. | 5/– | 35/– |
| | **Othello,** dark foliage, yellow flowers, August–September | 5/– | 35/– |
| | **Hessei,** massive spikes of bright orange flowers, a striking plant, 5 ft., July–September .. .. | 15/– | 100/– |

(The above three varieties of SENECIO like a damp situation.)

|  |  | doz. | 100 |
|---|---|---|---|
| | **SIDALCEA Brilliant,** bright deep rosy-red, 2 ft., July–August .. .. .. .. .. | | |
| | **Elsie Heugh,** tall spikes of satiny-pink flowers, 3 ft. .. | 5/– | 35/– |
| | **Elstead Crimson,** fine deep crimson, 3 ft., July–August .. | 5/– | 35/– |
| | **June Rose,** light rose-pink, 2 ft., early .. .. .. | 4/– | 28/– |
| | **Lindbergh,** ruby-red .. .. .. .. .. .. | 4/6 | 30/– |
| | **Monarch,** fine rose-pink, late-flowering, 3 ft. .. .. | 4/– | 28/– |
| | **Mrs. H. Borodaile,** rich crimson, new .. .. .. | 7/– | 50/– |
| | **Pink Beauty,** deep pink, strong growing .. .. .. | 4/– | 28/– |
| | **Pompadour,** bronzy-red flowers with a double centre .. | 6/– | — |
| | **Rev. Page Roberts,** pale pink, large flowers .. .. | 4/6 | 30/– |
| | **Rose Queen,** rich rose-pink, strong grower .. .. .. | 4/– | 28/– |
| | **Scarlet Beauty,** hardly scarlet, but a good bright colour .. | 4/– | 28/– |

BLOOMS' HARDY PLANTS        doz.   100

**Sidalcea—continued.**

| | doz. | 100 |
|---|---|---|
| **Sussex Beauty,** large soft pink flowers, 3 ft., July–August | 6/– | 42/– |
| **Wensleydale,** very deep rose-pink .. | 4/– | 28/– |
| a **SILENE acaulis saxatilis,** pink flowers on green mats .. | 3/6 | 25/– |
| a **alpestris flore pleno,** erect sprays of double white flowers, 4 ins. .. | 3/6 | 25/– |
| a **Elizabethæ,** bright rosy-crimson, 4 ins. .. | 5/– | — |
| a **Schaftæ,** valuable late Alpine, bright pink, 6 ins. .. | 3/6 | 25/– |
| a **SISYRINCHIUM bellum,** violet flowers, rush-like growth, 4 ins. .. | 3/6 | 25/– |
| a **Bermudianum,** resembles a miniature Iris in growth, violet .. | 3/6 | 25/– |
| a **boreale,** bright yellow, 4 ins. .. | 3/6 | 25/– |
| a **Californicum,** pretty yellow-flowered species .. | 4/– | 28/– |
| **SOLIDAGO Ballardi,** giant plumes of golden flowers, late | 3/6 | 25/– |
| a **brachystachys,** fine dwarf species, yellow, 8 ins., August.. | 3/6 | 25/– |
| a **robusta,** a little larger than the foregoing, but in every way an improvement, new .. | 12/– | 90/– |
| **Fruhgold,** stiff stems with arching sprays .. | 4/6 | 30/– |
| **Gold Elfe,** erect plumes of brightest golden-yellow .. | 4/6 | 30/– |
| **Golden Wings,** yellow, 6 ft., showy, October .. | 3/6 | 25/– |
| **Goldstrahl,** fine deep yellow variety, 3 ft., August–October | 4/6 | 30/– |
| **Mimosa,** golden-yellow, heads nearly flat, 3 ft. .. | 4/– | 28/– |
| **Peter Pan,** very dwarf variety with feathery yellow heads | 4/6 | 30/– |
| **virgaurea præcox,** valuable June-flowering variety, 3 ft. | 3/6 | 25/– |
| **SPIRÆA aruncus,** noble plumes of creamy-white, 6 ft. .. | 5/– | 35/– |
| **aruncus Kneiffi,** pure white, finely cut foliage, 2 ft. .. | 8/– | 60/– |
| a **bullata,** tiny shrubby species, heads of rosy-crimson, 6 ins., June–August .. | 5/– | 35/– |
| a **decumbens,** creamy-white, 4 ins. .. | 5/– | 35/– |
| **filipendula plena,** heads of double white flowers .. | 4/6 | 30/– |
| **palmata elegans,** clusters of pink and white flower heads, 2½ ft. .. | 5/– | 35/– |
| **venusta magnifica,** fine spikes of deep carmine-red, 4 ft. | 5/– | 35/– |
| a **STATICE bellidifolia,** very dwarf, sprays of mauve flowers, 9 ins. .. | 5/– | 35/– |
| **incana,** white everlasting, valuable for drying .. | 4/– | 28/– |
| **dumosa,** neat dwarf form of the above .. | 4/6 | 30/– |
| **latifolia,** the mauve *Sea Lavender,* fine for cutting.. | 4/– | 28/– |
| **Perezii multiflora,** deep blue, 2 ft. .. | 5/– | 35/– |
| **STOKESIA cyanea præcox,** light blue, 1 ft., July–September .. | 4/6 | 30/– |
| a **cyanea purpurea,** large rich mauve-blue flowers .. | 6/– | — |
| a **TEUCRIUM chamædrys,** neat shrubby growth, lilac-pink | 4/– | 28/– |
| a **polium** (syn. *aureum*), attractive grey woolly hummocks | 3/6 | 25/– |
| a **pyrenaicum,** pretty heads of creamy flowers in summer, 4 ins. .. | 3/6 | 25/– |

**45**

BLOOMS' HARDY PLANTS

|  |  | doz. | 100 |
|---|---|---|---|
| **THALICTRUM adiantifolium minus,** like Maidenhair fern | | 4/6 | 30/- |
| **aquilegifolium,** shades of rose and mauve, very showy, 5 ft. | | 4/- | 28/- |
| **dipterocarpum,** violet-mauve, fine border plant, pot-grown | | 4/6 | 30/- |
| **album,** pretty white form | | 6/- | 42/- |
| **flavum,** showy spikes of yellow flowers, 4 ft. | | 4/- | 28/- |
| **glaucum,** yellow, greyish foliage, 4 ft. | | 5/- | 35/- |

**THYMUS**

| | | | doz. | 100 |
|---|---|---|---|---|
| a | **argenteus Silver Queen,** a really good foliage plant, aromatic | | 3/6 | 25/- |
| a | **aureus,** golden lemon-scented Thyme | | 3/6 | 25/- |
| a | **azoricus,** forms green mats with purple flowers | | 3/6 | 25/- |
| a | **Doerfleri,** grey woolly mats, rose-pink flowers | | 5/- | 35/- |
| a | **ericæfolius,** tiny bushes of golden-green, 4 ins. | | 4/- | 28/- |
| a | **Herba-Barona,** flowers pink, foliage caraway-scented | | 3/6 | 25/- |
| a | **micans,** pink flowers on close hummocks | | 3/6 | 25/- |
| a | **nitidus,** little bushes covered in pink flowers, 6 ins., May–June | | 4/- | 28/- |
| a | **serpyllum,** close mats, pink flowers.. | | 3/6 | 25/- |
| a | **albus,** showy white form | | 3/6 | 25/- |
| a | **Annie Hall,** flesh-pink | | 3/6 | 25/- |
| a | **aureus,** lemon-scented mat, forming golden foliage | | 3/6 | 25/- |
| a | **coccineus,** bright rosy-red, makes a fine show | | 3/6 | 25/- |
| a | **lanuginosus,** mats of grey woolly foliage | | 3/6 | 25/- |
| a | **minus,** the smallest of all, pink | | 3/6 | 25/- |

**COLLECTIONS of THYMUS, our selection: 24 in up to 6 sorts for 7/-; 50 in up to 10 sorts for 13/-; 100 for 24/-.**

**TRADESCANTIA.** Very useful dwarf herbaceous plants in flower from June to September.

|  |  | doz. | 100 |
|---|---|---|---|
| **virginica alba,** pure white | | 3/6 | 25/- |
| **cœrulea,** clear blue.. | | 3/6 | 25/- |
| **plena,** double form of the above.. | | 4/6 | 30/- |
| **J. C. Wequelin,** large Cambridge-blue flowers | | 4/6 | 30/- |
| **Leonora,** large rich Oxford-blue flowers.. | | 4/6 | 30/- |
| **purpurea,** rich violet, 1½ ft. | | 3/6 | 25/- |
| **Richardsonii,** light blue | | 3/6 | 25/- |
| **rubra,** rosy-red | | 3/6 | 25/- |

**TRITOMA** (see *Kniphofia*).

**TROLLIUS.** These are becoming increasingly popular, especially for cut flower purposes, and our stock of strong one-year plants is one of the best in the country.

|  |  | doz. | 100 |
|---|---|---|---|
| **Canary Bird,** light yellow, very fine for cutting, 2½ ft. | | 4/6 | 30/- |
| **Commander-in-Chief,** deep orange flowers of perfect form, outstanding | | 9/- | 70/- |
| **Earliest of All,** yellow, 2½ ft... | | 4/- | 28/- |

46

BLOOMS' HARDY PLANTS doz. 100
**Trollius—continued.**

| | doz. | 100 |
|---|---|---|
| **Empire Day,** fine deep orange, 2 ft... | 5/- | 35/- |
| **Etna,** beautiful deep glowing orange.. | 4/6 | 30/- |
| **Europæus superbus,** large pale yellow, 2 ft. | 4/6 | 30/- |
| **Fire Globe,** rich glowing orange | 5/- | 35/- |
| **First Lancers,** bright orange, deeper centre | 6/- | 42/- |
| **Golden Wonder,** deep orange, very compact | 6/- | 42/- |
| **Goldquelle,** golden-yellow, large flowers | 5/- | 35/- |
| **japonicus fl. pl.** (syn. *Fortunei plena*), orange, semi-double | 6/- | 42/- |
| **ledebouri Golden Queen,** distinct, late-flowering variety | 5/- | 35/- |
| **Orange Crest,** large open flowers with deep orange stamens | 5/- | 35/- |
| **Orange Globe,** rich deep orange, one of the best .. | 5/- | 35/- |
| **Orange Princess,** lovely golden-yellow, strong grower, 2½ ft. .. | 5/- | 35/- |
| **Princess Juliana,** large deep orange-yellow | 5/- | 35/- |
| **T. Smith,** clear yellow | 6/- | — |

| | | doz. | 100 |
|---|---|---|---|
| a | **TUNICA saxifraga,** like a miniature pink *Gypsophila*, 6 ins. | 3/6 | 25/- |
| a | **saxifraga rosea flore pleno,** a beautiful form, large double pink flowers, one of the finest late summer-flowering Alpines | 5/- | 35/- |
| | **VALERIANA** (*Centranthus*), pink and red flowers .. | 3/6 | 25/- |
| | **Braggs' Variety,** a new variety with intense deep red flowers .. | 10/- | — |
| | **VERBASCUM Caledonia,** fine spikes of rosy-buff, 4 ft. .. | 5/- | 35/- |
| | **C. L. Adams,** a fine tall yellow variety | 5/- | 35/- |
| | **Cotswold Beauty,** biscuit-yellow with lilac centre, 4 ft. | 4/6 | 30/- |
| | **Cotswold Gem,** soft amber colour with purple centre .. | 4/6 | 30/- |
| | **densiflorum,** handsome spikes of deep bronzy-yellow .. | 4/6 | 30/- |
| | **Gainsborough,** grey woolly foliage, strong spikes of rich yellow flowers, a striking variety .. | 5/- | 35/- |
| | **vernale,** deep yellow, large flowers and good spike.. | 5/- | 35/- |
| | **VERBENA Bonariensis,** strong bushes of deep lavender flowers, very showy .. | 4/6 | 30/- |
| a | **chamædrifolia,** trailing stems of brightest scarlet flowers, always popular although somewhat tender | 3/6 | 25/- |
| a | **tenera Mahoneti,** mauve and white striped flowers, trailing .. | 4/6 | 30/- |
| | **VERONICA** | | |
| | **amethystina,** short spikes of deep blue, 1 ft., June .. | 4/- | 28/- |
| a | **Balfouriana,** flowers lilac, dwarf shrubby habit .. | 3/6 | 25/- |
| a | **Bidwilli Vera,** very minute growth, white flowers, 3 ins. | 4/- | 28/- |
| a | **corymbosa stricta,** deep blue, late-flowering, 6 ins. .. | 3/6 | 25/- |
| | **gentianoides,** spikes of pale blue flowers in spring, 1 ft. .. | 3/6 | 25/- |
| | **incana rosea,** silvery-grey foliage, short bright pink spikes, very free-flowering, 1 ft. .. | 7/- | 50/- |
| a | **Loddon Blue,** a very bright and attractive plant, 3 ins., May–June .. | 4/- | 28/- |
| a | **Miss Willmott,** small shrubby growth, pink flowers, 8 ins. | 3/6 | 25/- |

47

BLOOMS' HARDY PLANTS          doz.    100

**Veronica—continued.**

| | | doz. | 100 |
|---|---|---|---|
| a | **prostrata Mrs. Holt,** fine pink variety, recommended, 4 ins. | 4/– | 28/– |
| a | **rupestris,** fine blue Alpine, trailing habit | 3/6 | 25/– |
| a | **rosea,** pretty pink form of the foregoing | 3/6 | 25/– |
| | **Royal Blue,** very free, 9 ins., May–June | 3/6 | 25/– |
| a | **Shirley Blue,** rich blue, makes a fine show, 9 ins. | 3/6 | 25/– |
| | **spicata alba,** neat spikes of white flowers, 2½ ft. | 4/– | 28/– |
| | **alpina rosea,** short spikes of light pink flowers, very compact | 5/– | 35/– |
| | **Blue Peter,** bright deep blue, 18 ins., July–September | 4/6 | 30/– |
| | **Erica,** deep rose-pink, 1 ft., June–August | 5/– | 35/– |
| | **Romiley Purple,** an outstanding variety, producing neat spikes of deep violet-blue flowers over a long period, 18 ins. | 5/– | 35/– |
| | **Wells' Variety,** short spikes of rich blue, very free | 4/6 | 30/– |
| a | **Spode Blue,** large light blue flowers on trailing sprays | 3/6 | 25/– |
| | **subsessilis Hendersonii,** short branched spikes of deepest violet flowers ; a plant which can be strongly recommended, 1 ft. | 5/– | 35/– |
| a | **teucrium Skellumi** (syn. *Bastardi*), light blue, trailing | 3/6 | 25/– |
| | **Trehane,** pale blue flowers, golden foliage | 5/– | 35/– |
| | **True Blue,** 9 ins., May–July | 3/6 | 25/– |
| | **Wendy,** silvery-grey foliage, bright blue flowers, 18 ins., July–August | 4/6 | 30/– |

COLLECTIONS of VERONICA, pot-grown, our selection: 24 in up to 6 sorts for 8/-; 50 in up to 10 sorts for 14/-; 100 for 27/-.

**VIOLA** (Rock Varieties)

| | | doz. | 100 |
|---|---|---|---|
| a | **cornuta Jersey Gem Improved,** deep violet, recommended | 3/6 | 25/– |
| a | **gracilis Clarence Elliott,** pretty white variety | 4/6 | 30/– |
| a | **Devon Cream,** creamy-yellow | 4/6 | 30/– |
| a | **Dream,** light primrose-yellow | 4/6 | 30/– |
| a | **Golden Wave,** bright yellow | 4/6 | 30/– |
| a | **Grandeur,** fine deep royal purple | 4/6 | 30/– |
| a | **Major** (syn. *Payne's variety*), rich deep violet | 4/6 | 30/– |
| a | **Irish Molly,** a delightful effect of green, yellow and brown intermerged, the reverse of the petals being dull blue | 4/– | 28/– |
| a | **Jackanapes,** bright yellow and mahogany-brown | 5/– | 35/– |
| a | **King Henry,** a tiny hybrid, purple flowers, very free | 4/– | 28/– |
| a | **Olympica,** violet-purple, edge of petals flecked white | 6/– | 42/– |
| a | **T. E. Wolstenholme,** improved *Arkwright's Ruby* | 5/– | 35/– |

| | | doz. | 100 |
|---|---|---|---|
| a | **WAHLENBERGIA grandiflora Mariesi** (syn. *platycodon*), light and deep blue, 1 ft. | 4/6 | 30/– |
| a | **pumilio,** grey tufted foliage, large violet-purple cups, 1 in. | 6/– | 42/– |
| a | **serpyllifolia major,** close-growing variety, large shiny purple bells | 8/– | 60/– |

*"a" denotes pot-grown Alpines*

48

# Classified List of Alpines suitable for Special Purposes

## FOR CRAZY PAVING

ACÆNA Buchanani
AJUGA Rainbow
ANTENNARIA dioica
ARENARIA balearica
  cæspitosa aurea
CAMPANULA abietina
  pulla
  turbinata albescens
  and others
GLOBULARIA nudicaule
HELICHRYSUM bellidioides
HUTCHINSIA alpina
HYPSELLA longiflora
LINARIA æquitriloba
  globosa
  hepaticæfolia
LIPPIA repens
MAZUS reptans
NIEREMBERGIA rivularis
POTENTILLA verna nana
RAOULIA australis

SAXIFRAGA aizoon Baldensis
  rosularis
  and others
SAXIFRAGA (Mossy) Clibrani
  Stansfieldii rosea
  Whitlavii compacta
SEDUM Coral Carpet
  dasyphyllum
  Lydium
  and others
THYMUS azoricus
  Doerfleri
  serpyllum
  albus
  Annie. Hall
  aureus
  coccineus
  lanuginosus
  minus
VERONICA Spode Blue

## FOR DRY WALLS

ALYSSUM saxatile compactum
ANTHYLLIS montana rubra
ARABIS aubrietioides
ARENARIA montana grandi-
  flora
ARMERIA corsica
  Laucheana
AUBRIETIA Aubrey Prichard
CAMPANULA carpatica
  muralis
  Poscharskyana
CHEIRANTHUS Harpur Crewe
  Rufus
DIANTHUS cæsius fl. pl.
  deltoides Brilliant
  Little Jock
  Prichardi fl. pl.
  and others
FRANKENIA lævis
GYPSOPHILA fratensis
  repens rosea
HEDERA conglomerata
HELIANTHEMUM (in variety)
HYPERICUM polyphyllum

LINUM flavum compactum
MUEHLENBECKIA complexa
PHLOX subulata (in variety)
POTENTILLA Tonguei
SCABIOSA Parnassi
SEDUM Ewersii
  Maweanum
  murale
  rupestre
  sexangulare
SEMPERVIVUM triste
  and others
SILENE Schaftæ
TEUCRIUM polium
THYMUS argenteus Silver
                      Queen
  aureus
  Herba-Barona
  nitidus
TUNICA saxifraga
  saxifraga rosea fl. pl.
VERONICA rupestris
  Shirley Blue

For PRICES OF COLLECTIONS see page 50.

49

# COLLECTIONS OF ALPINES

## For your Garden Construction Work, Stock, or for any other Purpose

Hundreds of customers every year prove that these Collections represent the finest value offered to the Trade.

The selection must be left to us, but we are willing to include any varieties specially required, if stocks of same permit.

Only best quality pot-grown plants and really good varieties are selected.

| | | | |
|---|---|---|---|
| 100 in 10–50 sorts, labelled | .. | **24/-** |
| 250 „ 10–50 | „ | .. | **59/-** |
| 500 „ 20–100 | „ | .. | **116/-** |
| 1000 „ 25–150 | „ | .. | **230/-** |
| 100 „ 100 | „ | .. | **28/-** |

Carriage paid nett on 100 lots for C.W.O.

❖

# ALPINES SELECTED FOR
# SPECIAL PURPOSES

| | doz. | 100 |
|---|---|---|
| For CRAZY PAVING, in good variety | **3/9** | **26/-** |
| „ DRY WALL, etc. „ | **4/-** | **27/-** |
| „ SHADY POSITION .. .. | **4/6** | **32/-** |
| „ MORAINE, SCREE or Sink Gardens | **6/-** | **45/-** |

Carriage paid nett for C.W.O. on lots of 100 or more ; if under, add 10 per cent. for carriage. Not less than 1 doz. supplied, nor less than 25 at 100 rate.

50

# COLLECTIONS OF
# HERBACEOUS PLANTS

Specially selected for planting colour borders, etc., including tall and dwarf growing plants, in really good variety.

| From 3 to 8 plants of each sort. | From 9 to 16 plants of each sort. |
|---|---|
| **30**/– per 100. | **28**/– per 100. |
| **72**/– for 250. | **68**/– for 250. |
| **138**/– for 500. | **130**/– for 500. |
| **270**/– per 1000. | **250**/– per 1000. |

Specially selected for cut flower purposes :—

| **28**/– per | 100 in up to 10 sorts. |
| **68**/– for | 250 ,, 25 ,, |
| **130**/– for | 500 ,, 50 ,, |
| **250**/– per | 1000 ,, 50 ,, |

Carriage paid nett for cash with order on 100 lots.

———— ❖ ————

# ALPINES IN BUD AND FLOWER
# FOR SHOP SALE

Available from March to July in really good selling varieties. Details and prices of these will be seen in our Spring List issued in March.

———— ❖ ————

# ALPINES IN FLOWER
# FOR SHOWS

Available in extra good quality from April to September.

51

# SOME OF THE ADVANTAGES
# OF BLOOMS' SERVICE

(1) Having no retail connections whatsoever, all our energies are devoted to supplying the needs of the Trade.

(2) **DESPATCH.** Knowing how important it is that trade orders should be executed promptly, we make it a rule to despatch all orders wherever possible within 24 hours of receipt.

(3) **SITUATION.** Oakington is centrally situated as regards railway connections, which can be easily made to all parts of the country.
Risks of delay in transit are thereby minimised.

(4) **CLIMATIC CONDITIONS.** In this part of the country the climate is such that plants grown here stand the best possible chance of surviving removal, especially to northern districts.

(5) **SOIL.** The soil, too, is of a nature that ensures safe transplanting, as it is neither too light nor too heavy, but is a good medium light loam.

(6) We say in all sincerity that we do our utmost to satisfy and please our customers in every way possible.

W. HEFFER & SONS LTD., CAMBRIDGE, ENGLAND

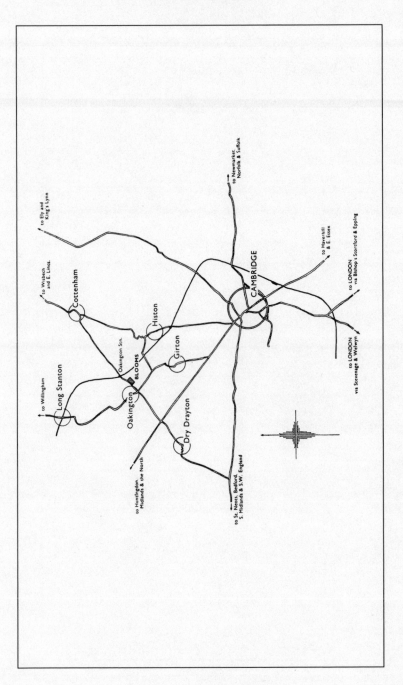

# APPENDIX 1

## CHECKLIST OF PLANTS RAISED AND NAMED BY THE AUTHOR

| Genus | Species | Cultivar name | Approx. raising date |
|---|---|---|---|
| Achillea | *taygetea* | Moonshine | 1954 |
| | | Anthea | 1982 |
| Aconitum | *napellus* | Bressingham Spire | 1957 |
| | | Blue Sceptre | 1957 |
| | *septentrionale* | Ivorine | 1958 |
| Agapanthus | *campanulatus* | Bressingham Blue | 1972 |
| | | Bressingham White | 1972 |
| | | Bressingham Bounty | 1981 |
| Anemone | *japonica* | Bressingham Glow | 1968 |
| Aster | *novi-belgii* | Royal Velvet | 1959 |
| | | Royal Ruby | 1966 |
| | *amellus* × *thomsonii* | Flora's Delight | 1964 |
| Astilbe | | Bressingham Beauty | 1967 |
| | | Elizabeth Bloom | 1982 |
| | | Rosemary Bloom | 1981 |
| | *simplicifolia* | Sprite | 1969 |

| Genus | Species | Cultivar name | Approx. raising date |
|---|---|---|---|
| Astrantia | *major* | Ruby Glow | 1983 |
| Aubrieta | | Bressingham Pink | 1969 |
| | | Red Carpet | 1972 |
| | | Mary Poppins | 1969 |
| | | Lilac Time | 1933 |
| | | Oakington Lavender | 1933 |
| Bergenia | | Bressingham White | 1976 |
| | | Bressingham Salmon | 1978 |
| | | Bressingham Ruby | 1984 |
| Campanula | *cochlearfolia* | Oakington Blue | 1929 |
| | | Cambridge Blue | 1929 |
| | | Blue Tit | 1933 |
| Campanula | *lactiflora* | Pouffe | 1935 |
| | *latifolia* | Gloaming | 1957 |
| | | White ladies | 1957 |
| | *latiloba* | Percy Piper | 1959 |
| | *wockei* | Puck | 1961 |
| | | Constellation | 1974 |
| | *carpatica* | Blue Moonlight | 1969 |
| | | Bressingham White | 1969 |
| | | Blue Sheen | 1986 |
| | *glomerata* | Purple Pixie | 1967 |
| Chrysanthemum | | Autumn Melody | 1984 |
| | | Peter Pan | 1984 |
| | | Peter Sare | 1987 |
| | | Snowcap | 1978 |
| Crocosmia | | Bressingham Blaze | 1966 |
| | | Emberglow | 1966 |
| | | Firebird | 1966 |
| | | Lucifer | 1966 |
| | | Spitfire | 1966 |
| | | Vulcan | 1966 |

# APPENDIX 1

| Genus | Species | Cultivar name | Approx. raising date |
|---|---|---|---|
| | | Bressingham Beacon | 1979 |
| | | Jenny Bloom | 1979 |
| Dianthus | | Dubarry | 1928 |
| | | Oakington | 1928 |
| Dicentra | *formosa* | Adrian Bloom | 1978 |
| Echinacea | *purpurea* | Robert Bloom | 1954 |
| Erigeron | | Charity | 1951 |
| | | Dignity | 1951 |
| | | Felicity | 1951 |
| | | Festivity | 1951 |
| | | Frivolity | 1951 |
| | | Gaiety | 1951 |
| | | Prosperity | 1951 |
| | | Serenity | 1951 |
| | | Sincerity | 1951 |
| | | Unity | 1951 |
| | | Vanity | 1951 |
| | | Dimity | 1953 |
| | | Amity | 1962 |
| Euphorbia | *griffithii* | Fireglow | 1954 |
| Gaillardia | | Mandarin | 1953 |
| Geranium | *cinereum* | Apple Blossom | 1962 |
| | | Ballerina | 1962 |
| | *armenum* | Bressingham Flair | 1960 |
| | | Lawrence Flatman | 1980 |
| Geum | | Baby Tangerine | 1982 |
| Helenium | | Bruno | 1960 |
| | | Butterpat | 1960 |
| | | Coppelia | 1965 |
| Helleborus | *orientalis* | Heartsease | 1953 |
| | | Winter Cheer | 1953 |
| Heuchera | *brizoides* | Blooms Variety | 1924 |

| Genus | Species | Cultivar name | Approx. raising date |
|---|---|---|---|
| | | Pink Spray | 1924 |
| | | Coral Cloud | 1932 |
| | | Crimson Cascade | 1932 |
| | *sanguinea* | Apple Blossom | 1932 |
| | | Corallion | 1932 |
| | | Freedom | 1932 |
| | | Gaiety | 1932 |
| | | Mary Rose | 1932 |
| | | Oakington Jewel | 1932 |
| | | Jubilee | 1932 |
| | | Bressingham Blaze | 1950 |
| | | Carmen | 1950 |
| | | Gloriana | 1950 |
| | | Ibis | 1950 |
| | *brizoides* | Lady Romney | 1950 |
| | | Pearl Drops | 1950 |
| | | Pretty Polly | 1950 |
| | | Red Spangles | 1950 |
| | | Scintillation | 1950 |
| | | Sparkler | 1950 |
| | | Splendour | 1950 |
| | | Snowflakes | 1950 |
| | | Sunset | 1950 |
| | *cylindrica* | Hyperion | 1959 |
| | | Green Ivory | 1968 |
| | | Green Marble | 1973 |
| Heucherella | | Bridget Bloom | 1953 |
| Kniphofia | | Bressingham Comet | 1963 |
| | | Bressingham Flame | 1963 |
| | | Bressingham Torch | 1963 |
| | | Candlelight | 1975 |
| | | Ice Queen | 1979 |

| Genus | Species | Cultivar name | Approx. raising date |
|---|---|---|---|
| | | Ivory Pinnacle | 1981 |
| | | Percy's Pride | 1975 |
| | | Shining Sceptre | 1975 |
| Ligularia | | The Rocket | 1973 |
| | | Sungold | 1976 |
| Mertensia | | Blue Drops | 1972 |
| Mimulus | | Firedragon | 1982 |
| | | Mandarin | 1985 |
| Omphalodes | | Anthea Bloom | 1961 |
| Penstemon | | Amethyst | 1980 |
| Perovskia | | Blue Haze | 1965 |
| Phlox | *subulata* | Blue Eyes | 1929 |
| | *maculata* | Omega | 1966 |
| | *paniculata* | Eva Cullum | 1978 |
| | | Bill Green | 1978 |
| | | Franz Schubert | 1980 |
| | | Harlequin | 1959 |
| | | Mary Fox | 1975 |
| | | Mother of Pearl | 1954 |
| Polygonum | *affine* | Dimity | 1977 |
| | *amplexicaule* | Firetail | 1966 |
| | | Redstart | 1985 |
| Potentilla | | Blazeaway | 1971 |
| | | Flamenco | 1973 |
| Pulmonaria | | Green Marble | 1983 |
| Pyrethrum | | Ariel | 1961 |
| | | Bellarion | 1961 |
| | | Inferno | 1961 |
| | | Prospero | 1961 |
| | | Taurus | 1961 |
| | | Vanessa | 1961 |
| | | Venus | 1961 |

| Genus | Species | Cultivar name | Approx. raising date |
|-------|---------|---------------|----------------------|
| Salvia | | Indigo | 1962 |
| Saponaria | | Bressingham | 1956 |
| Saxifraga | Mossy | Carnival | 1952 |
| | | Dubarry | 1952 |
| | | Elf | 1962 |
| | | Fairy | 1962 |
| | | Gaiety | 1962 |
| | | Pearly King | 1962 |
| | | Sprite | 1962 |
| | *apiculata* | Gold Dust | 1959 |
| Scabiosa | *caucasica* | Bressingham White | 1955 |
| | *graminifolia* | Pincushion | 1968 |
| *Schizostylis* | *coccinea* | Major | 1964 |
| | | November Cheer | 1969 |
| Sidalcea | | Oberon | 1963 |
| | | Puck | 1963 |
| | | Titania | 1963 |
| Thymus | *doefleri* | Bressingham | 1966 |
| Tradescantia | *virginiana* | Isis | 1953 |
| Trollius | | Bressingham Sunshine | 1979 |
| Veronica | *prostrata* | Blue Sheen | 1977 |
| | *teucrium* | Blue Fountain | 1965 |
| | | Blue Eyes | 1967 |
| | *spicata* × *incana* | Barcarolle | 1952 |
| | | Minuet | 1952 |
| | | Pavane | 1952 |
| | | Saraband | 1959 |

# APPENDIX 2

## CHECKLIST OF PLANTS DISTRIBUTED MAINLY BY THE AUTHOR

| Genus | Species | Cultivar name |
|---|---|---|
| Aconitum | *japonicum* | |
| | *vilmorinianum* | |
| Adenophora | *tashiroi* | |
| Adonis | *amurensis* | |
| | *a.* | 'Plena' |
| | *vernalis* | |
| | *volgensis* | |
| Agastache | *anisata* | |
| Agropyron | *magellanica* | |
| Anaphalis | *yedoensis* | |
| Andropleion | *scoparius* | |
| Anemone | *rivularis* | |
| Aquilegia | *vulgaris* | 'Nora Barlow' |
| Aruncus | *dioicus* | 'Glasnevin' |
| *Campanula* | *alaskana* | |
| | *alliarifolia* | 'Ivory Bells' |
| | × 'Stella' | |
| | *trachelium* | 'Bernice' |
| Carex | *morrowii* | 'Evergold' |
| Centaurea | ? *hyperleuca* | |

| Genus | Species | Cultivar name |
|---|---|---|
| Cerastium | *columnae* | |
| Chelone | *obliqua alba* | |
| Chrysanthemum | *corymbosum* | |
| | *parthenium* | 'Snowstorm' |
| Cichorium | *intybus roseus* | |
| Deinanthe | *bifida* | |
| Diascea | *rigescens* | |
| | *elegans* | |
| Disporum | *flavum* | |
| Doronicum | *caucasicum* | 'Spring Beauty' |
| Echinacea | *purpurea* | 'White Lustre' |
| Epimedium | *sagittifolium* | |
| Erysimum | | |
| (Cheiranthus) | | 'Constant Cheer' |
| Euphorbia | *longifolia* | |
| | *wulfeni* | 'Burrow Silver' |
| Filipendula | *ulmaria aurea* | |
| | *u. variegata* | |
| Fuchsia | × 'Oetnang' | |
| Gentiana | *doeringiana* | |
| | × 'Blackboys' | |
| Geranium | × 'Anne Folkard' | |
| | *wvlossovianum* | |
| Helianthemum | 'Annabel' | |
| Heuchera | *cylindrica* | |
| | *villosa* | |
| Hosta | *rectifolia* | |
| | *sieboldiana* | 'Bressingham Blue' |
| | *ventricosa* | 'Variegata' |
| Houttuynia | *cordata* | 'Chameleon' |
| Hydrangea | × 'Preziosa' | |
| Hyssopus | *aristatus* | |
| Inula | *barbata* | |
| Kirengeshoma | *koreana* | |

APPENDIX 2

| Genus | Species | Cultivar name |
|---|---|---|
| Liriope | *muscari* | |
| Lychnis | *chalcedonica* | 'Plena' |
| Macleaya | *cordata* | 'Flamingo' |
| Melittis | *melissophyllum* | |
| Meum | *athamanticum* | |
| Miscanthus | *sinensis* | 'Silver Feather' |
| Nepeta | *grandiflora* | 'Blue Beauty' |
| | *govaniana* | |
| Oenothera | *linearis* | |
| | *kunthiana* | |
| Ononis | *antiquorum* | |
| Ophiopogon | *planiscapus nigrescens* | |
| Origanum | *vulgare* | 'Herrenhausen' |
| Paeonia | *tenuifolia* | 'Early Bird' |
| | × *woodwardiana* | |
| Pennisetum | *orientalis* | |
| Penstemon | *hartwegii* | 'Firebird' and 'Garnet' |
| | *utahensis* | |
| Phlox | *paniculata* | 'Nora Leigh' |
| Polemonium | *foliosissimum* | |
| Polygonum | *campanulatum* | |
| | *amplexicaule* | 'Inverleith' |
| | *macrophyllum* | |
| | *milettii* | |
| | *regelianum* | |
| | *sphaerostachyum* | |
| Potentilla | *alba* | |
| | *thurberi* | |
| Primula | *auricula* | 'George Edge' |
| | × 'Johanna' | |
| | *vulgaris sibthorpii* | |
| Rheum | *kailense* | |
| | *alexandrae* | |

| Genus | Species | Cultivar name |
|---|---|---|
| Roscoea | *procera* | |
| | × 'Kew Beauty' | |
| Rudbeckia | *laciniata* | 'Goldquelle' |
| Salvia | *ambigens* | |
| | *bulleyana* | |
| | *verticillata* | |
| Sanguisorba | *sitchense* | |
| | *magnifica* | |
| Scabiosa | *lucida* | |
| | *ochroleuca* | |
| | *rumelica* | (Knautia *macedonica*) |
| Schizostylis | *coccinea* | 'Snow Maiden' |
| Sedum | *cauticolum* | 'Ruby Glow' |
| | *aizoon aurantiacum* | |
| | *heterodontum* | |
| | *pulchellum* | |
| Selinum | *tenuifolium* | |
| Senecio | *dorenicum* | 'Sunburst' |
| Serratula | *macrocephala* | |
| Silene | *schafta* | 'Robusta' |
| Solidago | *caesia* | |
| Stachys | *densiflorum* | |
| Strobilanthes | *atropurpurea* | |
| Stylophorum | *diphyllum* | |
| Symphytum | *rubrum* | |
| | *uplandicum* | 'Variegatum' |
| Thalictrum | *rochebrunianum* | |
| | *angustifolium* | |
| Tiarella | *collina* | |
| | *polyphylla* | |
| | *trifoliata* | |
| Tovara | *virginiana* | 'Painter's Palette' |
| Trollius | *yunnanensis* | |
| Veronica | *filifolia* | |

| Genus | Species | Cultivar name |
|---|---|---|
| | *longifolia* | 'Lilac Beauty' |
| | *virginica* | 'Alba' |
| Zauschneria | | 'Glasnevin' |
| Zigadenus | *nutallii* | |
| | *muscitoxicum* | |

# APPENDIX 3

## CONVERSION TABLE

These tables are designed to facilitate quick conversion between metric and imperial units. Bold figures in the central columns can be read as either metric or imperial: e.g., 1 kg = 2.20 lb or 1 lb = 0.45 kg.

| mm | | in | | cm | | in | | m | | yds |
|---|---|---|---|---|---|---|---|---|---|---|
| 25.4 | 1 | .039 | | 2.54 | 1 | 0.39 | | 0.91 | 1 | 1.09 |
| 50.8 | 2 | .079 | | 5.08 | 2 | 0.79 | | 1.83 | 2 | 2.19 |
| 76.2 | 3 | .118 | | 7.62 | 3 | 1.18 | | 2.74 | 3 | 3.28 |
| 101.6 | 4 | .157 | | 10.16 | 4 | 1.57 | | 3.66 | 4 | 4.37 |
| 127.0 | 5 | .197 | | 12.70 | 5 | 1.97 | | 4.57 | 5 | 5.47 |
| 152.4 | 6 | .236 | | 15.24 | 6 | 2.36 | | 5.49 | 6 | 6.56 |
| 177.8 | 7 | .276 | | 17.78 | 7 | 2.76 | | 6.40 | 7 | 7.66 |
| 203.2 | 8 | .315 | | 20.32 | 8 | 3.15 | | 7.32 | 8 | 8.75 |
| 228.6 | 9 | .354 | | 22.86 | 9 | 3.54 | | 8.23 | 9 | 9.84 |

| g | | oz | | kg | | lb | | km | | miles |
|---|---|---|---|---|---|---|---|---|---|---|
| 28.35 | 1 | .04 | | 0.45 | 1 | 2.20 | | 1.61 | 1 | 0.62 |
| 56.70 | 2 | .07 | | 0.91 | 2 | 4.41 | | 3.22 | 2 | 1.24 |
| 85.05 | 3 | .11 | | 1.36 | 3 | 6.61 | | 4.83 | 3 | 1.86 |
| 113.40 | 4 | .14 | | 1.81 | 4 | 8.82 | | 6.44 | 4 | 2.48 |
| 141.75 | 5 | .18 | | 2.27 | 5 | 11.02 | | 8.05 | 5 | 3.11 |
| 170.10 | 6 | .21 | | 2.72 | 6 | 13.23 | | 9.65 | 6 | 3.73 |
| 198.45 | 7 | .25 | | 3.18 | 7 | 15.43 | | 11.26 | 7 | 4.35 |
| 226.80 | 8 | .28 | | 3.63 | 8 | 17.64 | | 12.87 | 8 | 4.97 |
| 255.15 | 9 | .32 | | 4.08 | 9 | 19.84 | | 14.48 | 9 | 5.59 |

| ha | | acres | Metric to imperial conversion formulae | |
|---|---|---|---|---|
| 0.40 | **1** | 2.47 | | multiply by |
| 0.81 | **2** | 4.94 | cm to inches | 0.3937 |
| 1.21 | **3** | 7.41 | m to feet | 3.281 |
| 1.62 | **4** | 9.88 | m to yards | 1.094 |
| 2.02 | **5** | 12.36 | km to miles | 0.6214 |
| 2.43 | **6** | 14.83 | $km^2$ to square miles | 0.3861 |
| 2.83 | **7** | 17.30 | ha to acres | 2.471 |
| 3.24 | **8** | 19.77 | g to ounces | 0.03527 |
| 3.64 | **9** | 22.24 | kg to pounds | 2.205 |

# INDEX

# INDEX

# INDEX

# INDEX